The Wom[...]
Catholic R[...]...[...]
In England 1540–1680

The Women of the Catholic Resistance:
In England 1540–1680

Roland Connelly

The Pentland Press Limited
Edinburgh • Cambridge • Durham • USA

© Roland Connelly 1997

First published in 1997 by
The Pentland Press Ltd.
1 Hutton Close
South Church
Bishop Auckland
Durham

British Library Cataloguing in Publication Data.
A Catalogue record for this book is available
from the British Library.

ISBN 1 85821 509 9

Front cover illustration: Saint Margaret Clitherow.
Typeset by George Wishart & Associates, Whitley Bay.
Printed and bound by Antony Rowe Ltd., Chippenham.

Contents

FOREWORD

By Cardinal Basil Hume OSB, Archbishop of Westminster

It has been noticed by many people that among those English and Welsh Martyrs officially recognised by the Church there are very few women and the purpose of this book is to emphasise that despite this formal lack of recognition,Catholic women did indeed play a full and important role, side by side with the men, in the defence of the Church in England at the time of the Reformation.

In these brief biographies, Father Roland Connelly has carefully selected a rich variety of Catholic women from all parts of the country and from all walks of life. He includes children and teenage girls as well as ladies of more mature and advanced years. Some were royal or aristocratic and others more humble servants or housewives. In these pages there are nuns and single laywomen as well as wives and mothers and widows. But all were united with the Martyrs in the community of the Church and all were one in their fierce determination to preserve the Faith for themselves and their families and for their children's children for all time. It was for that purpose that they risked their lives to protect their priests in order to ensure the continued celebration of the Mass and we today are only able to practice our Faith in peace and freedom because of what they suffered and endured so long ago.

We have every reason to be proud of our Martyrs and we honour them in our prayers and devotions. We should also be proud of those other brave souls of the larger community, who may not yet be recognised as Martyrs but who stood firm in the shadows beside our Martyrs and helped them and quietly suffered with them. They should not be forgotten. They too deserve our recognition, our thanks and our prayers.

Basil Hume

INTRODUCTION

Much has been written about the heroism of the English Catholic Martyrs of the sixteenth and seventeenth centuries. Not so much has been written about their companions, who shared with them in their sufferings and endured the same dangers but who were not, in fact, called upon to die for their Faith. And very little indeed has been written about those extraordinary Catholic women who lived and died within the Martyr community as active members of the Catholic Resistance and who made their own distinctive contribution to the Catholic cause.

This book then is an attempt to describe the role and importance of these women, who came from all parts of the country and from all walks of life. They rejoiced in a common Faith and applied themselves with equal determination to the same task of religious resistance to the dictates of the powerful State, but in these biographies, each one is her own woman, making her own response in her own way to the difficulties of her day. Some died on the scaffold; others were condemned but reprieved. Some died cruel, lingering deaths in foul prisons; others avoided the extremities of the law and spent their whole lives working secretly for the Church they loved. All deserve the praise and plaudits of succeeding generations and many were fully worthy of the Martyr's crown.

Sadly, only four of these women have been officially recognized by the Church as true Martyrs but Saint Margaret Clitherow, Saint Margaret Ward, Saint Anne Line and Blessed Margaret Pole are worthy representatives of their sisters as well as of the whole Catholic community. That only these four women have received canonical recognition is due in part to the circumstances of those times when civil authorities (and most especially Queen Elizabeth) were reluctant to execute women, but is also due to the fact that the persecution was aimed deliberately at the priests and only indirectly were lay people involved when they tried to protect or defend their priests.

But if only a few Catholic women actually died for their Faith, many, many more were ready to offer their lives if that sacrifice should be demanded of them, and many, many more took every risk in defiantly opposing the machinations of the Protestant forces. The glory of those who died should not be allowed to overshadow the achievements of those who lived and in these pages, it is hoped, proper attention and appreciation will be offered to all.

The importance of women in the Catholic community was clearly observed by John Knox, the fiery founder of Presbyterianism and obliquely

1

he paid them his own tribute when he attacked several Catholic ladies in his famous diatribe, 'The First Blast of the Trumpet Against the Monstrous Regiment of Women'. Certainly he had no doubts that the Catholic women were the major opponents of his Reformation.

The same point of view has also been expressed, albeit in more charitable terms by A.L. Rowse, the eminent historian and acknowledged expert on the Tudor period, who does not hesitate to describe the Catholic community, at least in its early days, as a matriarchy. And another distinguished historian, Professor John Bossy, has written, 'On few points in the early history of English Catholicism is there such a unanimous convergence of evidence as on the importance of the part played in it by women and specifically wives' (*The English Catholic Community*, p. 153).

Contemporary evidence from English Government statistics serve to demonstrate the pattern and clarify the composition of the community. According to Mr Brian Magee's summary, the Diocesan Returns for 1603 show that more women than men were officially named as Catholics. He states for example that in the diocese of Chichester 153 Catholic women were recusants and only 109 men; in the diocese of Norwich there were 177 women and only 147 men; in the diocese of Chester there were 1,520 women and only 992 men; in the diocese of York there were 420 women and only 300 men. The only dioceses in the whole country to have more men than women on their Recusant Rolls were Gloucester, Rochester and London and the totals for all the dioceses of England and Wales were 4,593 women and 2,986 men. In other words, these figures show that 60 per cent of the known Catholics of 1,603 were women (Brian Magee, *The English Recusants*, p. 83).

To claim that these percentages remained constant throughout the years of persecution is not realistic but to postulate a significant number of women within the Martyr community is reasonable and it is perhaps not extravagant to add the rider that frequently the women outnumbered the men.

In 1580, both the Privy Council and the Anglican Bishop of Winchester were struggling with the Hampshire problem of the high incidence in that county of weak, conformable husbands and strong Catholic wives (Bossy, *The English Catholic Community*, p. 154). At the same time, in York, it was accepted by the civic authorities that 'a large proportion of the York recusants were the wives of Protestant tradesmen husbands' (J.C.H. Aveling, *Catholic Recusancy in York*, p. 59). There is reference in the State Papers of 1592 to the presence of Father John Mush 'about York' and the priest himself is quoted as having said, 'the gentlemen hereabouts had fallen away from the priests but the gentlewomen stood steadfastly to them.' In 1595, Archbishop Hutton of York acknowledged that the 'most part' of the Catholics in his very extensive diocese were women.

All this evidence suggests very strongly the numerical importance of Catholic woman but a fuller understanding of the nature and extent of the female contribution to the Catholic cause depends upon a wider examination of the conditions under which they lived and the strategies employed by the whole community.

In all parts of the country, Catholic men and Catholic women worked together for the good of the Church but each made a distinctive and characteristic contribution. Women could not tramp the lanes as guides and bodyguards to the priests as Blessed Ralph Grimstow and Blessed Robert Hardisty did; women could not scale the prison walls to take food to starving Catholic prisoners as Blessed Edward Fulthrop and Blessed William Andleby did; women could not attempt dramatic horseback rescues of captured priests as Blessed Thurstan Hunt and Blessed George Errington did; women could not draw their swords or fire off blunderbusses to defend the priest as Blessed John Talbot and Blessed John Norton did. All such swashbuckling heroics were unthinkable for the women of that time. But what women could do was to achieve the same purposes by ways more acceptable to the sensitivities of their contemporaries and the most important and most valuable thing they could do was to stay at home within their own recognized sphere of domestic responsibility and there make adequate provision for the reception and safety of the priest visitors delivered to them by the men. And this seemingly humdrum task required a strength of purpose and a courage of the same calibre as that shown by the men in their more spectacular exploits.

The reception of the wandering priests within the Catholic household was very much a woman's affair. Frequently the catholic husband was away; he might be in prison, he might be 'riding up and down' to avoid the pursuivants or he might be trying to establish a secondary residence in a safer parish, diocese or county. Such absences imposed additional burdens on his wife but even when he was at home it was still the wife who looked after the family and organized the household. In domestic affairs the wife reigned supreme and in the kitchen and the nursery at least, husbands never interfered. Nobody, then, was in a better position than the wife to welcome the unexpected or fugitive priest and keep his presence secret. She knew how to feed an extra mouth without raising comment; she knew which servants to trust and which neighbours were reliable; she knew how to disguise the presence of an additional guest. At a later date, other people and especially skilled craftsmen such as Saint Nicholas Owen SJ and Father Richard Holtby SJ would design and build intricate hiding holes for priests at risk but at first it was the woman of the house who improvised primitive accommodation in isolated rooms, frequently in attics, sometimes even in the rafters of the house, so that priests spoke about 'living like sparrows on the housetops', and carefully cultivated the habit of walking on that part of the floor actually supported by the beams so that no creaking floorboard should betray their presence.

In time, these houses became much more than merely places of refuge for the hunted priest. They were also places of rest and recuperation. The dangers and hardships of the priest's life tested all his physical and moral strength. Of no fixed abode, continually on the move, harassed by spies, pursuivants and informers, sleeping rough in hail, rain and snow, eating what little be could find, the priest was subjected to frequent attacks of chronic exhaustion and nervous strain and when he did reach the safe house, he frequently presented himself to his hostess as a very sick man.

She it was who nursed him back to health and strength and the valuable experience she had gained from attending to illness within her own family and household stood her in good stead as she worked with great respect and loving care to help the suffering priest to return to his apostolate as soon as possible.

Yet even as the priest subjected himself to the tender nursing of the lady of the house, he continued his priestly work. He celebrated Mass and distributed Holy Communion; he baptized the babies, reconciled the schismatics and heard confessions; he preached and gave religious instructions; and always he encouraged his congregation to fidelity, courage and personal holiness. At first his visits to a particular house were very short. It was dangerous to be too static; safety was perceived to be on the road. Lay Catholics grew accustomed to an intensity of religion for a few days and then the void for weeks or months as the priest disappeared to attend to the needs of other families on his extensive circuit. It was during these absences of the priest, when there could be no Mass that the faithful gathered every Sunday to conduct their own prayer services and developed a lay participation in those pastoral activities which were normally regarded as the preserve of the priest. In such quasi-liturgies, it was always the head of the house, the father of the family, who presided but the arrangements were usually made by the women and women continued to play a very important part in religious affairs.

By the earlier years of the seventeenth century, priests had begun to settle down in the more welcoming houses. They continued to move from place to place but now they covered their district from a more permanent base. Certain houses such as Grosmont on the North Yorkshire Moors or Harrowden in Northamptonshire or Battle Abbey or Cowdray in Sussex became missionary headquarters while many others became regular Mass centres with a resident priest as chaplain to the family and to the local Catholics. Wherever there was an available priest and a willing householder, Catholics gathered together for Mass and instinctively formed those special communities of Faith, which they called congregations or missions, but which were, in fact, the embryonic parishes of post-Reformation England.

Recusant chapels and Mass centres attracted Catholics from large areas whenever Mass was celebrated but for those people who actually lived in the house, a special religious way of life presented itself. Of course, the community depended on the priest and the defence and protection of the priest was always of paramount importance but within each community women occupied another place of special importance The customs of the time decreed that many young unmarried women should come together in certain houses to help with the general education of the children of the house but also to put the final touches to their own cultural education. It was a splendid opportunity for young Catholic women to live together without exciting any comment or criticism and as they gathered in a Catholic house they were able to teach the children their catechism and at the same time to develop their own spiritual lives in close proximity to the Mass and the priest.

In many ways these women lived like nuns. Of course, they could wear no distinctive habit and take no public vows but they were together in community, followed a strict religious rule of life and applied themselves wholeheartedly to the the the pursuit of holiness.

Lady Grace Babthorpe has left her own account of life at Osgodby in Yorkshire and seems at times to be describing the life of a convent rather than a family home. Father William Palmes (or Palmer), the Jesuit chaplain to the widowed Mrs Dorothy Lawson at Saint Anthony's, Heaton on the banks of the Tyne, has given an eye-witness account of a similar Catholic establishment. And the following pages show the existence of many other unofficial 'convents' with devout 'nuns' in other parts of the country.

It was to these houses especially that dedicated Catholics looked as they wrestled with the problems of Catholic education for their children and from these rudimentary convents and schools came an amazing progression of young people across the seas to the convents, schools and seminaries established for the English refugees on the continent of Europe. In due time, many of these pupils returned home as the well-educated laymen and laywomen who became the strength and glory of the Church in England, but it is a matter of continual surprise and edification that so many of these boys offered themselves as missionary priests and so many of these girls became nuns either as cloistered exiles overseas praying for their unfortunate country or as members of Mary Ward's new and vibrant congregation of pastoral sisters at work in England.

This extraordinary flowering of vocations in the late sixteenth and early seventeenth centuries was a distinctly English phenomenon and was of major importance for the survival of the Church. Priests and nuns were produced in plenty just when they were most needed and least expected. Of course, as always, numbers seemed small and insufficient to contemporary observers but later generations may contemplate with pride and gratitude and not a little pious envy the tremendous strengths of that seemingly bedraggled, downtrodden community, so small in numbers, so lacking in resources and yet so blessed by God with abundant vocations. And if reasons are sought for this unusual state of affairs then they lie in the holiness of the community and the holiness of the individual members, but many of these priests and nuns would not hesitate to attribute their vocations, under God, to the guidance and encouragement which they had received in their early years from those devoted women who risked their lives to teach the Faith to succeeding generations of children in the country houses of England.

Here then are brief, factual biographies of some of the more remarkable Catholic women who lived during those difficult years between 1540 and 1680 when the threat of martyrdom was a grim reality for every Catholic. These are the women who were tested by hardship, cruelty and injustice as they defied the law of the land and applied themselves to the defence of the Church. These are the women of courage, strength and determination who, with God's grace, persevered and endured and never surrendered. These are the women who helped to win the victory and who shared in the glory.

They conversed with saints and walked with martyrs. They deserve to be better known and honoured for what they were and for what they accomplished.

ELIZABETH BARTON

Elizabeth Barton, known to her contemporaries as the Holy Maid of Kent, or more simply the Nun of Kent, was the first person in England to raise her voice in loud and public protest about the divorce plans of King Henry VIII and she was, in consequence, the first loyal Catholic to be executed for religion's sake. Her death was the prelude to the deaths of many Martyrs but it seems very unlikely that she herself will ever be recognized by the Church as an authentic Martyr.

In her own time and among her own people, Elizabeth Barton enjoyed an extraordinary reputation for sanctity, and was widely acclaimed as a living saint; but others were convinced that she was a fraud and a political agitator. She remains to this day a woman of mystery and historians are careful to treat her with great caution. Perhaps she has been badly misunderstood, but no scholar seems willing to acknowledge her wholeheartedly as a saint or to condemn her wholeheartedly as a charlatan.

Elizabeth Barton was not an educated woman; perhaps she was not even a highly intelligent woman. She was born to a life of toil and poverty in the small parish of Aldington on Romney Marsh about the year 1506. As a very young girl she was already working as a domestic servant when she suffered a severe illness which brought her close to death and left her debilitated and subject to fits. Modern scientists have suggested that she was an epileptic but her Catholic friends and neighbours preferred to recognize in her affliction the hand of God. In her convulsions, she expressed herself wildly and vehemently about sin and evil and condemned the vices of her day. Then periodically, usually about the beginning of December, she would sink into a deep trance for two or three days at a time and emerge to describe the wonders she had seen in heaven under the guidance of an angel. She told people about the other visions she claimed she had received and she made many prophecies to local people about local affairs; it was generally accepted that her prophecies came true. Her fame spread beyond her immediate surrounds and pilgrims came from far and near to view her, listen to her words, seek her advice personally and ask for her prayers.

It was inevitable that the life of the village should be disrupted and the effect of all this adulation on an immature girl could only be harmful. In his wisdom, the Parish Priest, Richard Masters, reported the whole affair to Archbishop Warham of Canterbury who accepted responsibility and arranged for the girl to enter the convent of Saint Sepulchre in his own city of Canterbury. But pilgrims are persistent folk and even in her convent Elizabeth Barton could not escape from their importunities. Her ecstacies and revelations continued and a Benedictine monk, Doctor Edward Bocking, was appointed by the Archbishop to protect her from the crowd and to help and instruct her. For several years, Dr Bocking took note of all she said and did and reported it faithfully to his Archbishop who in his turn kept King Henry fully informed.

At first, Elizabeth had little to say about national affairs and the King therefore took little interest but after some eight years in the convent, it became evident that this young woman, now in her early twenties, was concerning herself more and more about the King's affairs and in particular expressing herself most forcibly about the royal plans for divorce.

Perhaps the religious instruction she was receiving from Dr Bocking made her more aware of the evil implications of the King's divorce; perhaps the powerful Dr Bocking was using her to express his own views; perhaps the Holy Spirit really was working through her. Whatever the cause, she began to speak out with vehemence and even to issue threats. She claimed that she had received a letter from Saint Mary Magdalene in heaven and informed King Henry that this letter told her that he would cease to be king one month after marrying Anne Boleyn, that he would not be king in God's eyes one hour after doing so and that he would die a villain's death. She terrified Archbishop Warham with her predictions of doom and warned Cardinal Wolsey that her angel had told her that if he dared to grant the King's petition for divorce, God would inflict on him terrible punishments. Nor did she hesitate to send similar warnings to the papal envoys and even to the Pope himself. In 1532 she forced herself before the King at Canterbury and openly upbraided him for deserting his lawful wife.

King Henry had to recognize a very dangerous situation. He was afraid of Elizabeth Barton because his fractured faith told him that she might be a messenger from God, but he was also afraid of her because she had so many followers who listened to her. Nor could he fail to notice her close friendship with such leading opponents of his divorce plans as Sir Thomas More, Bishop John Fisher, the London Carthusians and the Friars Observant from Greenwich. He realized that she was the figurehead, if not the living centre, of a hostile multitude and he saw the possibility of using her as a scapegoat in order to attack the others.

In November 1533, King Henry called together a carefully selected group of privy councillors, judges and nobles and for three days they debated what should be done about the Nun of Kent. Henry wished her to be condemned at once as a heretic and traitor but was persuaded to a greater subtlety. Elizabeth and her six principal supporters were taken to the Tower and initiated into those Tudor methods of interrogation which were so successful in procuring comprehensive confessions and instant conversions.

Accordingly, on 23 November, Elizabeth Barton was taken before the scaffold at Saint Paul's Cross and forced to listen to a long diatribe of a sermon from Dr John Capon, Abbot of Hyde, and soon to be promoted bishop in Henry's schismatical Church. The preacher denounced her as a fraud and a harlot, claimed she was the victim of her own vanity and the unworthy intrigue of monks, and roused the rabble to indignation. The insults, ridicule and humiliations heaped upon her by the mob were too much for the young girl (not yet thirty years of age) and she broke down and publically confessed that she was an imposter and that her visions and heavenly messages were all make-believe. Then, when prompted, she tried to justify herself by betraying her friends and seeking to lay the blame for her misdemeanours on the six priests who had supported her through thick and thin and who now stood accused beside her near the scaffold.

All were condemned to death as traitors by a Parliamentary bill of attainder on 30 March 1534 and sentence was carried out on 21 April. No distinction was made between man and woman. All were hanged, and then beheaded, and their severed heads displayed in various parts of London.

The importance of the Elizabeth Barton affair is not that she condemned herself as a religious fraud. Her crime was speaking out, for whatever cause, against the King, and for this, she and her party were ruthlessly destroyed. In fact, King Henry was giving notice that he would brook no interference in his private affairs and that loyal Catholics who dared to speak out against the royal divorce could expect to be treated harshly. No doubt some of his religious opponents were cowed by this show of force; others derived strength and encouragement from the bravery of a young girl, who might or might not have been holy, who might or might not have been a mystic, who might or might not have been disturbed, but who died for what she believed in: the Holy Catholic Church.

CATHERINE OF ARAGON

Princess Catherine of Aragon, fourth daughter of King Ferdinand and Queen Isabella of the united kingdoms of Aragon and Castile, belonged by birth to the most powerful and influential family in Europe. Her betrothal in 1497, when she was twelve years of age, to the relatively obscure Arthur, Prince of Wales was an occasion of some surprise to interested observers in many European courts, but this carefully arranged marriage was a significant acknowledgement of the new stature of an England growing in power and wealth under the wise and prudent rule of the first Tudor, King Henry VII.

The marriage was solemnized on 14 November 1501, but within five months the sickly Prince Arthur was dead and Catherine became a teenage widow before she had reached her seventeenth birthday. King Ferdinand and King Henry were both hard-headed businessmen as well as loving fathers and each recognized the dangers of personal material loss in the break-up of the marriage. The consequent financial wranglings over the payment of her dowry did nothing to alleviate the great distress of Catherine and she was left virtually abandoned in a strange country with unfamiliar people whose language she struggled to understand. Even more humiliating for the young girl were the determined efforts of the two kings to preserve something of their investments by marrying her off immediately to Henry, Duke of York, the second son of King Henry and heir to the throne of England but at that time only eleven years of age.

The marriage treaty was agreed and signed on 23 June 1503, and an immediate request was made to the Pope for the necessary dispensation for Henry to marry his deceased brother's wife. This dispensation was granted at once but there was then a long delay of six years before the marriage was solemnized on 11 June 1509. By this time, Henry had succeeded to the throne as King Henry VIII and no doubts whatsoever were raised about the legitimacy of the union. It was said to be a marriage made in heaven and for the next eighteen years Henry and Catherine lived happily together as man and wife.

The King loved his Queen very much and boasted of his good fortune in having such a talented and virtuous wife. Indeed, Catherine was so devout and holy, and practiced such an extraordinary and austere religious life, that she had to be restrained by the Pope from binding herself by vow to a rigorous rule of prayer, fasting, abstinence and pilgrimage. Her character, her piety and her religious observance made her a fitting Catholic consort for the young king, who in his turn seemed to possess all the virtues and whose theological studies won for him the papal title of 'Defender of the Faith'.

There was however one sadness which Henry and Catherine experienced throughout their marriage and that was the absence of a male heir. Catherine had several miscarriages and actually gave birth to three sons and two daughters, but all except the Princess Mary died in infancy. It was Henry's concern for a legitimate male heir which induced him to contemplate marriage to Anne Boleyn, who might otherwise have been just one of his several mistresses. But in order to marry Anne he had first to rid himself of Catherine and by 1527 the King's 'Great Matter' was no longer a secret of state, and his plan to divorce his Queen was the subject of scandalous gossip and anxious speculation throughout the kingdom.

Once more, Henry put his case to the Pope but this time to demand that Pope Clement VII should retract the dispensation of his predecessor and declare that the marriage of Henry and Catherine was invalid. A rather hesitant Pope found himself in the unenviable position of having to decide between the powerful King Henry VIII of England on one hand and on the other Catherine, his Queen, daughter of Aragon and Castile and beloved aunt of the reigning Holy Roman Emperor, Charles V. Diplomacy demanded delay, compromise and inaction and Pope Clement was an accomplished master of such arts. He appointed two Legates, Cardinal Thomas Wolsey, Archbishop of York and Cardinal Lorenzo Campeggio, the Italian Bishop of Salisbury and Cardinal protector of England, and formally empowered them to set up a Legatine Court in London to hear the opposing arguments and make a decision. At the same time, the Pope gave secret instructions to both Cardinals to use every opportunity for delay and to put off any decision for as long as possible.

It took Cardinal Campeggio some time to make the journey to England but on his arrival he proposed to Queen Catherine the rather dubious theological opinion of the time that if a wife should enter a nunnery then her husband was free to marry somebody else. He therefore offered his services to solve all the problems of the proposed divorce if only Catherine would play her part and become a nun. The Queen listened politely and said nothing. King Henry added his support and bluster to Campeggio's suggestion and told Catherine that if she did not enter a nunnery of her own free will then he would force her to do so. Again Catherine listened politely and said nothing. Cardinal Wolsey presented himself on his knees and begged her to surrender, and a deputation of English bishops came on the same mission. Still Catherine listened politely and still she said nothing. Then boldly and bluntly, she informed the assembled potentates that come what may she would live and die as the lawful wife of King Henry in that vocation of matrimony to which God had called her. So obvious was her determination that the Papal Legates gave up all hope of persuading her to withdraw and had no alternative but to summon the ecclesiastical Court over which the Pope had authorized them to preside.

The Court opened at Blackfriars on 18 June 1529. King Henry was present only by proxy but to the surprise of all, the courageous Catherine made a personal appearance. She expressed herself with great clarity, made a vehement protest against the proceedings of the Legates and lodged her formal appeal directly to the Holy Father in Rome. Her words were ignored and the Court continued in session, but on the third day King Henry attended in state and was seated in full splendour on his throne when Catherine burst in and threw herself before him to plead once more for justice. She begged him to save her honour and the honour of their daughter by withdrawing at once his petition for divorce. The King made no reply and Catherine, with all the dignity and poise of a true Queen of England, walked solemnly out of the hall and steadfastly refused to return.

Now, at last, the Pope had to give his personal attention to the matter and the officials of the Roman Curia began their slow, laborious examination of Henry's petition for divorce and Catherine's protest. The case dragged on for four years and Henry grew more and more impatient until in January 1533 he could wait no longer. Already, Anne Boleyn was pregnant with his child, and on 25 January he attempted marriage with her in a private and bigamous ceremony without benefit of divorce. On 23 May Thomas Cranmer, the new Archbishop of Canterbury, declared by the King's authority that Henry's marriage to Catherine of Aragon was null and void and the King, in effect, granted himself a divorce. To the rest of Catholic Europe it was an empty and futile gesture, but to the King of England it was the fulfilment of his immediate desires and ambitions.

In his Consistory of 11 July 1533, Pope Clement VII took note of these happenings in England and ordered King Henry, under pain of excommunication, to put away Anne Boleyn and take back Catherine as his lawful wife. It was of course all too late. King Henry had proclaimed himself 'Supreme Head of the Church in England', and at Whitsun Anne Boleyn was crowned Queen in Westminster Abbey, the folds of her robes concealing the signs of her pregnancy.

For the true Queen, Catherine, it was the ultimate humiliation. She was spared no pain. She was deprived of the title of Queen and King Henry insisted that she be known as the Princess Dowager, widow of Arthur, Prince of Wales. Their daughter, Princess Mary was also deprived of her rank and declared to be illegitimate and worthy only to be called the Lady Mary. Catherine's households and income were drastically reduced and she was obliged to live quietly away from Court on one of the royal manors. And then most cruelly, the King decreed that mother and daughter should be separated so that what he chose to call 'Catherine's harmful influence' over Mary would be minimal.

Queen Catherine's time of suffering was mercifully short. She lived only three years after the King's 'divorce'. Physically she was not a strong woman. She had endured debilitating illnesses all her life. Now she had to bear the added burden of insult, uncertainty and anxiety. She never acknowledged the King's divorce and constantly offered him her love, loyalty and devotion as his real wife, but to maintain herself as the Queen Consort of England was to deny the King's supremacy and Catholic Martyrs were being executed for lesser offences against the King. Perhaps Queen Catherine never knew how close she herself came to martyrdom but she must have known that she was dicing with death in opposing the King.

Of course, she was fighting a personal battle for her own dignity and for her marriage but she was also fighting a much more important battle for her Catholic Faith, and in so doing was giving comfort and encouragement to countless other Catholics who looked to her for leadership and inspiration.

From her deathbed, Queen Catherine wrote to her 'most dear lord, king and husband'. She forgave him all the wrongs he had done to her and commended their daughter, Mary, to his paternal protection. For once, the hard heart of Henry was touched and he sent her in reply a message of kindness, but before the messenger could reach Kimbolton Castle, Catherine was dead. She died from natural causes, probably from cancer, but she died as she had lived: a valiant and dedicated Catholic. It was 6 January 1536.

MARGARET BULMER

Dedication to the Catholic Cause is not necessarily a sign of interior holiness and it is possible for sinners as well as saints to be called to martyrdom. Margaret Bulmer does not appear to have lived a saintly life and indeed many of her contemporaries were scandalized by her outrageous behaviour but, like Saint Mary Magdalene, she lived to repent and she gave her life courageously for the Church she had grown to love.

In her own day, Margaret was widely recognized as the illegitimate daughter of Edward Stafford, Duke of Buckingham. Her father proudly acknowledged her, loved her dearly and ensured that in her early childhood at least she had every possible advantage. Unfortunately, the high lineage, wealth and power of the Duke inevitably aroused the envy and fear of King Henry VIII and it was only a matter of time before the expected accusations of treachery were made and Edward Stafford was brought to trial before his peers. He was condemned to death on 15 May 1521 and the eleven-year-old Margaret was left on her own as a penniless orphan with very limited prospects.

Nevertheless, as the girl grew older, the nobility of her birth allied to her extraordinary beauty attracted the attentions of many eligible men of rank, but not one was prepared to overlook her illegitimacy and offer her the honourable security of marriage. In her distress, Margaret rushed into a loveless marriage with Master William Cheyne, an insignificant but wealthy vintner of London. To the delight of the city gossips, Margaret did not allow this marriage to impede in any way her special relationship with Sir John Bulmer, who was himself married to another lady and was already the father of five children.

These marital entanglements intensified when, in the most sordid manner, Sir John determined to buy Margaret from her husband and offered the grasping merchant a sum of money which he at once accepted. This infamous deal is recorded in *The Chronicles of the London Greyfriars* (quoted by Father Godfrey Anstruther, 'The Rime of John Pickering', *Dominican Studies*, vol. II (January 1949), p. 28): '...the Lady Margaret Bulmer, wife unto Sir John Bulmer, and he made her his wife, but she was the wife of one Cheyne, for he sold her unto Sir Bulmer...'

When Sir John Bulmer returned north to his ancestral home at Wilton Castle on the south bank of the river Tees in Cleveland, Margaret Cheyne accompanied him and he installed her as his leman in Pinchinthorpe Hall which was about five miles away from his castle and from his wife. Margaret was not pleased with these arrangements and Sir John's wife, Lady Anne

Bulmer, was even less pleased when she discovered Margaret's presence in the neighbourhood. Such tensions however did not last very long because quite fortuitously Lady Anne died and Sir John was free to marry Margaret.

Sir John was free to marry but was Margaret free? Certainly they went through a wedding ceremony and did all they could to ensure its legality but if William Cheyne was alive then all was null and void. Margaret was called Lady Margaret Bulmer and lived as Lady Margaret Bulmer, but the London Greyfriars were not alone in expressing their doubts. Charles Wriothesley expressed contemporary opinion when he referred to her in his Chronicle as 'Margaret Cheyne, other wife to Bulmer called...' and the modern historian, J.D. Mackie, in the *Oxford History of England*, vol. VII (1952), p. 392, uses inverted commas when he calls Margaret Bulmer 'wife' to Sir John. At this stage, the matter cannot be resolved and charity at least demands acceptance of the marriage until definite evidence to the contrary is forthcoming.

Lady Margaret Bulmer was a very efficient chatelaine for Wilton Castle and attended to all her duties with skill and efficiency. Her character and strength of personality impressed themselves on the tenants and local inhabitants to such an extent that in the early years of the nineteenth century she was still remembered in Cleveland folklore as 'Madge Wildfire' and some have remembered her in less complimentary terms as 'Black Meg'. Such fame or notoriety is all the more remarkable in view of the fact that she spent so few years in Pinchinthorpe and Wilton. She was only about twenty-seven when she died and her time of residence in the north could not have exceeded ten years, and was possibly very much less.

In 1536, when the great religious rebellion called the Pilgrimage of Grace broke out in Yorkshire, Lady Margaret Bulmer felt called to take an active part in the defence of her Catholic religion. Of course, as a woman she could not bear arms and she could not fight, but as soon as news arrived from the East Riding that Robert Aske's men were marching on York, Margaret Bulmer took to horse and rode at a furious gallop to every village and hamlet on the huge Wilton estate in order to gather together (and if necessary to persuade) all able-bodied men to take up arms. When Sir John Bulmer rode out of Wilton Castle at the head of this citizen's army, he had Lady Margaret Bulmer riding by his side.

The Pilgrimage of Grace was the largest rebellion in English history but it was a glorious failure. Robert Aske and his captains were tricked into surrender when victory was almost within their grasp. The King did not hesitate to take his vengeance but surprisingly there were not as many executions as was formerly believed. For the leaders, however, there was no royal mercy and sixteen of them were brought to London for trial. Among them was one woman. Lady Margaret Bulmer had played too prominent a role in the insurrection for her activities to be overlooked and she faced exactly the same charges as the men.

On 16 May 1537, Lady Bulmer and Sir Robert Constable were brought from the Tower to the Guildhall and then on to Westminster where all the accused were tried together, and Margaret and thirteen others were condemned to death. On 25 May Sir John Bulmer was among those who were hanged and beheaded, and later that day Lady Margaret Bulmer was drawn on a hurdle from the Tower to Newgate prison and then on to Smithfield where she was burnt to death.

The late Father Godfrey Anstruther OP took a great interest in these trials and executions and published the results of his scholarly investigations in *Dominican Studies* of January 1949. In this article, Father Anstruther pointed out that the official indictments of that time were 'enormously verbose documents' but that it was always the first charge which was the real one. For the sixteen Pilgrims, the first charge was that they had denied the King his title of Supreme Head of the Church on earth. They were executed therefore not as political rebels but as religious martyrs.

Father Anstruther then noted that John Pickering, (the secular priest of Lythe and not the Dominican of the same name) was the only one of the accused to save his own life by formally acknowledging the King's supremacy. On 21 June he received his pardon from the King.

Father Anstruther therefore reasons, 'Thus we have fifteen people condemned to death, and the main charge against them all is that they denied the king his title of supreme head of the church. One of them acknowledged the king's supremacy and thereby saved his life. It is surely reasonable to argue that the others could have saved their lives in the same way.'

Father Anstruther's conclusion therefore is this: 'Whatever view we may take of the Pilgrimage of Grace, it seems clear that these victims could all have purchased their lives, as one of them did, by denying their religion. There is therefore at least a prima facie case for regarding John Pickering OP and his companions as martyrs in the strict sense of the word.'

It is sad that the Church has not recognized any Martyr from among those who died as a result of the Pilgrimage of Grace. Father Anstruther's powerful arguments and his great scholarly authority give rise to an optimism that in due time the Church will be able to honour Robert Aske and his companions as true Martyrs. And when that time comes, Lady Margaret Bulmer, in spite of all the vicissitudes of her life, will take her rightful place as one of the Martyrs of the Church.

MARGARET POLE

When Margaret Pole was born at Castle Farley near Bath in August 1473, the prospects for her future success and prosperity seemed bright and well assured. She was a princess of the royal blood of England. Her mother was Isabel Neville, the daughter of the Earl of Warwick, better known as the Kingmaker. Her father was George Plantagenet, Duke of Clarence, the younger brother of the reigning monarch, King Edward IV. But such proximity to the throne and centres of power cannot prevent natural misfortunes and indeed in those days brought its own special dangers, so that, quite contrary to all expectations, the Clarence baby was to know suffering, sadness and tragedy throughout her life.

In fact, Margaret was only three years old when her mother died, and before she was five years old she had to be told the dreadful news that her father had been executed or murdered by being drowned, at the King's command it was widely believed, in a 'barell of Malmsey wine' in the Tower of London.

By Act of Attainder, Margaret and her younger brother, Edward, now Earl of Warwick, were deprived of their rank and possessions and obliged to live privately as penniless orphans in the care of their grandmothers. After the battle of Bosworth Field, however, the Lancastrian victor, Henry Tudor, recognized the dynastic threat that the children posed as true descendants of the House of York and took immediate steps to minimize the danger. The eight-year-old Edward was locked up in solitary confinement in the Tower until, it was said, he was so confused that 'he did not know a goose from a capon'. Margaret was married off in 1491 to a 'safe' husband, Sir Richard Pole, who had strong Lancastrian connections but who was determined to love, cherish and protect his wife.

Even in the midst of this happy marriage, Margaret could not forget the torments of her small brother in the Tower and suffered intensely from the pains of separation. In fact, she was never to see her brother again. On 28 November 1499, the young Earl of Warwick, who had spent sixteen of his twenty-four years in prison was mercilessly executed by King Henry VII in order to reassure King Ferdinand of Aragon-Castile that the English throne was secure so that the projected marriage of Catherine of Aragon to the English heir could go ahead.

This 'marriage made in blood' was a source of profound disquiet to the Princess of Aragon and troubled her conscience so much that she endeavoured to do all in her power to make restitution to Margaret Pole. At first, she was in no position to do much but she offered her friendship and support and the two women were brought closer together by their abhorrence of a crime which was always a source of grief to them both. But in later years, this friendship forged in such pain enabled each one to help the other in their times of greatest need.

Death was never far away from Margaret Pole. Her husband, Sir Richard died in 1505 and she was left in poverty to bring up her five small children. But another death was advantageous to the hard-pressed widow when King Henry VII died on 22 April 1509. His successor, King Henry VIII, immediately married Catherine of Aragon and with Catherine crowned as Queen Consort, Margaret at last received justice and her own royal status was recognized.

King Henry VIII was as ready as his wife to undo, as far as it was possible, the injuries done to Margaret Pole and her family. One of the first acts of his reign was to bestow on her an annuity of £100. In 1512, the King undertook to pay for the education of Margaret's scholar son, Reginald, and on 14 October 1513 he created her a Countess with her deceased brother's secondary title of Salisbury and returned to her all the confiscated lands of the Earldom. At her petition, moreover, the Earl of Warwick's attainder was reversed and the injustice of the attainder fully acknowledged.

On Wednesday, 20 February 1516, Lady Margaret Pole, Countess of Salisbury, took her rightful place among the royal family at the christening of the Princess Mary and shortly afterwards she was appointed Governess to the Princess. Now, indeed, the Duke of Clarence's daughter had returned to Court and a full-blooded Plantagenet exercised power from within the royal household.

For four or five years Margaret Pole was honoured with the King's favour but by 1520 there were ominous signs that the fickle King was turning against her. Henry demanded universal approval and support as he struggled with the Pope for the divorce which would allow him to abandon his queen, Catherine of Aragon, and then to take in her place Anne Boleyn. As a loyal Catholic, Margaret Pole felt herself obliged to resist the royal pretensions and did not hesitate to condemn the King's actions. She was, accordingly, in 1533, summarily dismissed from her post of special responsibility at Court and her charge, the Princess Mary, was sent to Hatfield to serve her half-sister, the infant Elizabeth.

Eustace Chapuys, the Imperial Ambassador in England, reported to the Emperor, Charles V, that the Princess Mary had been removed from her mother and added, 'Her Governess, Lady Salisbury, daughter of the late Duke of Clarence and near kinswoman to the King, a lady of virtue and honour, if there be one in England, has offered to follow and serve her at her own expense, with an honourable train, but it was out of the question that this would be accepted; for in that case they would have no power over the Princess whom it is to be feared they mean to kill, either with grief or otherwise, or make her renounce her right.' (Letter written by Chapuys, 11 February 1544.)

Margaret Pole no longer enjoyed the confidence of King Henry but the King reserved his most bitter hatred for her son Reginald. This young man had returned to England from his studies in Padua in 1527 and had been commissioned by the King to produce a favourable decision on the Divorce question. But the young scholar refused to support the King and used all his erudition and courage to oppose him to his face before fleeing to safety overseas. The fury and frustration of the King knew no bounds as Reginald Pole rapidly established himself as one of the foremost Catholic scholars of Europe, and by 1536 was widely recognized as the Pope's theological champion against the King of England. In that year, Pope Paul III strengthened Pole's authority by creating him a Cardinal of the Church and Henry realized that nothing could be done to silence the powerful voice of the roaring Plantagenet. Cardinal Reginald Pole was beyond the power of the King but the Cardinal's mother and his brothers were still in England and at the King's mercy.

King Henry therefore determined to attack the Cardinal by attacking his family. On 29 August 1538, Sir Geoffrey Pole, the youngest of Margaret's sons and in fact the weakest in character, was arrested on a charge of corresponding with his outlaw brother overseas. In prison in the Tower, Sir Geoffrey was 'interrogated' fifty-nine times and foolishly made wild accusations of high treason against his mother.

Margaret Pole was examined in her house at Warblington by the King's Commissioners, the Earl of Southampton and Thomas Goodrich, Bishop of Ely. She was then removed in custody to the Fitzwilliam house at Cowdrey. In their report to Thomas Cromwell, the Commissioners declared that although they had 'travailled with the Lady of Salisbury all day till almost night, entreating her well both sorts, sometimes with doul and mild words, now roughly and asperly, by accusing her and her sons to the ninth degree of treachery, yet would she utter nothing but maketh herself clear'. Their conclusion was that she knew nothing of any treasonable practices, 'or else she is the most arrant traitress that ever lived'. (Martin Haile, *Life of Reginald Pole*, p. 240.)

Arrested at the same time as Margaret Pole was her eldest son, Henry, Lord Montague. Together, mother and son were condemned to death. Lord Montague was beheaded on Tower Hill on 9 December 1538 and has been widely regarded as a true Catholic Martyr. Margaret Pole's execution was delayed and she mourned her son even as she had mourned the equally cruel deaths of her father and her brother.

When Cardinal Pole heard about these events, he expressed himself in a letter to Cardinal Contarini:

> You have heard, I believe, of my mother being condemned to death by public council, or rather to eternal life. Not only has he who condemned her, condemned a woman of seventy, than whom he has no nearer relation except his daughter, and of whom he used to say that there was no holier woman in his kingdom; but at the same time, her grandson, the son of my brother, a child, the remaining hope of our race. See how this tyranny has grown, which began with priests, in whose order it only consumed the best, then went on to nobles, and there too destroyed the best. At length it has come to women and innocent children. (*Ibid.*, p. 267.)

19

In the spring of 1539, Margaret Pole was removed to the Tower of London where she remained under sentence of death for more than two years. Even Henry VIII hesitated to execute a noble woman of such innocence of life and it was only in 1541 that a suitable opportunity presented itself. In the aftermath of the Yorkshire rebellion in April of that year many of the leaders were put to death. Amid these multiple executions, it was King Henry's hope that the beheading of Margaret Pole would not be noticed. The martyrdom took place on 27 May and the venerable lady was put to death at an hour's notice. Marillac, the French Ambassador, reported to King Francis I that she was beheaded 'yesterday morning before seven o'clock, in a corner of the Tower, in the presence of so few people that till the evening the truth was still doubted'.

Kennet's *England* (vol. II, p. 277) has presented a lurid and disedifying account of the death of Margaret Pole and depicts her in the throes of hysteria, refusing to lay her head on the block and being pursued around the scaffold by the executioner swinging his sword at her. It is unfortunate that this unlikely story has received some credence in subsequent ages. A Plantagenet princess would not behave in such fashion and there is every reason to believe, from other more reliable sources, that Margaret Pole upheld the honour of her house and the dignity of her person as she submitted herself to a cruel and violent death and secured the Crown of a true Martyr for her Faith.

Eustace Chapuys, the Imperial Ambassador, wrote to the Queen Regent of Flanders and his letter is preserved in the Spanish Calendar, (VI, I, 166). He describes how the 'lamentable execution of the Countess of Salisbury' took place:

> at the Tower, in the presence of the Lord Mayor and about 150 persons. When informed of her sentence, she found it very strange, not knowing her crime; but she walked to the place in front of the Tower, where there was no scaffold but only a small block. She there commended her soul to God, and desired those present to pray for the King, Queen, Prince and Princess. The ordinary executioner being absent, a blundering youth, garconneau was chosen, who hacked her head and shoulders almost to pieces...

Cardinal Reginald Pole was at Capranica when he received the information about his mother's death. He read the letter and then told his secretary, Ludovico Beccatelli, who was his biographer and later Archbishop of Ragusa,

> ...the news it contains is good; until now I had thought God had given me the grace of being the son of one of the best and most honoured ladies in England, and I have gloried in it, returning thanks to His Divine Majesty; but now He has vouchsafed to honour me still more, by making me the son of a Martyr. That King, for her constancy in the Catholic Faith, has had her publicly decapitated, thus rewarding her for her many labours in the education of his daughter. (Quoted in Martin Haile, *op. cit.*, p. 282.)

Margaret Pole was unofficially regarded as a Martyr from the time of her death until the late nineteenth century. In 1874, her name was one of the first to be proposed to the Holy See by the English Bishops for more formal recognition in the Calendar of the Saints. On 29 December 1886 she was solemnly beatified by Pope Leo XIII and is now revered by the Church as Blessed Margaret Pole.

MARGARET ROPER

One of the most touching and tender features of the harsh imprisonment of Sir Thomas More was the loving support he received from his eldest daughter, Margaret Roper. 'Meg', as he so affectionately called her, was his favourite child and closest confidante. Throughout her life she enjoyed an amazing rapport with her father and to see him so cruelly treated in the Tower evoked in her a strong sense of indignation and a determination to help him in every way she could.

Sir Thomas was not allowed to have visitors in his cell, but Margaret persuaded his keepers to allow her to visit him regularly. She became the courageous messenger to carry his secret messages back and forth. She brought him the little delicacies and material comforts which did so much to alleviate his suffering. She assured him of the love of his wife, Alice and all his family and all his friends. She kept his mind active and his spirits alive with stimulating conversations and words of hope. And all this she accomplished despite the sad fact that she herself could not share her father's understanding of the cause for which he suffered. Sir Thomas had never imposed his own opinions even on his own family and his dutiful daughter-disciple made no attempt to persuade him now to change his mind. Their differing conclusions implied no loss of confidence or of affection.

Margaret Roper had been born in 1505 to Sir Thomas More and his first wife, Jane Colt. She was said to have resembled her mother in appearance but to have inherited her father's intellect. She was brought up in the academic atmosphere of the More household and met and impressed many of her father's friends who were among the great scholars of the day: Erasmus, Colet, Grocin, Linacre. From an early age, she was coached in the New Learning and was particularly proficient in Greek and Latin. Sir Thomas had very strong views on education and in his domestic school allowed no distinction between boys and girls. In fact of the ten pupils, eight were girls but all were taught the 'boys' subjects of Latin, Greek, Logic, Philosophy, Theology, Mathematics and Astronomy. By about 1529 Margaret and her sisters, Elizabeth and Cecily, were so advanced in their studies that they entertained the King by providing a lively and fluent Latin disputation before the assembled Court. It is not surprising that in Holbein's famous painting of the More family, Margaret is depicted with a copy of Seneca's *Oedipus* on her lap.

Margaret was married to William Roper in 1525 and bore him two sons and three daughters. It was a happy marriage. William had come to live with the Mores in 1518 when he was a student at Lincoln's Inn but was more a man of affairs than a scholar. Harpsfield records (c. 1550) that in 1521 William Roper was a 'marvellous zealous protestant' but could not stand up to the intellectual power and especially the combined prayer of Margaret and her father. He never wavered again and was a strong and active Catholic until his death in 1578.

Sir Thomas More was brought to trial in Westminster Hall on 1 July 1535. There is no evidence that any of his family were present in court but William Roper has left his own eyewitness account of the scenes at the Tower as the condemned man was returned to his cell. Perhaps an unfavourable tide prevented the barge journey to Traitor's Gate; certainly Sir Thomas arrived at Old Swan Steps on Tower Wharf and would have the symbolic axe carried before him. There was no doubt that he had been sentenced to death and as soon as Margaret saw her father,

> after his blessing on her knees reverently received, she hasting towards him, and, without consideration or care of herself, pressing in among the throng and company of the guard that with halberds and bills went round about him, hastily ran to him, and there openly in the sight of them all, embraced him, took him about the neck and kissed him. Who, well liking her most natural and dear daughterly affection towards him, gave her his fatherly blessing and many godly words of comfort besides. From whom after she was departed, she, not satisfied with the former sight of him and like one that had forgotten herself, being all ravished with the entire love of her dear father, having respect neither to herself, nor to the press of the people and multitude that were there about him, suddenly turned back again, ran to him as before, took him about the neck and divers times together most lovingly kissed him, and at last with a very full heart, was fain to depart from him; the beholding whereof was to many of them that were present thereat so lamentable that it made them for very sorrow thereof to mourn and weep. (William Roper, *Life of Sir Thomas More*, Paris (1626), pp. 97–9.)

Once more Sir Thomas was kept in solitary confinement but this time Margaret was unable to gain access. From his death cell, he wrote his last letter to his daughter, 'I never liked your manner toward me better than when you kissed me last for I love when daughterly and dear charity hath no leisure to worldly courtesy. Farewell, my dear child and pray for me, and I shall for you and all your friends that we may merrily meet in heaven.' With this letter, the condemned man sent also his instruments of penance: his hair, shirt and his scourge. (E.F. Rogers (ed.), *Correspondence*, (1947), p. 563.)

Sir Thomas More was beheaded on Tower Hill on 6 July 1535. Margaret Roper was permitted to claim the body and to bury her father in the little chapel of Saint Peter ad Vincula which had just been rebuilt within the Tower. She was not allowed however to have the head which was put on a stake on London Bridge for all to see and deride. A month later, when

Margaret heard that the head was to be thrown away into the river, she bribed the executioner to obtain possession. She carefully preserved throughout her life this precious relic of her father and when she died she left it in her will as a family heirloom to her daughter Elizabeth Bray.

The More family suffered much misfortune as a consequence of Sir Thomas's conviction as a traitor. All his goods and property were confiscated by the King, but William Roper led the family into a series of legal disputes to preserve what little they could of their inheritance. Sadly, there was disagreement within the family. The widow, Lady Alice, strenuously resisted most of William's proposals and Margaret found herself in the unenviable position of peacemaker between her husband and her stepmother. Nor was she free from the attentions of the officers of the Government. Her closeness to her father was well known and she had to spend some time as a prisoner in the Tower where they questioned her very carefully about her father's papers and associates.

All this strain took its toll and affected her health so that when Giles Heron, her sister Cecily's husband, was accused of high treason and hanged, drawn and quartered in company with four priests at Tyburn on 5 August 1540, she was a very sick woman. Worn out by all these family troubles and sorrows she lingered on until just before Christmas 1544 when she died at the age of thirty-eight.

ELIZABETH FISHER

It was a sign of Saint John Fisher's great love for his sister, Elizabeth, that even as he lay in the Tower of London awaiting his Martyr's death, he should think of her and write for her two valuable treatises on the religious life which she herself had espoused as a Dominican nun in the convent at Dartford.

Both these treatises are very significant. They are obviously the work of a saintly and experienced spiritual guide who knows he is writing for someone who is equally dedicated and devoted to that pursuit of God's love for which he was prepared to die. The first treatise was entitled, 'A Spiritual Consolation, written by John Fisher to his sister Elizabeth, at such time as he was a prisoner in the Tower of London', and it begins as follows, 'Sister Elizabeth, nothing doth more help effectually to get a good and virtuous life than if a soul when it is dull and unlusty without devotion, neither disposed to prayer, nor to any other good work, may be stirred or quickened again by fruitful meditation. I have therefore devised unto you this meditation that followeth.' (Quoted from E.E. Reynolds, *Saint John Fisher*, Burns and Oates (1955), p. 247.)

The second treatise, 'The Ways to Perfect Religion', was also written for his sister 'to the health of your soul and the furtherance of it in holy religion'. (Reynolds, *ibid*.)

The existence therefore of this sister Elizabeth is undoubted but it is not easy to trace her exact relationship with Saint John Fisher. Some historians, such as Michael Macklem, are satisfied that Elizabeth was the fourth child and only daughter of Robert and Agnes Fisher of Beverley in East Yorkshire, but other historians such as E.E. Reynolds claim a confusion and maintain that this Elizabeth was married to Edward White and that the Elizabeth who became a nun was in fact the daughter of Agnes Fisher and her second husband, who was also called White. Nevertheless, whatever the relationship, sister or half-sister, she was commonly known in the fashion of the times as John Fisher's sister and all sources are agreed that she was very close to him.

Elizabeth was well established as a Dominican nun in the convent of Dartford when King Henry VIII's edict took effect and all were expelled. By 1539 she was receiving the royal pension for ejected nuns but this did little to help her to adjust her life and make her way in the world she had abandoned so many years before. For almost twenty years she remained faithful to her vocation, in spite of all the dangers and difficulties of living outside her community, and then in 1557 she was able to return to regular

25

observance when Queen Mary and Cardinal Pole restored to the Dominicans their old community house at King's Langley, and the following year Sister Elizabeth and her community were able to take up residence and recommence the practice of their Rule in their own house at Dartford.

Unfortunately, the corporate existence of the Dominican nuns at Dartford did not last very long. Within twelve months of repossessing their house they had to acknowledge the accession of Queen Elizabeth and within another twelve months they were faced with the imposition of the new oath of supremacy which no loyal Catholic could accept. Once more the individual sisters were scattered, but this time Sister Elizabeth and some of her companions felt unable to endure the sufferings of isolation in England and banded themselves together to go into voluntary exile overseas as a living, religious community.

The remnants therefore of the Dominican convent at Dartford crossed the seas in secret and settled as best they could in Antwerp. They had no money and no visible means of support; they were prepared to live on casual alms and the generosity of the local people. But Faith alone was not sufficient and they had to seek hospitality in other convents. In 1560 it was reported that 'the sister of the Bishop of Rochester, now in the island of Zeeland' was 'in a very poor monastery and an unhealthy locality' (Father L.E. Whatmore, Blackfriars, December 1945). Eventually according to Father Robert Bracey OP (Catholic Record Society, vol. 24, p. 176) the English Sisters found refuge in a Bruges convent where they were assimilated and so died out. Nothing more was ever heard about Sister Elizabeth Fisher.

MARY TUDOR

The traditional view of Mary Tudor is that she was a tyrant and a bigot. She is still depicted in many history textbooks as the cruel Catholic Queen, who spent her life wreaking vengeance on innocent Protestants and in popular folklore she is remembered as 'Bloody Mary' who burned countless heretics in the fires of Smithfield. Seldom, indeed, has so much hatred and vituperation surrounded an historical character and the small voice of Catholic indignation and protest has not been able to overcome the myths and exaggerations of John Fox on whose *Book of Martyrs* the whole anti-Mary case is based.

Of course this is not the place to attempt a detailed defence of Mary Tudor but it must be stated that in recent years historians have come to a much more sympathetic understanding of her life and character. Works published by H.F.M. Prescott, Milton Waldman, Jasper Ridley, Carolly Erickson and David Loades depict her in a new light and many scholars today see her as a woman of strength, integrity and determination who suffered misfortunes throughout her life, but who ruled her country wisely as well as she was able, and might well have been remembered as a greater queen than Elizabeth had she surrendered her conscience to Protestant persuasions.

In fact, Mary remained staunchly Catholic throughout her life and in her early days at least prepared herself for martyrdom. When she became Queen she no longer feared the power of those who disagreed with her in religious affairs but her zeal for her own religion drove her to persecute others. In this, she was no different from her immediate predecessors on the throne, and indeed from her immediate successors, and she was behaving as any European monarch of that time would have behaved. To understand, however, is not to condone and to explain is not to attempt a blanket defence, but it is quite unrealistic to expect a twentieth-century appreciation of religious toleration in a sixteenth-century world, where heresy was the ultimate crime because it was judged to kill a man's soul and deprive him of eternal life.

Mary Tudor was born in the Palace of Greenwich on 18 February 1516. She was the only surviving child of King Henry VIII and Queen Catherine of Aragon. The King was disappointed that his only legitimate heir should be a daughter but he treated her well and instigated negotiations for powerful marriage alliances throughout Europe. She was about ten years of age when the King, in the summer of 1525, sent her with her own household to the Welsh Marches and gave her the unofficial title of Princess of Wales. At the same time it was significant of the King's plans for the succession that he sent his natural son, the six-year-old Henry Fitzroy, to the north of England and gave him an even greater household and the title of Duke of Richmond. Henry seemed to prefer the claims of his undoubtedly illegitimate son to the claims of his daughter, whose legitimacy at that time nobody doubted.

Mary returned from Wales in 1528 and resolutely associated herself with her mother in the struggle against the King's plans for a divorce. Neither woman would admit the King's claim to be the Supreme Head of the Church in England and both denied his competence to effect his own divorce. For these attitudes both Queen and Princess suffered. When King Henry went through his form of marriage with Ann Boleyn on 25 January 1533 it was his final rejection of his wife and daughter. If the marriage between King Henry and Catherine of Aragon was in fact null and void then Catherine was no longer Queen and her daughter was debarred from the throne by illegitimacy. Mary and her mother were dismissed from Court and separated. In fact, they were never to meet again in this life because the ailing Catherine died within three years. Mary, on her own and with a diminished household, was known simply as the Lady Mary, and when Ann Boleyn gave birth to King Henry's child, it was the Lady Mary who was appointed to serve her half sister, Princess Elizabeth, in a menial and humiliating capacity.

And yet Mary remained adamant. She continued to call her mother Queen Catherine of England; she ignored the coronation of Ann Boleyn and refused to accord her royal honours; she insisted that she herself be addressed as Princess and refused to answer any who dared call her 'My Lady'. Her uncompromising and forthright attitude upset her father and certainly did not endear her to her new stepmother. It was reported to the Emperor Charles V by his ambassador in London, Eustace Chapuys, that Ann Boleyn was trying to persuade King Henry to execute his own daughter but that this was too much even for King Henry who contented himself by applying such moral pressures as he could muster.

In her loneliness, Mary turned more and more towards her mother's family and especially to her powerful first cousin, the Emperor Charles V. She called him her 'only true friend' and gave him quasi-parental powers by promising not to marry without his consent. The Emperor in his turn was motivated as much by political considerations as by family love, but he was concerned to protect Mary's rights and through his ambassador he tried to afford her every protection.

In January 1535, Charles believed Mary to be in such danger that he began planning a method of escape for her, and Chapuys was instructed to take charge of detail. An intricate scheme was concocted in which Mary would be carried away on horseback from a recreational walk and then rowed out to sea in a small insignificant boat to a waiting ship which would deliver her safe and sound to the Emperor. It was a scheme riddled with risks and hardly likely to succeed, especially since Mary's health was not good and all lines of communication were strained. Eventually wiser notions prevailed and within a month the plan was aborted.

It seems likely that this prolonged period of stress and danger inflicted lasting psychological damage on Mary. She was, after all, only in her late teens for most of this time, and just turned twenty when her father again demonstrated his cruel powers and terrifying inhumanity by executing his beloved Anne Boleyn on 19 May 1536, and marrying Jane Seymour on the next day. Mary was strongly advised by both Thomas Cromwell and Eustace Chapuys that she must make some gesture in order to save her own life and, accordingly, against her better judgment, she accepted the draft of a grovelling letter of submission prepared for her and sent it, duly signed and sealed, to the King.

It has been suggested that when Mary signed this letter she was so panic-stricken that she signed it without having read it. Certainly, she surprised everyone by her abject surrender. She acknowledged the invalidity of her mother's marriage and thereby admitted her own illegitimacy. She renounced the Pope and professed her belief in the ecclesiastical supremacy of the King. She had given in on all those points of doctrine which might have made her a Martyr. Of course, unbeknown to the King she had made all her statements with mental reservations to preserve her Roman orthodoxy and had also written urgently to the Pope begging for immediate absolution to ease her burdened conscience. But as far as King Henry was concerned, Mary was once more restored to favour as a daughter and was well treated for the rest of the reign.

When King Henry VIII died on 28 January 1547, Mary had no difficulty in recognizing his son, Edward V1, as the legitimate heir and continued to live quietly in the Queen Dowager's household. By the summer of that year, however, the Protestant forces were already working upon the young and sickly King and the traditional practices of religion were coming under attack. A report of 16 June 1547 from Van der Delft in London to the Emperor Charles V commented specifically on Mary's adherence to the ancient faith and mentioned that she was hearing as many as four Masses every day.

The Protestants on the King's Council realized that they were on a collision course with Mary, the King's half-sister and his heir.

Henry VIII's schismatical Church was lead further into heresy and Catholic loyalists looked to Mary as their champion. She did not disappoint them. Parliament banned the Mass by an Act of Uniformity in 1549 but when the new prohibition came into force on Whit Sunday, Mary had her Mass celebrated with special pomp and ceremony in her chapel at Kenninghall. The Council remonstrated with her and she defied them. Privately supported by her brother, the King, Mary kept her Mass and constantly proclaimed by her actions that she was a convinced Catholic.

On 17 March 1551, she was summoned once more to London to explain herself to the Council. Her entry into the capital was a triumph. She was preceded in her procession by fifty knights on horseback and in her train were eighty ladies and gentlemen from East Anglia. Hundreds of Londoners ran out to greet her and noticed with awe that all the members of her household and her entourage were wearing rosary beads around their necks in that most conspicuous fashion that the young Catherine of Aragon had first brought with her in those distant days when all England was Catholic.

And so this running battle between Mary and the Council continued. She was allowed a private Mass; she made it as public as possible; in so doing, she risked her life but she won the plaudits and respect of Catholic Europe. Only the diehard Protestants of the English Government hated her and despised her, but they also feared her because they knew that she was the lawful heir to the throne.

King Edward VI ended his sad, consumptive life on 6 July 1553 in the sixteenth year of his age. In his later years he had become as convinced a Protestant as Mary was a Catholic and therefore willingly succumbed to the Duke of Northumberland's machinations to alter the succession in favour of his daughter-in-law, Lady Jane Grey, who was innocent, learned and a dedicated Protestant.

Mary at once showed her mettle. She had herself proclaimed Queen in Norwich on 13 July and marched on London to claim her throne. She was received with acclamation and accepted warmly by the general populace. She was crowned in Westminster Abbey on 1 October and applied herself immediately to what she considered to be her sacred task: the restoration of England to the Holy See.

As Queen, Mary made some grave errors of judgement. Her Spanish marriage was universally unpopular and her over-dependence on the Emperor Charles V was resented in England. The loss of Calais was regarded as a national disaster and Mary was held responsible. But on the whole, Mary governed her kingdom with wisdom and justice and Carolly Erickson has paid the following tribute to her ability: 'Visitors to Mary's Court found her intelligence and competence impressive and judged her to be "more than moderately read in Latin literature, especially with regard to Holy Writ". To ambassadors she spoke Latin, French and Spanish; she understood Italian, though she did not speak it, and displayed a quickness of mind and an eloquence of expression which left no doubt of her capacity to rule.' (C. Erickson, *Bloody Queen Mary*, (1978), p. 305.)

Mary's major concern, however, in government as in life was to repair the damage done to the Church by her schismatical father and her heretical brother. In this work she succeeded admirably by persuasion and example rather than by coercion and bullying. On 29 November 1554, a petition for England to be received once more into the Universal Church was passed by Parliament. In the Commons there were two votes against; in the Lords none. Next day, Saint Andrew's Day, the King and Queen and the members of both Houses humbled themselves before the Papal Legate, Cardinal Reginald Pole, and on their knees begged forgiveness from the Pope for themselves and all their compatriots. Mary's mission, it would seem, had been completed and not one heretic had been consigned to the flames. At Cardinal Pole's first synod in England it was decreed that the feast of Saint Andrew, on 30 November, should 'be for ever kept as a day of rejoicing, with processions and prayers to celebrate the Reconciliation of the Realm with the Catholic Church'. Alas, this celebration could only be observed for the next three years. Mary died on 17 November 1558 and the Church she had restored so laboriously collapsed at the same time.

If only Mary had had a Catholic heir, the future would have been so different and Catholicism could have prospered. Mary had accomplished much but the five short years of her reign were insufficient to achieve a deep and lasting transformation. If only she had had more time. If only she had had a child to succeed her. If only Mary Stuart's right to the throne had been respected. If only Elizabeth had been a Catholic. But all such empty hopes have no place in reality and from the Catholic point of view Elizabeth destroyed what Mary had built.

And yet Mary exercised a profound influence on succeeding generations of Catholics. Her courage, determination and constancy in resisting the religious demands of the King, her father and the King, her brother were noted and admired, and served to strengthen the Faith of some who might otherwise have wavered. Nor did her undoubted piety and devotion to the Holy See escape the attention of her many Catholic supporters, who recognized in her a holiness and fidelity which they sought to emulate. Queen Mary's bishops, Queen Mary's priests and Queen Mary herself all made major contributions to the defence of the Catholic Faith and the value of their work demands more investigation and better appreciation.

MARGARET CLEMENT (GIGGS)

The daughter of a Norfolk gentleman, Margaret Giggs was orphaned at a very early age and unofficially adopted by Sir Thomas More, who educated her with his own daughters and welcomed her into his family.

As a scholar, Margaret Giggs was as brilliant as that other Margaret, who became Margaret Roper, and being of the same age the girls became close friends and keen rivals. Having mastered Latin and Greek, Margaret Giggs proceeded to the study of medicine and achieved such success that Sir Thomas More made reference to her in his Dialogue of Comfort as 'the young girl, very wise and well learned and very virtuous too' who diagnosed Anthony's fever by reference to the works of Galen.

In 1526, Margaret Giggs married Doctor John Clement who had been her first tutor in the More household school but who was now one of the foremost medical doctors of his day, personal physician to Cardinal Wolsey and consultant for the King.

Sir Thomas More had a special affection for Margaret Clement and recognized the extraordinary spirit of charity which motivated her. They shared a deep concern for the poor and Father Thomas Stapleton has described in 'Tres Thomae' (1588) how Sir Thomas used to go 'into the dark courts and visit the families of the poor, helping them not with small gifts but with two, three or four pieces of gold' and that in this work he enlisted the willing services of Margaret Clement who often took his place when he was busy upon other affairs.

Margaret Clement was with her best-loved friend Margaret Roper when the two ladies bade farewell to Sir Thomas More after his condemnation, and she too received the doomed man's blessing. From his prison cell, Sir Thomas returned to 'my good daughter Clement' the algorism stone which he had borrowed from her and sent to her 'and my godson and her husband and all hers, God's blessing and mine'. She was privileged to be the only member of the More household present at Sir Thomas's execution on Tower Hill and again she was with Margaret Roper to help with the burial arrangements for the Martyr in the church of Saint Peter ad Vinculum.

All these are potent signs of a very special relationship between Margaret Clement and Sir Thomas More but her services to Saint Thomas were as nothing compared to the amazing efforts she made to help the ten Carthusian monks who were imprisoned in Newgate and deliberately starved to death by their gaolers. The facts of this sordid but heroic affair have been preserved in the 'Chronicle of Saint Monica's Convent, Louvain' and are quoted by Father John Morris SJ in his *The Troubles of our Catholic*

Forefathers (1872), but the basis is the account given by Margaret Clement herself to her daughter, that other Margaret Clement, who was the Prioress of Saint Ursula's Convent in Louvain and lived in exile as an Augustinian nun for more than fifty years.

The monks of the London Charterhouse were among the first to refuse the Oath of Supremacy which King Henry VIII sought to impose on all his people. By 18 May 1537 eight Carthusians had already been executed, but on that particular day the King's Commissioners again visited the monastery for what they planned to be the last time. Twenty of the brethren were forced to surrender; but ten still resisted and these ten were sent in chains to Newgate prison. Here, according to Margaret Clement's account, they were confined to one cell and, still chained together, 'they were not able to stir nor to help themselves'. Deprived of food they were deliberately killed by 'slow starvation combined with the stench and misery of their dungeon'.

It was to these monks in their extreme of suffering that Margaret Clement brought succour. Having bribed the gaoler, she disguised herself as a milkmaid, 'with a great pail upon her head full of meat, wherewith she fed that blessed company, putting meat into their mouths, they being tied and not able to stir, nor to help themselves, which having done, she afterwards took from them their natural filth.'

This great work of charity the courageous woman continued for several days but the King grew impatient that the monks were taking so long to die and demanded that a closer watch be kept over them. This so frightened the gaoler that he refused to allow Margaret Clement any further access to the prisoners. Nevertheless by force of pleading as much as by force of money, the keeper did allow her to climb on to the roof of the prison where she removed some tiles to form an aperture through which she could pass her basket. Unfortunately, the prisoners could not feed themselves and Margaret Clement's further efforts were all in vain. One by one the monks died and all are now revered by the Church as Blessed Martyrs.

Margaret Clement and her husband and family continued to live in England for several years and endured all the perils of those difficult times. But by 1549, with King Henry dead and his Protestant son, Edward VI, leading the country from schism to heresy they could no longer endure the religious conditions and set out for the Low Countries as voluntary exiles. At first, they stayed in Bruges but then moved on to Malines and were one of the first Catholic families to settle permanently on the Continent as refugees.

At Malines, both John Clement and Margaret acquired a reputation for holy living. They frequented the services and the Masses at the Cathedral and welcomed to their home as honoured guests the many impoverished English priests who needed material sustenance and spiritual comfort.

Eventually, in 1570, Margaret Clement was taken seriously ill and her husband, the doctor, recognized the signs of approaching death. She received all the sacraments with great devotion and then summoned all her children to her deathbed for her last blessing. But one daughter was delayed and could not come immediately. Margaret called her husband and told him that she could not wait any longer because the monks of the

Charterhouse were standing around her bed and calling her to join them in heaven. And so she died. And who could doubt that she was carried to heaven by the Fathers of the London Charterhouse who owed her so much on earth.

ELIZABETH WOODFORD

Elizabeth Woodford is a very significant link between the old religious life of pre-Reformation England and the later religious life of the exiled English nuns in continental convents, and in her personal life, she emphasizes most clearly the unbroken continuity of her manner of fulfilling her vocation, first in the ancient convent of the Augustinians at Burnham in Buckinghamshire and then in the more recent foundation of Saint Ursula's in Louvain.

Elizabeth Woodford was born probably about 1498 and was the daughter of Sir Robert Woodford and Alice, his wife, who lived at Brightwell Hall in Buckinghamshire. The child was probably educated at the local convent of Burnham Abbey as was the custom of the times and in 1519 became a nun herself when she was professed on the feast of Our Lady's Conception, 8 December. For twenty years, she lived her quiet, religious life of piety and devotion and never suspected that the day might come when she would be rudely ejected back into the world she had so firmly renounced.

The sisters were all alarmed in 1536 when the Royal Commissioners came to inspect the abbey but the old Abbess, Margaret Gibson, obtained a respite for her house by signing a deed recognizing the King's prerogative. This act of weakness troubled her so much that she resigned and Alice Baldwin succeeded her as Abbess in that same year.

Three years later, on 19 September 1539, Abbess Baldwin surrendered her abbey to the King and she and nine other nuns were expelled to seek a living as best they could. The Report of the King's Visitors declared very clearly that no charge could be brought against the lives of the Sisters and that all desired to go into other religious houses if any other religious house could be found.

Elizabeth Woodford was more fortunate than most of her sisters. Like them she received a pitifully small pension from the King but her old home was not far away and she was able to stay with her brother, Sir Thomas Woodford, at Brightwell Hall until such time as she could find a more suitable residence and occupation.

C.S. Durrant has suggested in *A Link between the Flemish Mystics and the English Martyrs* (p. 178) that Elizabeth Woodford might not have found it easy to maintain the spirit of her vocation in her childhood home surrounded by members of her own family. Certainly her time at home seems to have been very short and she went to live with the family of Dr Clement at Marshfoot in Essex, and again C.S. Durrant suggests she may have helped with the education of his eleven children.

This Dr Clement, of course, was the learned medical doctor who was so close to Saint Thomas More and who married Margaret Giggs from the More household. With this family, Elizabeth Woodford was able to live out her vocation in privacy and for almost ten years she continued the struggle to fulfill her monastic obligations despite the distractions of domestic affairs and the ever-present dangers of the outside world.

In 1547, with the death of King Henry VIII and the accession of his son, King Edward VI, Dr John Clement decided that the time had come to escape from the dangers of England and he took his whole family into exile in Flanders. Elizabeth Woodford moved with the family, first to Bruges and then to Louvain, where she found a convent of her own Order and immediately applied for admission.

The 'Chronicle of Saint Monica's Convent, Louvain' states,

> In the year of Our Lord, 1548, under the reign of King Edward the Sixth of that name, religious houses being put down, and religious persons, both men and women, thrust out to lead their lives in great danger of the world, and the face of the Church of England turned to heresy, Elizabeth Woodford, leaving her native soil, who before had left the world by religious profession, came into Brabant, and offering herself to the Monastery of Saint Ursula's in Louvain, of the same Order of Saint Augustine that she was of, there to end her life in religious observance as she had vowed, was graciously received.

It cannot have been easy for Elizabeth Woodford to return to her religious observance after a break of almost ten years and in such a different environment. She was now about fifty years of age. She was for some time the only Englishwoman in the community. She knew only a few words of Flemish and the Canonesses of Saint Augustine knew no English. The Convent was very poor; food was in short supply and prepared in the Dutch manner; manual labour was extremely hard; prayers were unfamiliar and silences prolonged and very strict. All in all, it was a particular type of heroism for the English nun to adapt herself to her new surroundings, but she did adapt and she prepared the way for many of her countrywomen to follow her.

Perhaps Elizabeth Woodford's most important 'follower' was Margaret Clement, the youngest child of Dr John Clement and Margaret Clement, his wife. In 1548, when Elizabeth Woodford entered Saint Ursula's Convent, little Margaret Clement was with her sisters in the school. Later she was professed as a nun and in due time became Prioress and then a founding member of the new English Convent of Saint Monica's. In writing her biography, Sister Elizabeth Shirley points out that as a schoolgirl Margaret Clement had her problems, for Sister Elizabeth Woodford 'being the chiefest cause that her parents placed her in this monastery, though she was not her mistress, yet she did exercise her after the sharp manner which had been in England in the bringing up of youth'. And in quoting this passage, C.S. Durrant recalls 'Lady Jane Grey's complaints of "the pinches, nips and bobs" she received from her "sharp and severe parents" who required her to do

36

all "in such weight, measure and number even as perfectly as God made the world".'

Elizabeth Woodford had a profound effect on the religious education of Margaret Clement. The old nun was severe but she gave the young sister the benefit of her experience of English observance and if at times that involved a certain severity, Margaret Clement was not one to bear grudges and Sister Elizabeth Shirley insists without hesitation that 'she loved the old English nun.'

Elizabeth Woodford lived in community at Saint Ursula's for twenty-five years. She was held in high esteem by the Dutch sisters and as more and more Englishwomen joined the Convent, she would probably give them details of her life as a nun in their own country. It is likely therefore that some of the terms and customs still practiced in modern convents owe their origins to Saint Ursula's and have thus been handed down from pre-Reformation England.

Sister Elizabeth Woodford died on 25 October 1573. Even in her obituary notice she is described as 'the old nun'; she must have passed her seventieth year. The obituary pays her two special compliments. It says, 'She was a substantial woman and a strict observer of religion, although somewhat severe, as they used in old times to be towards youth in England.' The obituary also says, 'She was of so good a judgement, that the Prioress of Saint Ursula's would often ask her counsel and follow her advice in matters of moment.' Certainly the observance and fidelity of this old nun of Burnham Abbey were sources of encouragement and inspiration to all those Englishwomen who had no experience of the tranquility of pre-Reformation monasticism but who learned from her amid all the terrors of persecution and found for themselves havens of refuge in the convents of foreign lands.

Anne Foster

In her biography of Saint Margaret Clitherow, Mary Claridge has quoted from the 'Chronicles of the Canonesses of Saint Augustine at Saint Monica's in Louvain' (vol. 1, p. 168) to show that Mrs Anne Foster was one of the friends and active associates of the Saint in York in the 1570s and that in the late autumn of 1577 she was arrested with two of her daughters, Anne and Frances, and put in prison on the Ouse Bridge.

Mrs Foster did not live long in prison. The 'Chronicle' reports that she died within twelve months 'from the divers infirmities occasioned by her prison'. Her death, however, caused more trouble to the authorities than she had ever been able to cause during her life. When the Anglican minister came to arrange for her burial, he found to his amazement that she was clutching in her lifeless hands a document in which she formally professed her Catholic Faith, demanded Catholic burial, and resolutely refused any religious service from any Anglican minister.

All this, of course, posed very serious problems about her burial. The only graveyards were attached to churches, all of which were now Anglican. No Catholic priest would dare to appear in public and he would certainly never be allowed to openly conduct a burial service in a city like York. Nor for that matter, was it now possible for the Anglican minister to bury the lady. By her act of Catholic Faith she had excommunicated herself from the Church of England and could not therefore be buried in Anglican consecrated ground.

The whole situation was infuriating for the Anglican ministers and they smarted under what they regarded as a gross insult. 'It is almost incredible how they chafed at it' remarks the 'Chronicle',

> but especially the minister, who put the whole city in an uproar, and also complained to the Queen's Council and to the Earl of Huntingdon... He complained also to the Archbishop and the Dean and Chapter, and not only so, but most unhumanly caused the dead corpse to be brought out of prison and laid openly on the bridge in the common street for all the world to gaze and wonder at. In the mean season, the President and Council, Archbishop and Chapter, were assembled about the bold and traitorous act, as they termed it, of writing her last will.

Immediately Anne's husband, John Foster, was summoned and they attempted to blame him for 'this heinous trespass of his wife'. But John

Foster had had some legal training. It would seem in fact that he was the city coroner. He insisted that he had not offended Her Majesty in anything, and that he was not there when his wife died. Nor, said he, was there anything else he could say in this matter.

The assembly was not satisfied. Some said she should be buried in a dunghill; others wanted her thrown into the river from the bridge on which she still lay. Reason seemed to have deserted the gathering and hatred was taking its place.

> Mr Foster besought their honours to consider that she was but a woman, and being now dead, never could offend them anymore; whereat the Council was discontented, and asked him how he durst entreat for such a papist, and began to call him in question for his conscience, affirming that they knew well enough what he was, and would then have committed him, if some commissioners on the bench had not favoured him. Notwithstanding all this, he replied thus: that whatever she was, she was his wife, and he bound by the law of God to love, honour and protect her, and this being the last and least thing he could do for her, he humbly besought them to give him leave to bury her; which request by friends present was at last agreed to in this manner, that he might take her out of the minister's power and bury her where he would, without any other solemnity than only to put her in the grave.

Mr Foster had won his case and proceeded to make sure that his wife received decent and honourable burial. He made his arrangements in complete secrecy but very obviously used his connections to enlist the support of unlikely friends in Anglican circles. Knowing 'very well the great love and devotion she had to the Earl of Northumberland, who was martyred in York and buried in Holy Cross Church', Mr Foster opened the Earl's grave and 'without any hindrance laid his wife's body with that Blessed Martyr's relics'.

CECILY STONOR

In 1581, the activities of Government spies and agents in London intensified so much that the very existence of the Jesuit mission was threatened and it became increasingly evident that a strategic withdrawal from the city was the only wise course of action. Of special concern to the missionaries, however, was the printing press which they had hidden at Mr Brinkley's house at East Ham and which they were using regularly for the production of Catholic books and papers. In fact, at that very moment the printers were awaiting the final proofs of Father Edmund Campion's book *Decem Rationes*, or his ten reasons to justify his Catholic Faith.

In these circumstances the Fathers searched anxiously for some place of seclusion and safety outside London and their earnest endeavours were rewarded when one of their active lay supporters, John Stonor, offered them the use of his ancestral home at Stonor in Oxfordshire.

Stonor was a large, empty manor house. It was situated forty miles away from the persistent dangers of London and was well hidden in the middle of extensive woodlands in an isolated hollow of the Chiltern Hills. A primitive printing press could rattle away there for months and never be heard by hostile ears, and over and above all that Stonor was the centre of a district where most of the people had preserved their loyalty to the Catholic Church and were prepared to practice a specially robust recusancy.

The owner of this house was Lady Cecily Stonor, the widow of Sir Francis Stonor. She had been born about the year 1520 and was a daughter of Sir Leonard Chamberlayne of Shirburn Castle, only a few miles from Stonor. Her father's family were staunch Catholics, and all her life Cecily remembered with pride that she was a niece of the Carthusian monk, Blessed Sebastian Newdigate, who had been martyred at Tyburn in 1535 when she was about fifteen years of age. Nor was that her only connection with the Martyrs because she had been living in Oxfordshire during the Catholic Rising of 1549 and had known, at first hand, about the many priests subsequently hanged from their own steeples.

It was therefore a union of two Catholic families when Cecily Chamberlayne married Francis Stonor in 1552. The marriage took place at a time of religious quiet. The young and unfortunate King Edward VI was dying and within twelve months the Catholic Queen Mary had come to the throne. The Stonors were able to live in peace at Stonor and educate their children in the traditions of their Catholic forefathers.

Sir Francis Stonor died in 1570 and his widow and her teenage children moved to a smaller house at Stonor Lodge in the village. Here, despite the persecutions of Queen Elizabeth, Lady Cecily Stonor continued to practice her Faith and protect her priests. She had a Marian priest, Father William Morris, as her resident chaplain and she allowed a seminary priest, Father William Hartley, to use her house as a base for his missionary work in the Thames Valley. Henry Clifford, who knew her personally, has written that she was 'generally noted for her rare devotion and marvellous abstinence' but the calibre of the lady is perhaps better illustrated by her words when she appeared before the Justices at Oxford and told them very plainly,

> I was born in such a time when Holy Mass was in great reverence and was brought up in the same faith. In King Edward's time this reverence was neglected and reproved by such as governed. In Queen Mary's, it was restored with much applause, and now in this time it pleaseth the state to question them, as now they do me, who continue in this Catholic profession. The State would have the several changes which I have seen with mine eyes, good and laudable. Whether it can be so I refer to your Lordships' consideration. I hold me still to that wherein I was born and bred, and find nothing taught in it but great virtue and sanctity, and so by the grace of God I will live and die in it. (Quoted by Father Robert Julian Stonor OSB in his book *Stonor*, (1951), p. 259.)

This was the Catholic lady who welcomed Father Edmund Campion SJ and Father Robert Persons SJ and their companions to Stonor in 1581. She knew what she was doing and she was fully aware of the risks she was taking in harbouring priests and permitting them to operate a printing press on her premises. Nevertheless, this elderly lady, already in her sixties, did not hesitate to commit herself and her fortunes to what she recognized as a task of paramount importance: the publication of Father Campion's masterpiece, the *Decem Rationes*.

It was no mean feat for the printers to convey the heavy printing press from London to Stonor and to accomplish the journey unobserved by spies. And yet they succeeded. The master printer, Stephen Brinkley, rode ahead and the artisan printers disguised themselves as gentlemen and applied themselves as best they could to the unfamiliar exercise of riding. Each carried a piece of the printing press and despite the awkward shapes and heavy weights managed to keep it out of sight so that all arrived at Stonor undetected.

Father Robert Julian Stonor has described the place where the press was reassembled. He has accepted the old family tradition that the printing room was in the attic in that part of the house known as Mount Pleasant. Here there is a large room above the Minstrels' gallery at the west end of the Great Hall.

> From the back of the room a concealed door leads into another small room, in the far corner of which a triangular piece of partition can be drawn inwards low down in the wall, making a hole through which a man of average size can just creep. From the other side of this aperture a ladder leads up into the central gable of the roof, whence it is possible

to reach any point in the immense attics which run the entire length of the buildings and from which, owing to the house being built on the slope of the hill, it is possible to escape into the woods at the back of the house. (*Stonor*, p. 246.)

For more than three months the printers laboured on Father Campion's book and by the end of June, four hundred copies were ready for distribution. It was a work of great erudition, written in Latin and addressed principally to his old friends and admirers in the University of Oxford. Father William Hartley, a former Fellow of St John's College, Oxford and a recently ordained seminary priest from Douai, now joined the group at Stonor and it was this intrepid young priest and future Martyr who sneaked into Oxford one dark night to hand over some of the books to Campion 's friends and to leave others in St Mary's Church for any graduates or undergraduates who might wish to take one.

The effects of Saint Edmund Campion's book were far-reaching and profound. Scholars and members of the University were impressed with his audacity in publishing such a work, and copies were passed from hand to hand. He was, of course still remembered as the most accomplished scholar of his day and the clarity and profundity of his thought and the beauty of his language in this new book excited much academic admiration and led many readers to a deepening appreciation of Catholic truth and practice. The University was shocked and impressed; the Government was shocked and horrified and all the more determined that this dangerous Campion must be captured as soon as possible.

On 11 July Father Campion and Father Persons decided that they could no longer endanger Lady Stonor's life by staying at Stonor and they took their permanent leave. The book was published, Lady Stonor had played her full part, the departure of the priests might at least divert attention away from Stonor.

The subsequent fate of Father Campion is well known. For some unknown reason, instead of moving away as quickly as possible from the Thames Valley, he moved southwards to Lyford Grange in Berkshire where Mrs Yates had given hospitality to a group of Bridgittine nuns who were seeking to perpetuate King Henry V's royal foundation of Syon Abbey. Father Campion said Mass and preached for the household and the nuns but a traitor was present in the congregation and reported his presence to the local magistrates. For several days, the priest played an incredible game of hide and seek in that moated manor house with its secret hiding places, but eventually he was caught and by 22 July was a close prisoner in the Tower of London. Saint Edmund Campion was martyred on 1 December 1581 and canonized as one of the Forty Martyrs on 25 October 1970.

The aftermath of Father Campion's arrest was a not-unexpected attack on Stonor. On 4 August the Privy Council wrote to Sir Henry Neville ordering him 'to search Lady Stonor's house for copies of the latin books, which Campion has confessed to have been printed there in a wood, and for other books of Persons, and the press thought also to be there remaining, and to examine such persons as they shall find in the house as to what Masses have been said there, what reconciliations used, and of their conformity in religion.'

In his memoirs, Father Robert Persons SJ has recorded that 'the house at Stonor was surrounded by Neville and his agents, and all those who had worked at the press were arrested on the spot – indeed they were at that time busy in printing another Catholic work. From this house at Stonor, Sir Henry Neville hastened to that where Lady Stonor dwelt, and there John Stonor, the son of the widow, was taken on the charge of having received a priest into his house and was put with the prisoners.' Altogether thirty-two persons were arrested but surprisingly Cecily Stonor was not among them.

Perhaps Lady Stonor's apparent immunity from arrest deserves some explanation. The blunt fact seems to be that she was the head of the most powerful family in Oxfordshire and nobody in the district or the county would wish to tangle with the Stonors. Everybody in the county knew that she was a practising Catholic but they also knew the power of her family and the power of her friends. And it did not escape general notice that her eldest son Francis was a personal friend of William Cecil.

Father Robert Julian Stonor is of the opinion that she was treated so leniently because this son, Francis, had conformed to the Established Church and because the influence of William Cecil was paramount in the Privy Council where the Stonors also enjoyed the patronage of their old family friend, Sir Francis Knollys. But it should also be remembered as he has pointed out that 'she was in very poor health and bore a name which was much loved at Court and which might be expected to have much influence on others in Oxford and its shire if she could be induced to recant.' (*Stonor*, p. 257.)

Lady Cecily Stonor was not arrested as a result of this raid of August 1581 but she did not escape unpunished. Sir Henry Neville handed her over to the custody of her son Francis at Blounts Court, and by order of the Privy Council dated 5 September, all her estates were confiscated and their administration granted to Francis. In fact, Lady Cecily was a prisoner in her son's house and he was ordered to ensure that she did not leave this house 'nor admit the resort of any other than of her ordinary servants, until Her Majesty's further pleasure shall be signified unto her'.

By November, the Privy Council seemed to have reached the conclusion that their policy was succeeding and that Lady Stonor was beginning to cooperate. Accordingly, they allowed her to return to Stonor and make her residence once more in her ancestral home. Indeed, the Councillors were so bold as to suggest to Sir Henry Neville that 'their Lordship's think meet they do appoint the parson of Henley or some other learned man to resort unto her from time to time to teach and instruct her in God's truth and thereby reduce her to conformity.' The parson of Henley must have been a very brave man or very foolish, if indeed he made this attempt. He certainly had no effect on Lady Cecily.

Nevertheless, the lady was in poor health and on 25 April 1582 the Privy Council gave her special permission to leave Stonor for two months and take the waters at Bath. Of course she had to pay for this privilege and this charge was in addition to her annual fine of £500 which she had been paying since 1577. Francis was reminded that he was responsible for his mother's behaviour and told peremptorily to watch her company and make sure 'that none be admitted that are corrupt in religion etc.' and that even her physician 'shall be of good religion and not apt to confirm her in her obstinacy by conference'.

Lady Stonor's continuance in the Faith was attested in 1584 when it was reported to the Government that her manservant had been found with other papists in a house in St Mary Overy's at Southwark and there is further evidence from Father Anthony Sherlock's confession to the Privy Council in 1606 that on first coming into England in 1586 he 'grew into acquaintance first with one lady Stonor near Henley-upon-Thames and continued there for the most part of three or four years, saying Mass in her house many times'.

Meanwhile her younger son, John, had escaped to the Continent. An entry in the Douai Diary for 10 February 1583 states, 'This day has come to us from Paris the noble Mr John Stonor, who because he was in charge of the printing of certain Catholic books, which he had printed in the house of that most noble lady, his mother, and because he greatly helped the Catholics both by circulating these books and by other works of zeal, has endured long hardships of imprisonment in the Tower of London.' Lady Cecily never saw this son again; he remained in exile for the rest of her life.

By 1590, to the great joy of his mother, Francis Stonor was reconciled to the Catholic Church. Perhaps he had always been a Church Papist while his wife Martha Southcote, the daughter of Judge John Southcote of Devonshire, openly proclaimed her Catholic Faith. On 28 February 1590, Francis was arrested and brought before the Privy Council as a recalcitrant Catholic but what transpired has not been recorded. What is known is that in 1591 he was having to pay the Government £30 a year for his own recusancy and a further £60 a year for his mother's recusancy.

At last, in 1592, Lady Cecily Stonor was committed to prison. Among the Cecil papers quoted by Father Stonor there is a list dated 1592 which gives the names of all those recusants in Oxfordshire who were at liberty, those who were kept upon bond and those who were in prison (Calendar of Cecil MSS, Part III). Lady Stonor is placed in the third category. By this time she was over seventy years of age and had been ill for many years. It is unlikely that she could long survive the horrors of an Elizabethan prison. It is therefore commonly accepted that this great heroine for the Faith died in prison about the year 1592.

MARGARET WEBSTER

Margaret Webster was the mother of a devout Catholic family in the West Riding of Yorkshire and for several years in the early 1580s her house was a Mass centre and place of refuge for the travelling priests of the county. Misfortune, however, came to the family unexpectedly when Margaret's husband engaged himself in an acrimonious dispute over the ownership of a piece of land, which had formerly belonged to Pontefract Abbey but which was now claimed by the Websters and by their immediate neighbours, the Withams. In fact, the head of the Witham family was known to be 'a hot Protestant' and he was so determined to win his case that he threatened to denounce the Websters to the authorities, for harbouring priests, unless they submitted to his demands.

The response of the Websters was totally unexpected. Both Mr Webster and his son, Arthur, renounced their Faith and then, safe from Mr Witham's deplorable attack, launched themselves into further infamy by seeking a commission for Arthur Webster as a pursuivant so that he could at once proceed against two members of the Witham family who were Catholics.

It was all a very sordid affair of greed and treachery and a childish tit for tat but much worse was to come. Mr Witham pointed out to Arthur Webster that in virtue of the commission by which he had arrested the two Withams, so was he bound now by the same commission to arrest the members of his own family who had remained Catholic, and that included his mother, Margaret Webster and his sister, Frances.

By this time, Arthur Webster had lost all control of his finer feelings and to the horror of his contemporaries, Catholic and Protestant alike, now took it on himself to apprehend his mother and his sister and have them taken to York as close-prisoners for the very Faith which he had so recently shared.

At first, Margaret Webster was in York Castle on her own and separated from her daughter but later they were allowed to come together, and anxious to make reparation for the infidelity and malice of the other members of their family, they devoted themselves to the service of the other prisoners. Nothing was too much or too humble for Margaret Webster to undertake in her efforts to help her fellow Catholics and she applied herself so wholeheartedly and so enthusiastically to her labours that she over-taxed her strength. Overwhelmed by her labours and sufferings, she died peacefully, still in York Castle, on 27 May 1585.

FRANCES WEBSTER

Frances Webster was the daughter of the valiant Margaret Webster, whose story has already been related. Betrayed and captured by her own brother, Frances was taken to York as a prisoner for her Catholic beliefs, and on arrival in that city was separated from her mother and placed in solitary confinement in Peter Prison, the Archbishop's special ecclesiastical prison, close to the Minster.

Frances, it would seem, was a very young woman. She might have been in her early twenties, she might have been younger. But whatever her age, she was a most extraordinary person of outstanding holiness and an amazing strength of character. An unknown author, writing probably in the 1590s, likens her to Saint Barbara and describes how in prison, 'she showed herself most constant, a bold confessor of Christ's Catholic doctrine, fervent, zealous, devout, patient, quiet, charitable, never ceasing to work good works with all her power'. (Paper III in Father Christopher Grene's Collection F.)

It is also related in this particular paper how Frances discovered that 'in a deep and darksome dungeon, underneath her own cell', a missionary priest, Father John Fingley, was being held in the most appalling conditions and how she managed to make a little opening to let some light and air reach him. 'But, O God,' exclaims the author of this paper, 'How lightsome and how joyful a heart had he, when he beheld her constancy, when he considered her purity, when he heard her comforting words proceeding from a chosen vessel of the Holy Ghost, when he felt also her true charity.'

It is not difficult to appreciate the effect which the very presence of Frances Webster had on Father Fingley in his isolation. She brought him the reminder that other people were concerned about him; she assured him that he was not forgotten; she restored his self-respect and honoured him as so many other Catholics would wish to do. In the person of this young girl he recognized the representative of the people he had come to serve and from her words of encouragement he derived a new strength and a new determination to persevere.

Frances was also able to help the suffering priest in a material way. His cramped cell was cold and damp and his clothing thin and inadequate. Somehow, she managed to obtain a gown which she passed down to him through the hole she had made and he was able to use it as 'clothing of his body in the days and to stand him instead of a bed in the night'. Later, she was questioned by the prison authorities about this act of mercy and she boldly told them that she had given it, and that if it were to give, she would give it and show any work of mercy to the anointed of God'. She was therefore removed from Peter Prison and Father Fingley was left on his own to prepare for his own martyrdom. He was hanged, drawn and quartered at York on 8 August 1586 and beatified by the Church on 22 November 1987 as one of the Eighty-five Martyrs.

Meanwhile, Frances Webster was taken across the city to join the other Catholic prisoners in York Castle. Here she had the great consolation of meeting up again with her mother and was able to nurse the older lady as the vile conditions of prison life sapped her strength and brought her close to death. As she watched her mother die from her sufferings, Frances prayed that she herself might be the next one privileged to give her life for Christ.

And indeed so it transpired. Within a month of her mother's death, Frances also was taken gravely ill. Conscious that her days in this life were numbered, she begged her companions to find her a priest. Her plea was heard by a young Catholic man, Mark Wraye who was in the habit of climbing into the prison in secret in order to relieve the prisoners. Now he used his expertise either to smuggle in a priest from outside the walls or to guide him from another part of York Castle. Certainly, the seminary priest, Father William Birkbeck, was able to visit Frances Webster and administer to her the Last Rites of the Church. She died, a prisoner for the sake of Christ on 29 June 1585.

MARGARET CLITHEROW

Saint Margaret Clitherow, the Pearl of York is well known to English Catholics and since her canonization as one of the Forty Martyrs in 1970, devotion to her has developed in many parts of the country and especially among organizations of Catholic women.

Fortunately, ample information about this truly remarkable woman is readily available to historians and many books and pamphlets have been published for the more general reader as well as for the specialist. Of vital importance is the 'True Report of the Life and Martyrdom of Mrs Margaret Clitherow' which was written certainly before 3 June 1586 (Morris, *Troubles*, vol. iii, p. 358) by her Spiritual Director, Father John Mush. Seven manuscripts of this valuable document are known to exist and they give an exciting if sometimes lurid account of the Martyr's life and death by one who was close to her and knew her well.

Margaret was born in the early years of Queen Mary's reign, possibly in 1553, the very year of the Catholic Queen's accession, and it is therefore highly likely that she was baptized as a Catholic during her infancy and educated as such until at least her eighth year. After that she was completely subjected to Protestant influences and as she grew up did not consider herself to be a Catholic.

On 16 May 1567 Margaret's father, Thomas Middleton, died and within a few months, according to the customs of the time, her mother had married again. Her new stepfather was Henry May, who has been described by his contemporaries as a 'foreigner', 'a southerner', and 'an adventurer'. He was certainly a young man of ambition with an eye for a wealthy widow and by means of this marriage, in Katherine Longley's words, 'he gate-crashed his way into the ruling oligarchy of the city, and rose with extraordinary speed'. The fact that Henry May proclaimed himself to be a convinced Protestant did nothing to impede his progress in civic affairs but had a profound effect on the religious atmosphere in which his fifteen-year-old stepdaughter was being educated.

Margaret was married in Saint Martin's Church on 1 July 1571 to a York butcher, John Clitherow. The bridegroom was much older than the bride and was in fact a widower with two children. Nevertheless, it was a happy marriage and the closeness of the couple was not marred by the developing religious differences between husband and wife.

The moment when Margaret decided to become a Catholic cannot be accurately ascertained and the circumstances are not known, but within three years of her marriage, she was undoubtedly a Catholic and her house in the Shambles was established as the principal Mass centre in York.

Father John Mush has described the extraordinary nature of her profession and expression of Faith, and has noted that her true love of God was reflected in three ways. 'First, that she had every day a hearty sorrow and humble repentance for her youth spent out of Christ's Catholic Church, in vain follies and schism'. The second mark of her love of God was 'her vehement desire to convert others, that God might be glorified in all his people'. Thirdly, she was resolved to do nothing, however slight, that she thought was offensive to God. (See Biography by Katherine Longley, p. 54.)

Whoever had prepared Margaret Clitherow for her reception into the Catholic Church had performed the task in exemplary manner. She knew her theology and she recognized very clearly the paramount importance of the Mass and the vital necessity of protecting the priests without whom there could be no Mass. And so, despite the fact that her husband was not a Catholic and despite the fact that her stepfather, Henry May, was an active persecutor of the Catholic Church, Margaret managed by June 1578 to 'provide place and all things convenient that God might be served (i.e. Mass said) in her house'. The unknown author of the 1619 Abstract of the Life and Martyrdom of Mistress Margaret Clitherow had access to other sources of information denied to Father Mush and is therefore able to state, 'knowing the persecution to be great, and the eyes of the state watchful over her, she ever kept her priest within a chamber of her neighbour's house (which she had hired for that purpose) and had made not only a passage from her own house unto that chamber, but means for the priest to escape (without coming to her house) upon the least notice of any danger.'

Father Mush tells us that almost all the priests who were captured and martyred in York in 1582-3 had been Margaret Clitherow's own confessors and spiritual directors. She was at home when Father William Lacey, Father Richard Kirkman and Father James Thompson were caught, tried and executed in 1582 and she was in the same prison with Father William Hart and Father Richard Thirkeld when they were taken out to be martyred.

Margaret Clitherow was living dangerously and she knew it but she continued to befriend and harbour the priests of York. Her 'criminal' record is indicative of her noble and courageous activities for the Church. On 6 June 1576 she is noted in the Housebook of York Corporation as 'detected' for recusancy. On 23 November 1576 she is certified as a recusant to the Council of the North and on 2 August 1577 the High Commission Act Book shows that she was put in prison in York Castle. She was certified as a recusant to the Privy Council on 28 October 1577 but was released from the Castle on 30 June 1578.

She managed to live in peace and freedom for a little over three months but then had to make a series of formal appearances before the High Commission on 6 October 1578, 1 December 1578, 8 April 1579, and 3 October 1580. On this last appearance, she was asked to take an oath of loyalty or 'to reform herself in religion now publicly received' and when she refused she was committed a close prisoner to the Castle where she remained until being released for childbirth on 24 April 1581. She was again convicted of recusancy at the Quarter Sessions of 3 August 1582 and was committed to the Castle at the Quarter Sessions of 8 March 1583. Twice in 1584 she was released on bond but then on 10 March 1586 was arrested for her final trial.

Nor should it be forgotten that while Margaret Clitherow was spending this period of about ten years in and out of prison, her husband, John, was also being obliged to suffer for his wife's conduct. He had to enter bonds for her release in 1577, 1578, 1581 and pay her fines in 1578, and 1581. He had to appear before the High Commission to answer for his wife's behaviour on 29 October 1577, 18 November 1577, and 30 June 1578. On 8 April 1579 he was ordered to pay twelve pence weekly to the Lord Mayor until 'further order be taken'. At the time of Margaret's final trial, John was summoned before the Council and sent as a prisoner to the Castle on 10 March 1586. Nine days later he was released but ordered to leave York for five days so that he could not be with his wife as she prepared for death. It is a powerful sign of his love that he was prepared to suffer all this for her sake and yet he never became a Catholic or shared in any of her alleged religious crimes.

It was on the afternoon of Thursday, 10 March 1586 that the sheriffs for that year, Roland Fawcett and William Gibson, raided the Clitherow house in the Shambles. John Clitherow was in prison; his wife was occupied in her household business. Father Mush has reported that the entire routine of the house was proceeding as usual. 'The priest was in his chamber... in the next neighbour's house, and some other persons with him, and being forthwith certified of the searchers, they were all safely shifted away.' The narrative continues: 'In a low chamber of her house – an attic – Mr Stapleton was quietly teaching his scholars, not knowing what was done in the house below.' When he realized that pursuivants were in the house, he slammed the door of his schoolroom and locked it, and so gave himself time to escape by the secret passage which the priest had already used.

The sheriffs had nothing to show for their troubles and therefore turned their attentions to the schoolchildren and to one ten-year-old boy in particular. This is the one whom Father Mush usually calls 'the Flemish boy' and he was stripped and terrorized. 'With rods they threatened him, standing naked amongst them, unless he would tell them all they asked. The child, fearing that cruelty, yielded, and brought them to the priest's room, wherein was a conveyance (a secret contrivance) for books and church stuff, which he revealed.'

Now indeed Margaret was in trouble. The existence of her Catholic school was proved and that in itself was against the law but much more importantly the discovery of the priest's room with the altar, the books, the vestments, the chalice and all the requisites for Mass was clear evidence that she had been harbouring a priest. The children and the servants were all taken away to different prisons in York and Margaret herself was taken immediately to the Manor and brought before the Council of the North who committed her to York Castle.

Meanwhile, the terrified Flemish boy had been talking and had given the Council a list of names of those people whom he had seen at Mass in Margaret Clitherow's house. He also named two priests whom Margaret had harboured: Father Francis Ingleby of Rheims and Father John Mush of Rome.

At the Lent Assizes, on 14 March, in the Guildhall at York, Margaret Clitherow was formally charged with the capital offence of harbouring a known Catholic priest, Father Francis Ingleby. She was allowed no counsel and had to conduct her own defence.

At the very beginning of the trial, Judge Clench asked her, 'How will you be tried?' Margaret replied, 'Having made no offence, I need no trial.' And that really was the end of the trial. There was much more discussion, argument, instruction and even mockery but the trial could not proceed until Margaret agreed to be tried 'by God and the country' but this she steadfastly refused to do. According to the law of the land, the judges had no alternative but to pronounce the dreaded punishment of *peine forte et dure*, and it was Judge Clench who uttered the fateful words of the sentence,

> If you will not put yourself to the country this must be your judgement. You must return from whence you came, and there, in the lowest part of the prison, be stripped naked, laid down, your back upon the ground, and as much weight laid upon you as you are able to bear, and so to continue three days without meat or drink, except a little barley bread and puddle water, and the third day to be pressed to death, your hands and feet tied to posts, and a sharp stone under your back.

Judge Clench was disposed to show mercy. The Law required that he should give the accused three warnings before passing sentence; in fact he gave Margaret Clitherow seven warnings and his provisional judgement was a personal act of clemency. But finally he was obliged to ask, 'How say you, Margaret Clitherow? Are you content to put yourself to the trial of the country? Although we have given sentence against you according to the law, yet will we show mercy, if you will do anything yourself.' His plea fell on deaf ears; Margaret still refused to plead. Her last words in court were: 'God be thanked; all that He shall send me shall be welcome; I am not worthy of so good a death as this is; I have deserved death for my offences to God, but not for anything I am accused of.'

There has been much discussion as to why Margaret Clitherow refused to plead. She knew such action could only lead to her own death. It has been suggested that she knew that whatever happened she was going to die and she knew that if her trial continued many people would get hurt. Her children and their friends and the little Flemish boy would be called to give evidence against her. They would inevitably mention the names of more priests and increase their danger. Nor could Margaret accept with any equanimity the invidious situation of the members of the jury who would have her blood on their hands because they dare not declare her innocence. To protect all these people she denied herself whatever justice might be forthcoming in the full process of a trial.

Margaret Clitherow was pressed to death at the Tollbooth in York on Friday, 25 March 1586. At the last moment she was allowed to wear the white shift she had prepared for herself. Her last words were, 'Jesu, Jesu, Jesu, have mercy on me.'

CECILY HOPTON

At first glance, the story of Cecily Hopton reads lightly like a gentle tale from Gilbert and Sullivan and could easily be sentimentalized in the pages of a romantic novel. In fact, her story is of sterner stuff and is set grimly in the Tower of London amid sordid scenes of blood, torture and death.

For Cecily Hopton was the young daughter of Sir Owen Hopton, who had been appointed by Queen Elizabeth as Her Majesty's Lieutenant for the Tower of London and the only home that Cecily knew was the Governor's residence within the walls of that forbidding prison. Here she had immediate access to all the prisoners and in many cases she was their only contact with the outside world and the freedom for which they all pined. Cecily could witness their sufferings and offer them such comforts as her stern, unrelenting father would authorize or permit.

Sir Owen, of course was a staunch Protestant and he had made sure that his daughter was of like persuasion. At first she had no time for the Catholic prisoners in the Tower but by 1581 she found herself singularly impressed by their religious behaviour and their courageous acceptance of adversity. Such men as Saint Edmund Campion, Saint Ralph Sherwin, Saint Alexander Briant and Saint Luke Kirby were impressive by any standards but Cecily saw their sufferings at first hand in their cells. She saw the effects of the rack on Alexander Briant and Edmund Campion in particular and she marvelled at their faith and determination. She found herself drawn inexorably towards the Faith for which all these men were prepared to suffer so much.

There was however one Catholic layman who caught the eye of Cecily Hopton and for whom she developed a particular affection. This was John Stonor of Stonor in Oxfordshire. He was the younger son of Lady Cecily Stonor and had taken chief responsibility for the presence of priests in the house in early August 1581. For this reason he had been sent to the Tower, as recorded in Father Edward Rishton's Diary for 13 August. At this time John Stonor was twenty-five years of age and Cecily Hopton fell deeply in love with him. With his encouragement she determined to join the Catholic Church and one of the priests, possibly one of the martyr priests, arranged for her reconciliation.

The formal account of this episode in the state papers is unfortunately very brief. It merely states, 'It was one Stonor that converted the Lieutenant's daughter; he was a prisoner in the Tower and she was far in love with him. She conveys messages and letters between the prisoners in the Tower and the Marshalsea.'

In fact, Cecily was able to do much more than just pass letters and messages. She became an invaluable link between the Catholics in prison and their friends outside. Free to come and go just as she wished, without let or hindrance she could smuggle into prison nourishing food and better clothing which did much to strengthen the resistance of men who had been subjected to so much physical deprivation. But she also brought in books and all the requisites for Mass. The Protestant Bishop Aylmer could complain to Lord Burghley on 5 December 1583 that 'those wretched priests do commonly say Mass in prison' and indeed Father John Gerard recounts that 'Father Hartley was discovered saying Mass in Mr Shelley's room.' It was due in no small measure to Cecily Hopton's courage and ingenuity that daily Mass was celebrated within the walls of the Tower and that many martyr priests had the great privilege and consolation of celebrating Mass as their final preparation for death.

Unfortunately for Cecily Hopton, her love for John Stonor was not returned. He honoured her and respected her as a friend, and indeed because of her conversion he regarded her as his spiritual child, but he felt no romantic attachment towards her. It was therefore a great sadness for Cecily when after eight months' imprisonment, John Stonor was released on bail on 25 April 1582. He stayed a short time at his mother's house and then crossed the seas to the Low Countries where he lived in happy exile for the rest of his life. He married a Flemish girl, Catherine de Lyere, and died eventually in Louvain in 1626.

John Stonor's release from the Tower had no effect on the dangerous and valuable activities of Cecily Hopton. She continued her underground work for the Church for another four years, but she was finally discovered in 1586. Her father, Sir Owen Hopton was immediately removed from office and Cecily was never again allowed access to the Tower.

ISOBEL WHITEHEAD

According to local information collected by Father John A. Myerscough SJ, Isobel Whitehead is believed to be one of the Whiteheads of Monkwearmouth in County Durham. If this is so, then she is related to Hugh Whitehead, the last Benedictine Prior and first Dean of Durham.

Isobel herself became a Benedictine nun in the Cluniac Priory of Ardinton but was rudely ejected from her convent at the time of King Henry's suppression of all monastic institutes. True to her vocation, she continued to observe, as best she could, all the duties of her religious state, and for the best part of fifty years lived on as a nun in the world. With no means of support, she was forced to wander from place to place, always seeking out friendly Catholics on whom she relied for food and accommodation. Like a missionary priest she assumed a false identity and moved stealthily by night and in disguise from one safe haven to another. Wherever she could, and especially in the north-east of England, she assisted the poorer Catholics, encouraging them in their resistance, teaching the catechism and preparing the way for the coming of the priest.

Eventually, in her old age and worn out by her sufferings she made her way back to Ardinton, where she was made welcome by Mr and Mrs Ardinton at what was now Ardinton Hall. Unable to care for herself, the sick nun was nursed by Mrs Ardinton but it soon became evident that she was too ill to leave her bed, and a priest was hastily summoned.

Unfortunately however, the priest himself was under surveillance by the pursuivants and his visit to Ardinton Hall excited their suspicions even further. They followed him at a distance until he entered the Hall and then they came out into the open and forced their way into the barricaded house. Destroying all in their path, they broke into the room of the sick nun and standing over her with drawn swords, threatened to murder her unless she told them of the whereabouts of the master of the house and of the priest they were pursuing.

Dame Isobel Whitehead, frail and weak as she was, refused to give them any information and she was accordingly dragged from her bed with violence and sent to York Castle as a close prisoner. At the same time, her hostess, Mrs Ardinton was also arrested and taken with her to York.

The two ladies were moved from prison to prison and were treated with great cruelty. Despite her age and her sickness, Dame Isobel did all she could to help the poor Catholic prisoners suffering with her and gave away all her money in order to help them. She was, however, too feeble to resist the physical torments of the Elizabethan prison, and Father John A.

Myerscough SJ has no hesitation in affirming that, 'The sufferings and privations killed her and she died a Martyr for the Faith in prison, on 18 March 1587.'

MARY STUART

Mary Stuart of the Royal House of Scotland was born in Linlithgow Palace, West Lothian on 8 December 1542. Her father, King James V, died just seven days later and the infant princess became the Queen of the Scots. At the age of ten months she was carried into Stirling Castle Chapel and solemnly crowned by Cardinal David Beaton, Archbishop of Saint Andrews.

It was a time of particular turmoil for Scotland. The English had just inflicted a decisive and humiliating defeat on the Scottish forces at Solway Moss. Internal divisions threatened the kingdom as over-powerful lords impeded efficient government in order to pursue their own selfish purposes. And over and above all this was the bitter religious struggle between Catholic and Protestant. It was no time for a minor to rule and as John Knox pointed out 'all men lamented that the realm was left without a male to succeed.'

Mary, the Queen, was looked after and protected by her mother, the Queen Dowager, Mary of Guise, who relied heavily on the help and support of the French Court and especially of her own ducal family within the House of Lorraine. It was no surprise therefore that when Mary was six years of age she was betrothed to the Dauphin of France and on 7 August 1548 she left the inhospitable shores of Scotland to sail to France where for the next thirteen years she was to enjoy the pleasures and influence of what was generally regarded as the most sophisticated of the European Courts.

On 24 April 1558, Mary, aged fifteen, was married to the fourteen-year-old Dauphin in a splendid ceremony in Notre Dame Cathedral, Paris. Fourteen months later she became Queen of France, when her husband unexpectedly succeeded his father as King Francis II.

At this stage in her life Mary was extremely happy. Young as she was, she had a devoted husband who gave her love and respect. She enjoyed being a queen and indeed had been treated with the deference due to a queen all her life. She had good and powerful friends who gave her every honour. She was renowned as a beautiful woman of wit and wisdom and was widely recognized and acclaimed throughout Europe as an exemplary Catholic of piety and devotion. The future seemed bright indeed for the teenage Queen and her royal spouse.

Alas, all was to change in 1560 and Mary's happy, carefree days were over. For the rest of her life she would know only sadness, anxiety and suffering, and become the lonely, forlorn but still romantic figure of Mary, Queen of Scots.

Mary's troubles began when her mother, Mary of Guise, died on 11 June

1560, but much worse was to follow when it was realized during the ensuing November that King Francis, Mary's husband, was so ill that any hopes of recovery had to be abandoned. The young King, still one month short of his seventeenth birthday, died on 6 December, and Mary was left a grieving and distraught widow at the age of seventeen.

Political affairs consequent on these deaths demanded the return of Mary to Scotland. As Queen Dowager of France she had no precise role to fulfill and her presence was resented at Court. On the other hand, Scotland was in turmoil. Royal government had been in abeyance since the death of Mary of Guise and the country was now ruled by a Protestant regime which contained John Knox as well as Mary's half-brother, Lord James Stewart. The people of Scotland had forgotten their Queen and what they remembered of her they did not like because she was a Catholic and because of her French connections. If Mary was to regain the power of her throne, her presence in Scotland was urgently required and she did not hesitate to follow where she thought her duty called her.

On Tuesday, 19 August 1561, the Queen of the Scots came back to her native land. She was still grieving for her husband and grieving for the delights of her beloved France. She landed in thick fog at the port of Leith and was welcomed warmly enough by a small group of lords. And then she began her impossible task as a dedicated Catholic queen of ruling a belligerent Protestant country dominated by John Knox.

Mary's attempt to rule Scotland lasted for almost seven years but she had to rule alone and was almost universally disliked by her people. She made a disastrous marriage with Henry Darnley who was an unsuitable husband in every way, and then when he was murdered at Kirk-o-Field, Edinburgh on 10 February 1567 she married James Bothwell, Earl of Hepburn, who had been accused and acquitted by his peers of complicity in this murder. Popular opinion claimed that Mary also was involved and the widespread indignation lead to a civil war in which Mary was defeated and further humiliated. Indeed, she was forced to abdicate in favour of her infant son, who thus became King James VI of Scotland and later King James I of England when the two nations came together in the United Kingdom. James never knew his mother; he was taken away from her immediately lest 'she corrupt the purity of his religion by her Romish ways' and he never saw her again.

For safety's sake, Mary fled from Scotland and threw herself on the mercy of her kinswoman, Queen Elizabeth of England. Perhaps she remembered the kindness that Elizabeth had shown her in 1561 when she secretly admitted the validity of Mary's claim to the English Crown and helped her find a husband, but she seems to have forgotten that it was always the policy of the Tudor monarchs to eliminate by execution all possible claimants to their throne.

Mary was a grave embarrassment to Elizabeth. She was an uninvited visitor and a most unwelcome guest, but the eyes of Europe were on the English Queen and any false move could provoke retribution from either France or Scotland who both regarded Mary as Dowager Queen. On the other hand, to allow Mary her freedom would seem to be an open invitation to her to engage in seditious activities which might well culminate in open rebellion and civil war. Elizabeth was cautious and she was suspicious. She had Mary closely questioned in Carlisle and then removed her as a prisoner to the magnificent isolation of Bolton Castle in Wensleydale.

For the next seventeen years, Mary Stuart was held prisoner in various parts of England, and just as Elizabeth had feared she was a constant source of unrest. From her first arrival in England in May 1568, English Catholics made her cause their own, and looked to her for inspiration and encouragement in their efforts to restore the Faith.

There were Catholic conspiracies to release Mary; there was talk of invasion by France to rescue her; there was the Rising of the Northern Catholic Earls in 1569; there were plots to kill Queen Elizabeth so that Mary could take her place. All such schemes were doomed to failure and came to nothing, but they did serve to keep Queen Elizabeth in a continual state of anxiety even though Mary had repeatedly assured her that she wished her no harm.

Eventually, in 1586, Mary was alleged to have involved herself in the plot of Anthony Babington, and to have encouraged him in his plan to assassinate Queen Elizabeth. Much of the evidence against Mary would seem to have been fabricated by Sir Francis Walsingham, Private Secretary to Queen Elizabeth, and Mary vehemently and consistently denied that she was guilty in any way. Nor could she as a queen in a foreign land concede to any court the right to bring her to trial.

To the Royal Commissioners who came to examine her at Fotheringay on 11 October 1586, Mary spoke out boldly,

I am myself a Queen, the daughter of a King, a stranger, and the true kinswoman of the Queen of England... As an absolute Queen, I cannot submit to orders, nor can I submit to the laws of the land without injury to myself, the King my son, and all other sovereign princes... For myself, I do not recognise the laws of England nor do I know or understand them as I have often asserted. I am alone, without counsel or anyone to speak on my behalf. My papers and notes have been taken from me, so that I am destitute of all aid, taken at a disadvantage. (Quoted in Antonia Fraser, *Mary, Queen of Scots*, (1969), p. 551.)

Despite her protestations, Mary was forced to present herself for trial, where she was found guilty of conspiring to kill Queen Elizabeth and duly sentenced to death. On Wednesday, 8 February 1587, in the Great Hall of Fotheringay Castle, Mary Stuart was beheaded.

The Protestants of England rejoiced that the Catholic threat to the throne had been removed but only in England was the death of Mary Stuart welcomed. The rest of Europe stood aghast and horrified that a queen of such doubtful lineage as Elizabeth should dare to lay violent hands on the undoubtedly truly-born and highly respected Queen of the Scots. In Scotland, King James VI resented the insult to his mother and his line, and there was an indignant uproar throughout the country. Nor had France forgotten that Mary was a Dowager Queen, very dear to many people who now showed anger and disgust with England. There was talk of war and talk of an invasion to exact satisfaction from the English Queen, but despite the noise of the protests no action was forthcoming. Only in Spain did King Philip II register his displeasure with the whole sordid business and intensify his preparations for the sailing of the Armada.

As for the English Catholics they had no doubts that Mary Stuart was a true Martyr of the Catholic Church. Throughout her long imprisonment, they had fixed their hopes on her and longed for the day when she would be free to rule England as the rightful Catholic Queen. They knew that she herself had never plotted the death of Queen Elizabeth but they knew also that Queen Elizabeth could never reign in peace as long as the Catholic menace of Mary Stuart persisted. The choice was clear-cut and the dilemma fully recognized: if Mary did not become Queen of England then she would become a Martyr.

Mary herself had no doubts that she had a vocation to be a Martyr. In prison she lived an exemplary Catholic life and was allowed her own Catholic chaplain most of the time. When she heard that she had been condemned to death she wrote at once to the Pope, Sixtus V, to assure him of her undying loyalty to the Holy See. In her last letter, written on the very day of her execution, she addressed herself to King Henry of France and told him of her conviction that it was her religion coupled with her place in the English succession which was the true cause of her death.

The circumstances of the execution also gave rise to the belief that it was a martyrdom. Mary spent the preceding night in prayer and then approached the scaffold with great dignity. She was dressed in black from head to foot except for the long white veil which flowed down her back to the ground like a bride's. She held a crucifix and a prayer book and had two rosaries hanging from her waist. When she disrobed to place her head on the block it was noticed that her petticoat and bodice were red, the liturgical colour for martyrdom in the Catholic Church. When Dr Fletcher, the Protestant Dean of Peterborough, attempted to harangue her on his own Christian beliefs, she said very firmly, 'Mr Dean, I am settled in the ancient Roman Catholic religion, and my mind to spend my blood in defence of it.' Her final prayer was in Latin, '*In manus tuas, Domine, confido spiritum meum*' (Into your hands, O Lord, I commend my spirit).

The executioners also seemed to give the impression that this was a religious martyrdom. The Dean of Peterborough tried to shout out his prayers so loudly as to drown Mary's Latin prayers but when the deed was done and the executioner held up the severed head of Mary Stuart, it was the Earl of Kent who let the cat out of the bag by proclaiming at the top of his voice, 'Such be the end of all the Queen's and all the Gospel's enemies'.

It was also significant that great care was taken by the executioners to make sure that no relics were left for Catholics to revere. The bloodstained block was burned; every article of the Queen's clothing and the ornaments of her person were burned. The Protestants knew the 'superstitious' practices of the Catholics; they knew that Mary would be recognized at once as the latest of the English Martyrs; and they were determined to prevent any manifestations of religious honour.

In fact, contemporary Catholic opinion immediately accepted Mary as a true Martyr for the Faith. In the very year of her death a book was published in Cologne describing 'The suffering and death for her most constant Catholic Faith of Mary Stuart, Queen of Scots, Catholic Prince, recently done to death by Queen Elizabeth and the nobility of England at Fotheringay Castle'. This book includes a poetic account of 'The Martyrdom of the Most Serene Mary, Queen of Scotland, killed in England because of her Catholic Faith' and also includes a synopsis of 'the life and glorious death through martyrdom of Mary Stuart, Queen of Scots, executed on account of her profession of the Catholic Faith by Queen Elizabeth of England'.

Another book published in 1587 was written by Adam Blackwood, Rector of the University of Paris, and had the simple title of *The Martyrdom of the Queen of Scotland*. Shortly afterwards, Robert Turner, who was later to become Rector of the University of Ingolstadt, published his spirited defence of Queen Mary which he called, 'Mary Stuart, Queen of Scotland, Dowager of France, Heir to England and Ireland, Martyr of the Church, Innocent of the Murder of Darnley'.

The evidence is overwhelming that the Catholics of her own time believed Mary to be a true Martyr and this devotion persisted until well into the eighteenth century. In his *Memoirs of Missionary Priests and other Catholics of both sexes*, published in 1741, Bishop Richard Challoner could write, 'In the beginning of this year, viz. February 8, 1587, Mary, queen of Scotland and dowager of France, was beheaded at Fotheringhey castle in Northamptonshire, after an imprisonment of eighteen years. As her constancy in the catholic religion was the chief cause of her death, whatever might otherwise be pretended; so is she usually reckoned amongst those who suffered for religion.'

Mary Stuart's cause has never been presented to Rome for official recognition and it is sad that devotion to her has diminished through the years. At times, especially in Scotland, her cause is given greater prominence but she is remembered more as a romantic heroine than as a religious martyr, and only time can tell as to whether Catholics will once more accord to her that special honour and reverence which could lead to her canonization as a Martyr of the Church.

MARY HUTTON

Mary Hutton was the wife of William Hutton, a draper in the city of York. In the early 1570s, they lived in the Christ Church parish, close to the Minster and close to the market place and business centre of the city. Even before the coming of the seminary priests in 1574, the Huttons were enthusiastic members of the secret Catholic community which flourished in that district and which depended on the ministrations of the old priests from Queen Mary's reign.

The strength of Catholicism in York at that time was a source of constant anxiety to the civic authorities, who seem to have been well informed as to what was going on but who were quite incapable of controlling the situation and persuading these hidden but formidable Catholics to obey the law and attend the Anglican Church services. Nor were the secular and Anglican authorities unaware of the important part that local women were playing in this determined Catholic resistance. In October 1573, the Council of the North complained to the York City Corporation that day by day the number of people refusing to attend the Anglican services was increasing, and in September 1576, the Lord President himself, the Earl of Huntingdon, reported to William Cecil, Lord Burghley, that not only was the 'decline in religion' continuing but that for the city of York, 'those that are in these matters most peevish, so far as I yet see, are in this town women'.

Certainly in the Christ Church parish, many of the Catholic men were lying low and the Catholic community seems to have been composed predominantly of women, and for some strange reason many of them were the wives of butchers. In the full list of recusants for 20 November 1576, in the York City archives (House Book XXVI), the names make interesting reading. For the Christ Church parish, the only man among sixteen women is William Hutton. The list reads,

> Dorothy, wife of Doctor Thos. Vavasour; Frances, wife of Geo. Hall, draper; Wm. Hutton draper (will come to church when excommunication on him is lifted) and wife Mary; Janet, wife of Percival Geldard, butcher; Janet, wife of Lancelot Geldard, butcher; Emot, wife of Richd. Halliday, girdler; Agnes, wife of Jn. Weddell, junior butcher; Alice, wife of Jn. Cowling, penyman; Jane West, servant to Geo. Hall, draper; and Anne Boyes, her fellow servant; Anne, wife of Chris. Kitchingman, carpenter; Margaret, wife of Jn. Clitheroe, butcher; Janet, wife of Wm. Bachelor, butcher; Agnes, wife of Jn. Chambers, innholder (gone to Newcastle); Janet, wife of Geo. Smithes, butcher

(says she now goes to church); Alice, wife of Tho. Rocke, butcher (says she now goes to church).

In this community, of course, the outstanding leader was Saint Margaret Clitherow but Dorothy, wife of Doctor Thomas Vavasour, also played an important part and Mrs Mary Hutton was closely involved with both. Together, these ladies ensured that Mass was celebrated regularly in one or other of their houses and that the fugitive priests on whom they depended were properly looked after and protected, and indeed it is another remarkable fact of these times that so many priests were able to engage themselves in this particular work and make their own essential contribution to the development of this womanly initiative.

Reference has already been made to Mrs Anne Foster, who was one of the ladies in this group and who was imprisoned on the Ouse Bridge in the late autumn of 1577. One of the official reasons given for this arrest was that she and her daughters Ann and Frances, 'with Mrs Clitherow and others their companions had already with their meetings and assemblies, and even at their gossiping and feasting done much hurt in York, and would do much more if they were permitted'. In her *Life of Margaret Clitherow* (p. 69) Mary Claridge explains that these 'meetings and assemblies' were in fact secret instruction classes given by the visiting priests, and that the Council was so suspicious of these gatherings that since 1576 committees had been set up in every parish to report on 'the occasions and causes' of the 'meetings and assemblies' of suspected persons and 'of such as wander from place to place to teach or instruct any in any point of religion contrary to the laws'.

As an active and enthusiastic member of this group, Mary Hutton joyfully proclaimed the great truths of religion to her friends and neighbours, or 'gossips' as they were more commonly called. Under the tutelage of Margaret Clitherow and Dorothy Vavasour, all these women came together, according to ancient custom at the childbirths, the christening parties, the wedding banquets and the funeral feasts and always they talked about religion. And so too, whenever they met other women in the shops or the market place or the street, this godly conversation continued as the Catholics encouraged each other to a more fervent observance of their devotions or stimulated their non-Catholic acquaintances to further consideration of the validity of the claims of Rome.

Such was the religious environment in which Mary Hutton lived and worked, and to these influences must be added the powerful example and encouragement of William, her husband. He too worked closely with the priests and never hesitated in his allegiance to the Catholic cause. He paid the religious fines for himself and his wife but he also spent long years as a prisoner for his Faith in York Castle. On many occasions he was able to alleviate the sufferings of the Catholic prisoners, but his greatest achievement was to publicize the plight of these poor prisoners by writing a series of reports on the iniquities of the system and the inhuman treatment which was accorded to so many simple people. Much of what is known today about the Catholic prisoners in York is based on the writings of William

Hutton and the humble draper has left vivid descriptions of what individual men and women had to endure.

As for Mary Hutton, she was in trouble with the law for her religion so often that it is difficult to produce her full record. On 20 November 1576, she was summoned before the Lord Mayor's Court and accused of non-attendance at church. She replied that she did not go to the Anglican Church because her conscience would not permit her. For this she was fined but she refused to pay the fine so in June 1577 some of her household goods were seized and then sold to pay off the penalties due. On 29 October 1577 she sent a message to the most important and most powerful man in the north of England, the Lord President of the Council of the North and told him very frankly that she would never come to church (York City Archives). On 4 March 1578 she appeared before the Lord Mayor's Court and promised that she would go to 'God's Church' but she did not specify which Church was God's Church and she certainly had no intention of attending the Protestant Church. On 19 August in that same year she was called before the High Commission and with Mrs Anne Cooke and Mrs Emot Halliday was sentenced to imprisonment in the Kidcote. Six months later she was released on a bond of £40 paid by her husband, but her period of freedom must have been very short because he was paying another bond on 17 June 1579 to secure her release again.

And so the story continues. The York City House Book reported on 4 March 1579 that 'Mary, wife of William Hutton, draper refuses to go to church', and according to her husband's notes, it was in this year that she was arrested while attending Mass in Doctor Vavasour's house and committed to the Ousebridge Kidcote in company with Mrs Dorothy Vavasour and Mrs Alice Oldcorne. And there she was to stay for the rest of her life.

One of the cherished customs associated with martyrdom was the preservation by devout Catholics of portions of the martyr's body as treasured relics to be honoured and revered. It was not a custom that had any appeal to the authorities, who, in their turn wished to display these bodies as objects of derision and formidable deterrents. In York, the heads of some of the martyred priests were gruesomely exposed on the roof of Saint William's Chapel on Ouse Bridge, close to where Mary Hutton was imprisoned. Inevitably, when the heads disappeared, Mary Hutton was accused of stealing them and she and the other Catholic women were punished by being placed in the dreaded lower prison where water from the river regularly flooded the cells.

Great efforts were made to prove Mary Hutton's involvement in this theft. She was told that she would be hanged unless she confessed to the crime; she replied that she would not accuse herself but would stand the consequences of anything proved against her. In his *Bibliographical Dictionary of English Catholic* (vol. III, p. 516), Mr Joseph Gillow has quoted a contemporary document to show that at that time, Mary Hutton 'had three of her youngest children with her in prison, the eldest being under nine years of age. The Magistrates caused them to be brought before them, and had the four beadles there armed with great birch rods to terrify the little children into an acknowledgement of any questions put to them. In this way, the eldest boy was forced to confess that his mother had made him take the heads off the stakes with the assistance of two girls named Margaret Lewtie and Alice Bowman.'

Meanwhile, the Christ Church community continued its Catholic activities even though numbers were depleted and dangers increased. On Christmas Eve, 1582, a priest Father William Hart was caught while saying Mass in the Hutton family home. He was condemned to death and executed for his priesthood and is included today in the Calendar of the Martyrs as Blessed William Hart.

And then, only ten days after this martyrdom, Father Richard Thirkeld was arrested while visiting the prisons on Ouse Bridge. And again there was a Hutton connection. When Father Thirkeld was searched by his captors, two keys were found upon his person. These keys were identified positively by the local locksmith, who could certify that he had made them for two chests belonging to the priest. At once, the search was on and in the house belonging to William and Mary Hutton the two chests were found in a secret place. The keys fitted the locks and proved ownership. Both chests were full of those forbidden Catholic books which were so necessary for worship and instruction among Catholics and so hated by the civic authorities. A great bonfire was made in the market place and all these valuable books were ruthlessly destroyed.

Father (Blessed) Richard Thirkeld was martyred on 29 May 1583 but his execution took place as privately as possible to prevent the Catholics obtaining his relics. Afterwards, for the same reasons, his body was burned and the ashes scattered.

Mary Hutton was still languishing in prison in 1587 when two bitterly anti-Catholic officials, Wedall and Beckwith were elected Sheriffs of York. It was their perverse pleasure to immediately increase the sufferings of the Catholic prisoners in the Kidcote by moving them all down to the lower levels beside and subject to the river. The place was already infected by a prisoner who had died there and nearly all the women contracted his foul disease. 'Whereupon,' wrote Mr Joseph Gillow, 'Mary Hutton, wife to William Hutton, a virtuous and constant young woman, died on 25 October 1587.' There seems no doubt that she died, not from natural causes but that she was killed by the loathsome conditions of her prison, and that in effect she chose to die for her Faith as a true Martyr.

DOROTHY VAVASOUR

Dorothy Vavasour, née Kent, was the wife of Doctor Thomas Vavasour, the fifth son of Sir Peter Vavasour of Spaldington in the East Riding of Yorkshire, where this cadet branch of the Vavasours of Hazlewood had settled in 1481.

Doctor Vavasour was perhaps the most outstanding lay Catholic in the North of England. He had been practising medicine in York since at least the 1550s but his full-time occupation was to serve the Church in whatever way he could, and as a doctor he had a good cover for his religious activities. He had graduated at Cambridge in 1535 but for the sake of his conscience had gone into exile during the reign of King Edward VI. He did not waste this period of his life but spent his time in study at the renowned medical school at Venice and qualified himself as a Doctor of Physics. He returned to England in Queen Mary's time but when Queen Elizabeth came to the throne, 'he openly professed and defended the Catholic faith' and had the unusual distinction of being named and excommunicated from the pulpit of York Minster.

Dorothy Vavasour was no less a Catholic than her husband. Her approach to religion has been described in one of the seventeenth-century papers in Father Christopher Grene's, Collection F:

> Knowing her husband's mind for faith and religion, and seeing him somewhat careful [i.e. worried] for her and his children, before his apprehension did desire him to cast away all care and fear for her and his children, and to do that constantly and nobly in God's cause which his conscience did teach and move him to do. Herewith, he being marvellously encouraged, did take heart and comfort unto him and prepare himself, with God's grace, to suffer what persecution soever God should suffer to fall on him. (Quoted in Father Philip Caraman's *The Other Face*, p. 200.)

Dorothy and Thomas Vavasour worked for the Church as equal partners. Their medical centre was also a religious centre. Patients visiting the doctor excited no suspicion and the scholarly doctor with all his books brought many wandering souls back into the Church. Meanwhile, his wife organized the maternity department where Catholic mothers-to-be could come together in safety and where in time, babies could be baptized and children educated. Priests were frequent and regular visitors to the Vavasour house and they celebrated Mass and the sacraments and received converts. Here

Margaret Clitherow came for her instructions and here she was received into the Church, possibly by one of the Marian priests in 1573 or 1574.

It is difficult to understand how this busy centre of vibrant Catholicism could be kept secret but Dr Vavasour and his wife were able to avoid detection for many years. It was rumoured that they had friends in high places, but it seems more likely that grateful patients were reluctant to betray their benefactors and other people recognized the value of the medical services that were available and were prepared to keep any other information to themselves. It was not until July 1568 that for the first time the High Commission issued a warrant for the doctor's arrest but by that time he had successfully disappeared. In 1570, unidentified correspondents reported to William Cecil that they had been 'hunting' Dr Vavasour for the last two years but had had no success. In fact, nobody had seen him in York since the Northern Rising of the previous year and it was strongly rumoured that as a loyal Catholic he had taken the field with the Earls in their Rebellion.

Meanwhile, with her husband on the run, Dorothy Vavasour continued the good work of the hospital-cum-Mass centre, but from 1570, the new Archbishop, Edmund Grindall, was more aware of what was going on and made his plans accordingly. In his Visitation Court Book (1571) it is reported that 'Thomas Vavasour, MD and wife Dorothy have been declared contumacious on three separate occasions, that Thomas cannot be found and is excommunicate and that Dorothy has been referred to the High Commission.'

For five years Thomas Vavasour remained in hiding but in 1574 a raid on his house brought his personal work to an end. Mary Claridge (*Life of Margaret Clitherow*, p. 61) has described how he usually lived away from his home in York. Apparently, he retired to his ancestral home at Spaldington but then coming home in secret to his wife and children,

> he was betrayed by a schoolmaster, who reported him to the Council, upon which immediate search being made by the Lord President's gentlemen and others, very fearfully raging about every place of the house with naked swords and daggers thrusting and porring in at every hole and crevice, breaking down walls, rending down cloths, pulling up boards from the floors, and making such spoil of their goods in such cruel manner, that the gentlewoman his wife and his children, being so frighted with fear lest they should have slain her husband that thereupon she lost her wit... The search lasted a whole day, yet the secret place being so politicly devised, they could not find him, and being certain that he was in the house, they did not depart until the Lord Mayor was willed to command watchmen with halberts to be set about the house, thereby to make him yield by famine, which so remaining that night and the next day, he yielded himself to the watch for saving a priest which was with him.

Thomas Vavasour was brought before the High Commission on 9 November and engaged himself in a spirited discussion with Archbishop Grindall on matters theological and spiritual and in effect, it was said, put the Archbishop to shame. Certainly, he refused to go to church or communicate 'and moreover' says the official report 'maintained openly papistical, unsound and idolatrous opinions, whereupon, and for that he is much inclined to seduce others and refused to appear until lately, by chance apprehended, he was committed close prisoner to Sheriff Brooke of York'. Later, Archbishop Grindall got his revenge for being beaten in the religious debate by sending Doctor Vavasour to the infamous Blockhouses in Hull. He reported to Lord Burghley, 'My Lord President and I, knowing his disposition to talk, thought it not good to commit the said Dr Vavasour to the Castle of York, where some other like affected prisoners remain; but rather to a solitary prison in the Queen's Majesty's Castle at Hull, where he shall only talk to the walls.'

Thomas Vavasour remained in prison for the rest of his life and suffered for eleven years before his death on 12 May 1585.

The shock of her husband's arrest and the frightening circumstances surrounding it imposed such a severe strain on Dorothy Vavasour that she suffered a complete breakdown. She was described as 'troubled, sick and disquieted' and for some time it seemed that her mind had been affected. But then, one day, quite suddenly, when she was reciting the Office of Our Lady, she was instantaneously restored to perfect health of mind and body in such fashion that she was convinced that it was a miracle of healing.

At once she reapplied herself to her apostolic work and Father Christopher Grene's contemporary paper points out that:

> she being the chief matron and mother of all the good wives of York, did in a manner addict and give herself wholly unto the service of God. Her house was a house of refuge for all afflicted Catholics, of what state, degree or calling soever, resorting thither. There God's priests, wandering in uncertain places for fear of imminent danger, had harbour and the best entertainment that she could make them. There gentlemen and poor men too, so that they were honest and Catholics, were well accepted. There women, their times of bearing and bringing forth their children approaching, had good and safe being, both for the time of their delivery, the christening of their children, and the recovery of their health again. There all good Catholics resorting thither had free access, with her good will, unto Divine Service and Sacraments.

On 15 August 1578 as the Catholics gathered at Dorothy Vavasour's house to celebrate the feast of Our Lady's Assumption, it was noticed by some, that armed men were in the vicinity and that the house seemed to be under surveillance. Those who recognized the warning signs were able to turn back or walk past the door innocently; for others already in the house, it was too late. The congregation was assembled for Mass and the priest was vested to begin, when Mr Andrew Trewe, the alderman and Mr Richardson, the sheriff, burst into the room and arrested all those who were present.

On 19 August, Dorothy Vavasour and her friends were brought before the High Commission, but of course they could claim that they had committed no offence because the Mass had not started. Dorothy was therefore 'referred to the order of the Lord Mayor and Sheriffs of York provided that no conventicles be used in her house nor any concourse of people'. She was then required to promise 'that she would remain in her own house as a prisoner except to go to her gardens and that she would behave quietly in matters of religion'. On these conditions, she was released from the Kidcote and allowed to return home.

This brush with the authorities did nothing to diminish Dorothy Vavasour's zeal or restrict her work for the Church. Her activities continued unabated and her house and maternity home beside the Minster remained a major centre for Catholicism in York. Here in February 1581, it is almost certain, according to Katherine Longley (*Life of Saint Margaret Clitherow*, p. 61) that Mrs Vavasour entertained Father Edmund Campion SJ, who had returned to England just six months before. That the future Saint Edmund should pay this visit during his preliminary tour of the north was a great honour for a lady who had suffered so much for the Faith but alas, it was a visit with unfortunate consequences. Within a few months of his visit, Edmund Campion was captured at Lyford Grange in Berkshire. Under the strain of torture, he sought some mitigation of his pain by giving the minimum of information but nevertheless revealed the names of some of the Catholic families who had given him hospitality. On 4 August 1581, the Privy Council instructed the Earl of Huntingdon, Lord President of the Council of the North, to search the homes of all these 'traitors', and on 15 August Dorothy Vavasour's house was again raided.

This time the raid was more carefully organized. The two sheriffs accompanied by three aldermen and 'many others' had the benefit of complete surprise and were able to interrupt a Mass in progress. Priest and people were taken with violence and Father William Wilkinson, an old Marian priest, former curate of Topcliffe, was taken 'through the streets with the vestment upon him, and two wax tapers carried before, being mocked and spitted upon with vagabonds; the rest of his company following next after, with a great troop following them'.

The Quarter Sessions Book for the City of York shows that Father Wilkinson and eleven lay people were convicted on 4 October 1581. All were fined one hundred marks and sentenced to one year's imprisonment in the Kidcote. It is interesting that in the list of convictions the name of Dorothy Vavasour occurs twice. The first entry is 'Dorothy Vavasour, wife of Thomas Vavasour, Doctor of medicine'. Then a little later, there is the entry, 'Dorothy Vavasour, spinster, daughter of Thomas Vavasour'. Mother and daughter went to prison together.

The prisoners were taken to the New Counter in the Kidcote on Ouse Bridge and here in the special section known as John Trewe's house, Dorothy Vavasour was to spend the remaining six years of her life. With her in this prison were two of her daughters, Anne and Dorothy and many of her friends including Mary Hutton, Audrey Wetherall, Elizabeth Brogden, Jane Elithorpe and Elizabeth Read. To this prison also in 1586 came Margaret Clitherow, already condemned to death, and despite the restrictions imposed on them Mrs Vavasour and her companions were able to do something to comfort the Martyr and help her in her preparations for her glorious death.

Like Mrs Hutton and Mrs Oldcorne, Dorothy Vavasour suffered at the hands of the bitterly anti-Catholic sheriffs Wedall and Beckwith, who inaugurated their term of office by cruelly thrusting into the 'low place of the Kidcote all the Catholic women prisoners'. It was an uncomfortable, mean place, close to the river and frequently flooded. It was also a place of infection where a prisoner had recently died from gaol fever. All the ladies contracted this vile disease and Dorothy Vavasour died in agony on 26 October 1587. She was not called to martyrdom on the scaffold but her deliberately accepted death in prison was in the true and noble tradition of all the Martyrs.

MARGARET WARD

Margaret Ward was born at Congleton in Cheshire and came to London in the service of Mrs Whittel, but she was herself a 'gentlewoman' as both John Stowe (*Annals of England*, 1605) and Dr Anthony Champney (*Annals of Queen Elizabeth*, c. 1612) have asserted. The Chalcedon Catalogue (1628) refers to her as a matron but no husband is ever mentioned and it would seem more likely that she was a young unmarried girl, attached to a Catholic lady as her companion and pupil rather than as a humble servant.

Mrs Whittel kept a Catholic house in London and was a great friend to the seminary priests. She offered them the safety and hospitality of her home and did all she could to protect and assist them in their dangerous apostolate. In the early summer of 1588, she was very concerned about the plight of Father William Watson. This young priest had been captured within four months of his arrival in England but through human frailty and inexperience had secured his freedom by agreeing to attend a service in the Anglican Church. Then, overcome by remorse for this grievous lapse, he had returned to the same church on the following Sunday and tried to make amends by disrupting the service and shouting out his repentance. At once, he was seized and dragged back to prison in the Bridewell, where, according to Bishop Richard Challoner (*Memoirs of the Missionary Priests*) 'they thrust him into a dungeon so low, and so strait, that he could neither stand up in it, nor lay himself down at his full length to sleep. Here they loaded him with irons, and kept him for a whole month upon bread and water; of which they allowed him so small a pittance, that it was scarce enough to keep him alive, not suffering anyone to come near him to comfort him or speak to him.' From this vile dungeon he was taken to a better cell, high up in the building, but 'the adversaries of his Faith made this lodging more troublesome to him than the former, by plying him continually, sometimes with threats, sometimes with prayers and promises, to engage him to go again to church, and to seem, at least outwardly, whatever he might inwardly believe to be of their religion, so that their continual importunities made him perfectly weary of his life.'

It was indeed a serious situation and a matter of some urgency. The Protestants were sure that a priest who had once denied his Faith could be induced to do so again, and the Catholics were painfully aware that in his weakened state, Father Watson might well succumb to the persuasions of his captors. It was a battle for the priest's soul and all his friends were aware that he desperately needed the support and encouragement of Catholic visitors if he were to remain faithful to his Church.

In these circumstances, Margaret Ward accepted the responsibility to attempt to save the priest from himself. Her first efforts to visit him were thwarted because he was allowed no visitors but Margaret used her charm to make a friend out of the gaoler's wife and so secured permission to talk with the priest and take him food and clothes. She had to submit herself to the humiliation of being searched before and after each visit and even the loaves and pies in her basket were broken open in the interests of a rigid security. Gradually, as she won the confidence of the officers, the strict rules were relaxed and Margaret was able to talk more freely to the priest, without being overheard. By her words and attitudes she gave him hope; she strengthened him in his resistance; and eventually communicated to him a daring plan of escape.

On her next visit, Margaret smuggled in a length of rope and in the middle of the night when all the guards were sleeping, Father Watson climbed out of the window of his cell and lowered himself on the rope. Unfortunately, through his own miscalculation, the rope was too short to reach the ground and the poor priest was obliged to summon all his courage and jump from a great height. He fell on an old shed with such force that he broke his arm and his leg and made such a noise that he brought the gaolers running from all directions. Nevertheless, an Irish boatman, John Roche had been commissioned by Margaret Ward to help in the escape and he was able to carry the badly injured priest to safety in his own house and later to set him on his way across the seas to exile in Liège.

Meanwhile, nothing could be done to retrieve the rope which was still hanging from the cell window and as soon as the authorities inspected it, they knew that only Margaret Ward could have provided it for the prisoner. Early next morning the constables and the justices surrounded her house. They found her on the point of setting out to change her lodgings but all her efforts at concealment were in vain and she was arrested and rushed off to prison.

Margaret Ward knew she could expect no mercy. She was at the heart of a painful controversy and her adversaries were infuriated that she had prevented the apostacy of a priest; but over and above all that, it was a time of powerful emotions and great hatreds. Earlier in the summer, the coming of the Spanish Armada, with its avowed aim of restoring the Catholic religion in England, had provoked, not unexpectedly, widespread resentment against the Catholics throughout the country. The fact that few English Catholics supported the attempted Spanish intrusion did nothing to alleviate the bitterness of the Protestants and as soon as the Spaniards had been defeated and dispersed in the first week of August, a mighty wave of anti-Catholic hysteria swept the country and the religious persecution was intensified. A new Proclamation against the Papists was published; six new gallows were erected in and about London; Robert Dudley, Earl of Leicester, the Queen's great favourite was heard to say that 'he desired to see all the streets of London washed with the blood of Papists'.

In these circumstances, Margaret Ward was denied the leniency usually shown to women. She was loaded with chains and ruthlessly tortured as if she were a man. The Spanish Jesuit, Father Pedro de Ribadeneira, writing in

1593, has described the efforts that were made to force her to talk and betray the whereabouts of the priest. She was flogged and then hung up by her wrists with only the tips of her toes touching the ground for so long that she was crippled. But she steadfastly refused to give away any information about the priest she had helped.

Oh 26 August 1588, Margaret Ward was brought to trial at the Old Bailey and openly admitted that she had helped Father Watson to escape from prison. Basing himself on the contemporary accounts of Father Anthony Champney and Bishop Diego de Yepes, Bishop Richard Challoner, in his *Memoirs of the Missionary Priests* has written a detailed account of the trial:

> ... being asked by the judges, if she was guilty of that treachery to the Queen, and to the laws of the realm, of furnishing the means by which a traitor of a priest, as they were pleased to call him, had escaped from justice, she answered, with a cheerful countenance, in the affirmative: and that she never, in her life, had done anything of which she less repented, than of the delivering that innocent lamb from the hands of those bloody wolves. They sought to terrify her by their threats, and to oblige her to confess where the priest was, but in vain; and therefore they proceeded to pronounce sentence of death upon her, as in cases of felony.

Even then, Margaret was offered her liberty if she would ask pardon of the Queen and promise to attend a service of the Established Church. Her reply was firm and unequivocal:

> ... as to the Queen, she had never offended Her Majesty; and that it was not just to confess a fault, by asking pardon for it, where there was none: that what she had done in favouring the priest's escape, she believed the Queen herself, if she had the bowels of a woman, would have done as much, if she had known the ill treatment he underwent. As to the going to their Church, she had, for many years, been convinced that it was not lawful for her so to do, and that she found no reason now to change her mind, and would not act against her conscience; and therefore they might proceed, if they pleased, to the execution of the sentence pronounced against her; for that death, for such a cause, would be very welcome to her; and that she was willing to lay down not one life only, but many, if she had them, rather than betray her conscience, or act against her holy religion.

It was a sign of the times that in the five weeks between 28 August and 1 October 1588 no fewer than twenty-two Martyrs were executed in England for their Faith and fifteen of these Martyrs suffered in London. Such were the consequences of the ill-judged Spanish Armada.

Margaret Ward was taken to Tyburn on 30 August 1588. With her in the cart were five companions: a seminary priest, Blessed Richard Leigh and four laymen, Blessed Edward Shelley, Blessed Richard Martin, Blessed John

Roche (the Irish boatman who had assisted Father Watson), and Blessed Richard Flower. As they began their final journey of triumph, the priest gave his solemn blessing to his saintly comrades and to 'all who stood about the cart'. Then they sang their hymns of joy all the way from Newgate to Tyburn. On the scaffold, according to a report from Saint Henry Walpole SJ, Father Leigh made a long, courageous speech of defiance and afterwards, as he began to pray again, seemed to fall into some sort of trance or heavenly ecstasy. The hangman had to pluck his sleeve to remind him of the business in hand and all this time the arch-spy, Richard Topcliffe, true to form, taunted them all with loud, vulgar shouts of vile abuse until all the executions were completed.

As befits a priest, Father Leigh was hanged, drawn and quartered; all the laymen were hanged; Margaret Ward was subjected to what was then regarded as the ultimate humiliation for a woman and was also hanged.

Margaret Ward was beatified by the Church in 1929 and on 25 October 1970, Pope Paul VI canonized her as Saint Margaret Ward, one of the Forty English Martyrs.

ANNE LAUNDER

Anne Launder has been variously called Lander, Landers, Lauder or Lawnder but by birth she was undoubtedly a Constable. Her father was Robert Constable of Easington in Holderness and her grandfather Sir Robert Constable of Burton Constable. She was married to John Launder of Naburn near York but as he was an attorney with a busy law practice in York they set up house in that city and raised their family of seven children in the parish of Saint Martin's, Coney Street. Here they were very close to the Clitherow house in the Shambles and a warm friendship developed between the two wives, Anne Launder and Margaret Clitherow. It was a friendship based upon the religion they shared and cherished, and Anne Launder became an enthusiastic member of that group of Catholic women which included Mary Hutton and Dorothy Vavasour as well as Saint Margaret Clitherow herself.

In this group of York matrons, however, Mrs Launder presented herself as a most unusual woman. Mary Claridge has described her as 'gay, extravagant, a trifle fantastic', and in her book on Margaret Clitherow has quoted a contemporary account (p. 76) of the appearance of the attorney's wife 'in her brave gown, trimly set out with fringe and lace, her golden coifs and shining cowls, her gorgeous hats adorned with gold, her fine frizzled locks, which were wont to be laid abroad by a show'. But beneath all her finery, Anne Launder was a strong, determined Catholic, completely dedicated to her Faith. She defied the religious laws. She resolutely refused to attend the services of the Church of England and she attended the forbidden Mass whenever she could.

In 1576, Anne Launder was arrested and committed with several other Catholic women to the Kidcote prison on Ouse Bridge and in the November of that year she was brought before the Lord Mayor to answer for her religious behaviour. She made no secret of her Catholicism and it is a measure of her courage that she told the Lord Mayor to his face that she did 'not like of anything' that was read in his church and declared 'her resolute mind to suffer all manner of crosses rather than to offend Him who had died upon a Cross for her'. She was clearly beyond the limited power of the Lord Mayor and she was therefore remanded to appear before the superior court of the Lord President and the Council of the North.

Once more in prison while awaiting this new trial, Mrs Launder was advised by her husband to claim her fundamental legal rights. Accordingly, she wrote a firm but respectful letter to the Lord President, the Earl of Huntingdon and made her formal request to be represented by learned counsel. Her request was brusquely refused and she was told in no uncertain terms that Catholics were outside the law and therefore had no right to any legal assistance whatsoever.

This ruling was not accepted by her lawyer-husband, John Launder, and when the case came to court, he made an immediate plea that his wife and her companions should be allowed legal representation. Indeed, he pressed this plea with such conviction and erudition that the Lord President was momentarily overcome and announced that he would accept Mr Launder's request and listen to any defence put forward by suitable counsel. Immediately, no doubt by prior arrangement, a renowned barrister presented himself to the Lord President and was granted the right to speak in defence of the accused. This barrister was a well-known Catholic, Leonard Babthorpe, son of Sir William Babthorpe of Babthorpe and Osgodby and, in fact, a cousin of Mrs Anne Launder.

But at this point in the proceedings of the High Commission, the Lord President began to regret the permission he had given and questioned Mr Babthorpe about the law. 'Are Catholics entitled to be defended in this way?' he asked. Mr Babthorpe assured him that they were. The Lord President repeated his earlier point that there was no law for Catholics. Mr Babthorpe claimed that he could prove that Catholics had the same legal rights as all their countrymen, but before he could elaborate his argument he was suddenly ordered to be silent. The Lord President had reached his decision. There was no law for Catholics. Mrs Launder could not be defended, and in seeking to defend her both lawyers had put themselves in contempt of the law and demonstrated an affection for Catholicism, which, maintained the Lord President demanded punishment.

Leonard Babthorpe and John Launder were arrested in court and sent to London as prisoners. The former was placed in the Counter and the latter in the Tower. As lawyers they were brought to the Star Charter and obliged to acknowledge that as a Catholic, Anne Launder had no legal right to be defended. They were accordingly rebuked and sent back to York for punishment. Mr Babthorpe, as a barrister of some importance was ordered to humiliate himself by going on his knees before the City Council and asking pardon. John Launder as the junior was sentenced to the pillory.

At this stage, John Launder lost heart and felt that he could take no more. The public ridicule of the stocks taxed him to the limit. Overcome by shame and fear, he wrote to his wife begging her to yield a little in religion that he might be spared this great humiliation. Yet even as he wavered in his determination, he knew what he had to do and certainly his wife would permit no compromise. Her reply to him was so persuasive that he never hesitated again. With renewed strength, he submitted himself patiently to the indignities of the pillory and for the rest of his life he remained a constant and faithful Catholic.

Anne Launder meanwhile was in prison in York and in 1579 was committed to York Castle, 'where she did much good by example of her godly life and charitable works'. For some time her husband and her children were with her in the same prison but the Launders were too important a family to be left in York and husband and wife were separated and sent independently to the infamous Blockhouse at Hull, where an unmerciful keeper had acquired a terrifying reputation for the extremes of cruelty which he practised on his Catholic prisoners.

A contemporary document, quoted by Father John Morris SJ in *Troubles of our Catholic Forefathers* (series III, p. 323) has described how Anne Launder endured on her own the torments and deprivations of the Blockhouse for five or six years, 'suffering with great constancy, patience and Christian fortitude, and comforting all other afflicted Catholics, her fellow prisoners, and relieving them with great alms'.

It is possible that Anne Launder never saw her husband again. From Hull, both were transferred to London, to the Counter or the Clink, but the authorities made sure that they were kept apart. And there Anne lingered for the remainder of her sorrowful life. She died in 1589, just one year before her husband. In the squalor of their prison, John and Anne Launder died gloriously for their Faith.

ANNE THWING

The ancient family of Thwing, once the powerful lords of Hilton Castle in the North Riding, settled in York in the early 1560s, when Thomas Thwing, a practising lawyer married the wealthy heiress, Elizabeth Hellet, and by this marriage the Thwings acquired the ownership of the large mansion, Heworth Hall, on the outskirts of the city.

Neither Thomas Thwing nor his wife seem to have been known as recusants but they certainly educated their children as Catholics. One of their sons, Edward, was fully a Catholic when he arrived at the English College at Rheims on 22 July 1583 and the Douai Diary makes no reference to the need for any form of reconciliation. Subsequently, Edward was ordained in 1590, martyred in 1600 and beatified by the Church in 1987.

By 1593 William Thwing, the son of Thomas, had inherited Heworth Hall, but in order to protect his property he had become a Church papist, conforming at least outwardly to the State Church and spending most of his time away from Heworth Hall in another residence within the city walls. The Hall itself was looked after by William's sister, Anne, about whose Catholicism there can be no doubt.

It was therefore Anne who took pity on a wandering priest, Father Anthony Page, and risked her life to offer him hospitality in January 1593. All might have been well had not a great hullabaloo broken out in the north of England on the night of 1/2 February, when Henry Hastings, 3rd Earl of Huntingdon and Lord President of the Council of the North, put into effect a grandiose scheme he had concocted to mount a sudden and simultaneous raid on as many Catholic households as possible and to destroy once and for all the Catholic Church in the northern counties.

Father Richard Holtby SJ, the Superior of the northern Catholic Mission, has left a detailed chronicle of events in a report which is now preserved among the Stonyhurst manuscripts (Anglia I, No. 74). He can report as an eyewitness that,

> This year, being the year of Our Lord, 1593, upon the first of February at night until the next day at nine of the clock, being Candlemas Day, there was a general search made for Catholics all over Yorkshire, Richmondshire, Cleveland, the Bishopric of Durham and Northumberland, wherein all the Justices of the Peace and others of authority with such as favoured the heretics' faction, together with the ministers themselves, did flock together, entering the houses of the Catholics and all such as were suspected to favour their cause, in so

great numbers that it is hard to say how many were abroad that night in searching. For there came to some houses above a hundred or seven score persons to search.

And yet despite all the huffing and puffing of Henry Hastings, his attempted pogrom was singularly unsuccessful. Father Holtby reports, 'Yet I could not perceive that it had any great effect, save that a few lay men were taken in sundry places'. He acknowledges that he and his brother, Father John Holtby SJ 'escaped very narrowly' and that 'many were forced to forsake their houses to escape the danger'. But instead of capturing many priests, as Henry Hastings had hoped, 'one only was apprehended' and that was Father Anthony Page at Heworth Hall.

It is perhaps significant that Father Page had been ordained only sixteen months and that he had spent but twelve of those months on the English Mission. He was not a man of great experience and although he had spent most of his apostolate in Yorkshire, he was not the regular chaplain at Heworth. Nor could it be said that Heworth was a safe house for priests. The practice of building hiding holes within the structures of recusant houses was not yet universal, and it would seem that this fugitive priest had made the elementary mistake of retiring to rest before identifying his escape route.

It must have been a frightening experience for Father Page, as it was for his hostess, Anne Thwing, when the house was surrounded by armed men during the hours of darkness. The priest was rushed away to the best hiding place that could be found at a minute's notice but the haystack that was chosen was so obviously a place of concealment that the priest hunters would look there first and Father Holtby's report explains how, 'A little hiding-place had been made in a place where the hay was laid, whither the priest was conveyed for avoiding the peril of the search, but the entrance thereof not being well stopped, one of the searchers climbing up upon the hay fell into the place wherein Mr Anthonie was, and so was he taken, whereat great joy was made...' (J. Morris, *Troubles of our Catholic Forefathers*, vol. III, pp. 137–43.)

Father Anthony Page was dragged to York where he was martyred on 20 April 1593. He has been officially recognized by the Church as one of the English Martyrs and was declared Blessed in 1987.

As for Anne Thwing, she also was guilty of high treason for harbouring the priest but the authorities seem to have overlooked her participation in the affair. The Thwings only became involved when the Lord President noticed the excellence of Heworth Hall and took steps to make it his own by bringing the owner to law. Father Richard Holtby has pointed out the manner in which the Lord President cast covetous eyes on the 'gentleman's house' because 'it stood in a very convenient place and was a pretty building'. If the owner could be indicted for harbouring a priest then the way was open for the crafty Lord President to take possession of his property.

Accordingly search was made in the city of York for William Thwing, the rightful owner of Heworth Hall in order to accuse him of the criminal offence of harbouring the priest and in Father Richard Holtby's words he:

was apprehended, committed, indicted, arraigned, and in great peril to be condemned, though he pleaded both his absence and ignorance of the matter; and certainly he had been condemned if his sister had not voluntarily and boldly come in before the Judges and jury, protested her brother's ignorance of the matter, and affirmed constantly with all that it was her own deed, and that she had received and kept the man of God without her brother's consent and knowledge. Upon which evidence, contrary to all men's expectation, the jury acquitted the gentleman and so he was dismissed. His sister was committed to prison in his place...

By this heroic gesture and courageous statement, Anne Thwing had saved her brother's life and protected the family inheritance, but the price she had to pay was enormous. Writing in 1594, Father Holtby reports that 'remaining constant in her profession, (she) still abides in prison, and (as I think) uncondemned...' Her eventual fate is not known. It is unlikely that she suffered a Martyr's death but how many years she languished in the miseries of a York prison and where and when she died are facts which so far have escaped the historians. She may have died in prison; she may have been released like so many other women on the accession of King James I or she may have been reprieved at an earlier date. Whatever her subsequent punishment, nothing can diminish the greatness of a woman who was ready to risk her life first to protect a priest and then voluntarily to save her brother from the gallows.

DOROTHY ARUNDEL

Dorothy Arundel was the wife of Sir John Arundel of Lanhern, near Bodmin in Cornwall. Both husband and wife were staunch Catholics, determined in their observance and proud of their religious heritage. An ancestor, Humphrey Arundel had given his life for the Church as a result of the Western Rising of 1549 and Sir John himself was one of the first Catholics to be formally denounced as a recusant in an official document of 15 October 1577. Later, in 1581, he spent time in prison for his Faith but by March 1588, Sir John and Lady Dorothy were living quietly together in their house at Muswell Hill in London, where they maintained a seminary priest, Father John Cornelius.

Father Cornelius too was a Cornishman. He had been born of Irish parents in poor circumstances at Bodmin in 1557 but the family had then moved to live on the Arundel estate at Lanhern. Sir John Arundel had recognized the talents and virtue of the boy and had paid his way through Oxford before encouraging him to study for the priesthood at Douai and Rome.

Sir John Arundel died on 17 January 1591 and his widow, accompanied by Father Cornelius, moved house to Chideock Castle, Dorset. It was here on 14 April 1594 that a sudden raid by the sheriff's men resulted in the capture of Father Cornelius; taken to prison with him were Thomas Bosgrave, a member of the Arundel family and two of the family servants, John Carey and Patrick Salmon.

Lady Dorothy Arundel, of course, was as guilty as her servants in harbouring the priest but the local constable hesitated to accuse so powerful and important a woman and her legal offence was ignored. A lesser woman might have used the opportunity to flee or hide herself away but Lady Dorothy was determined to do what she could to secure the release of the accused. Therefore she presented herself at the trial and spoke out boldly on their behalf. Courageously she acknowledged her own involvement but in doing so made a powerful plea for justice.

She told the judges, 'I alone concealed him. And so entirely was it my own act that I did not even name it to my mother; and hence the blame or the merit, whichever of these it is, belongs to me alone. And in doing this I have intended no offence to the Queen, nor to yourselves, nor to any one else, but have obeyed the laws of piety and of nature rather than those of men.'

Lady Dorothy then applied herself more directly to the so-called crime of Father Cornelius. She told the Court,

Father John has in our house a mother, a poor Irish woman, decrepit, aged and bed-ridden. You can satisfy your own eyes of this, if you please. Now, if it is a crime to afford a mother of such age, and under such circumstances, the extreme consolation of seeing her own child; if there is any generation of savages that would refuse it, then I give up, and will acknowledge that I have done wrong in inviting him to satisfy this duty of piety and to pay this debt of nature. Not because you reprehend me for it as for a crime, will that make it to be one; on the contrary, I esteem it as a meritorious act. (Quoted from 'The Other Face', edited by Father Philip Caraman SJ, p. 228.)

Sadly the eloquence and fine reasoning of Lady Dorothy were all in vain. Father John Cornelius and his companions were condemned for their Faith and duly executed at Dorchester on 4 July 1594. All were beatified as Martyrs in 1929, and are known as the Chideock Martyrs.

Lady Dorothy was not indicted. Her words of apparent self-condemnation were ignored. She was able to return home to Chideock Castle where she continued to lead her Catholic life to the full, and before her peaceful death she had the happiness on 11 July 1597 of seeing her two daughters, Gertrude and Dorothy, consecrate themselves to God as Benedictine nuns in the English Convent at Brussels.

URSULA TAYLOR

Ursula Taylor was born at Hebburn on the banks of the Tyne but as a young woman she had moved downstream to her own house on the Lawe Top at South Shields. Here, in the early 1580s she presented herself as a quiet, retiring gentlewoman but in point of fact her house was a thriving centre of intense Catholic activity and she herself was playing a most important part in the secret missionary organisation of her Church in the north of England.

South Shields was an ideal port for Catholics to use in all their communications with the Continent. Ships plied frequently between the Tyne and the Low Countries. The port was busy enough for illegal activities to be unnoticed and isolated enough to escape the close supervision of government agents. Catholics occupied key positions on land and of course many of the visiting seamen were Catholics too.

Miss Taylor's house was situated close to the port. It could therefore be used as the first place of refuge for the incoming priests from the ships and also as a safe place of assembly for the young men en route for the seminaries overseas. The financial arrangements and security of the house were the responsibilities of Mr Lawrence Kellam, a former student of the English College, Douai but he was very much an assistant to the lady of the house and helped her in every way he could. External affairs were looked after by Mr George Errington who acted as courier, guide and protector for all the Catholic travellers using the house. He collected boys and students from all over the north of England and delivered them safely to Miss Taylor so that she could arrange for their departure from the port. He also collected from Miss Taylor the newly-arrived priests and escorted them to their inland destinations.

In fact, with the encouragement of Father John Mush, the Superior of the Mission, George Errington had built up an extensive organization of enthusiastic young laymen to help him in his work. Together they had devised little-known routes from village to village and then used their local knowledge to select safe houses in the more inaccessible districts. Together these men formed their own company of the road and pooled their own experiences to make sure that their charges were protected at all times. In many ways they were similar to that society which had been solemnly blessed by Pope Gregory XIII in April 1580 for the assistance of Father Edmund Campion SJ and Father Robert Persons SJ in the London district. But in the north, the beginning or the end of every journey was Ursula Taylor's house at South Shields and it is established, in particular, that from there priests were conducted first to Thorneley near Durham and then to

Grosmont, or Nappa Hall, or Killerby, or Overton in Yorkshire and so on to the Midlands and beyond. The priests who entered England through the port of South Shields were priests for the whole of England.

Of course, in all this work, secrecy was a top priority, but government spies were always on the alert and by April 1585, one of them, Nicholas Berden, had acquired at least some generalized information about these Catholic activities. At this time, he was able to report to his masters that priests were landing at or near Newcastle upon Tyne. 'The priests most commonly do come over,' he wrote, 'in French boats that come to Newcastle for coals, which land the said priests either at Newcastle or in some creek near to the same.' Berden then goes on to add that 'they were then conveyed farther into the land' to various gentlemen's houses, where they changed their clothes and were provided with horses for their journey to London or elsewhere.

It was evident that Berden was on to something but he lacked the essential detail. He makes no mention of Ursula Taylor and he makes no mention of South Shields. Nor was the situation altered when quite by chance, George Errington was picked up at Sandgate on the Tyne just as he was about to embark for France in the company of at least one prospective Church student and with nine contraband letters in his pocket. From his examination before Sir Owen Hopton in the Tower of London it became clear that he was in the habit of breaking the law by making unauthorized trips to France and that he was unequivocally attached to the Catholic Church. He was kept a close prisoner in the Tower from 30 August 1585 until 3 February 1587 but was then released on bail. He returned north singularly unrepentant and resumed his work immediately with Ursula Taylor against whom there was still no suggestion of any suspicion.

This happy situation, however, was radically changed in 1589 when two seminary priests were shipwrecked off the South Coast and landed in Dover where they were arrested and interrogated. It is generally accepted that these unfortunate priests were the future martyrs, Blessed Francis Dickinson and Blessed Miles Gerard, but despite their undoubted sanctity they talked too much and gave away valuable information about Catholic activities on the Tyne.

In a letter written at a later date (27 June 1600), Tobie Matthew, Bishop of Durham, explained to Sir Robert Cecil that the Privy Council had passed on to him the information that the priests had provided:

South Shields, a port town in the mouth of the Tyne, near Newcastle, was the chief landing place for the most part of Jesuits and seminary priests that arrived in the north parts, and for bringing in of Mass books and other popish and traitorous books that came into the north of England, as the place where they were best befriended, and might most safely be concealed, until they were dispersed abroad elsewhere within the realm, and the like for passage outwards in conveying youths and others beyond the seas to the seminaries; having for this purpose a house at Shields, belonging to one Ursula Taylor, a recusant, to receive and lodge them; one Lawrence Kellam, a treasurer resident here, to furnish them with money and other needful provisions; and one George Errington, a lusty, tall gentleman, well-horsed and armed, to guide and convey them to such gentlemen's houses and other places as they were assigned unto.

It was indeed a damning and accurate document and one is left wondering what methods were used to extract such detailed information from holy priests who later proved by their actions that they were ready to die in defence of the Faith.

At the behest of the London authorities, Bishop Tobie Matthew appointed a special secret agent, Henry Sanderson, to enforce the full rigour of the law against the Catholics of South Shields and 'to break the nest of that popish and traitorous crew, thus settled in that place'.

As this government campaign was first launched and then intensified by Henry Sanderson, the pressure on Ursula Taylor's establishment became too great. She closed the house and she and her companions withdrew at once into hiding. Urgent warnings were sent across the sea to the Catholic authorities in Rheims in a desperate attempt to prevent any more priests travelling to South Shields, but communications were slow and uncertain and the messages were not fully understood. Very soon Bishop Tobie Matthew was able to rejoice that 'Henry Sanderson had so faithfully and diligently performed...as he forced the priests to seek elsewhere for landing places, so as some of them were taken, by two or three together coming unto Newcastle, by an unaccustomed way...'

But perhaps the saddest feature of this whole sorry affair was the fate that befell four newly ordained priests. Father Edmund Duke, Father Richard Hill, Father John Hogg and Father Richard Holiday were waiting in Rheims, about to cross the sea to England, when they heard the news from South Shields. Unfortunately they did not realize the full gravity of the situation. The young men were impatient to begin their ministry; they decided to brave the adverse circumstances and sail to the Tyne, where they arrived on 11 April 1590. They were not expected; there was no one to receive them; the whole mission was in disarray and Ursula Taylor was miles away. The inexperienced newcomers tried to move southwards where they hoped for better fortune but they were soon captured at Coxhoe near Durham and before they could even say one Mass in England, they were hanged, drawn and quartered at Durham on 27 May 1590. All four were beatified by Pope John Paul II on 22 November 1987.

During these dangerous times Ursula Taylor managed to keep herself well out of sight but as soon as she saw the opportunity she returned to her previous responsibilities at South Shields. Towards the end of 1590 she was in residence and prepared once more to welcome her priestly guests. Despite the increased danger she was harbouring a Welsh priest, Father George Williams, in February 1591 and also making plans with George Errington for the resumption of their special apostolate along the secret roads of Northumbria.

On 27 February, however, three Catholic laymen presented themselves unexpectedly at her door. Their names were Roger Ashton, Oliver Cotton and Robert Musgrave. All were sound and reliable Catholics and certainly above suspicion. They were most likely prospective ecclesiastical students trying to reach the Continent to prepare themselves for the priesthood. They had set sail from a Tyneside port but adverse winds had forced their ship to return and the Captain had obliged all his passengers to go ashore at South Shields and fend for themselves. Knowing that they were close to the house of Ursula Taylor, the three young men implored the protection of her hospitality and she, in her charity, willingly accepted them in the name of the Lord.

In fact, Ursula Taylor had taken one risk too many. The young men had not realized that they were under surveillance and that Henry Sanderson was not far away. The house was raided by pursuivants and the hostess and her four guests were all arrested and taken to Durham for trial. The presence of the priest in their midst was sufficient for all to be charged with the capital offence of harbouring.

According to Father John A. Myerscough SJ (*The Martyrs of Durham*, (1955), p. 68), Miss Taylor and her guests were first charged at Durham but,

> after this, they were all put into irons and taken to York Castle. Mr Roger Ashton was placed in the Kidcott, Mr Oliver Cotton was committed to the custody of Alderman Jackson, Father George Williams to York Castle, and Miss Ursula Taylor to the Peter prison, hallowed by the martyr, the Venerable (now Blessed) John Finglow, and by the saintly and noble girl, Frances Webster. At the present time, the Catholic Church of Saint Wilfrid stands on the site of the Peter prison.

Ursula Taylor was kept for only a short time in Peter prison. On 22 June she was removed to the Castle where she suffered much hardship. 'She was condemned to utter solitude in a dark cell, without heating of any kind, without water, and lacking even the bare necessities of life. Her gaoler did not live on the premises, and being some distance away from his charges, paid scant heed to the vital needs of his prisoner. Of her, Father Christopher Grene wrote: "She suffered all this for the love of Our Lord and for the sake of the Catholic Faith." ' (*Ibid.*, p. 69.)

In prison, Miss Taylor showed the same courage that she had demonstrated so clearly in her house of refuge at South Shields. She refused resolutely to change her religion and she was, therefore, classified as 'an incorrigible' and sent to Hull to endure the harsher conditions of the South Blockhouse. She suffered here for more than three years until 28 December 1594, when a number of her friends managed to collect sufficient money to secure her release upon bond.

Ursula Taylor does not seem to have returned to her former active missionary life. By the time of her release, George Errington was in prison. He would be martyred at York on 29 November 1596 and beatified by Pope John Paul II on 22 November 1987. Both the pioneers and organisers of the underground railway were out of action but the new Superior in York, Father Richard Holtby SJ recognized their achievement and built on their success, and throughout the 1590s priests continued to enter the country through South Shields and make their way south to Thorneley and to the thriving citadel at Grosmont on the North Yorkshire moors.

JANE WISEMAN (VAUGHAN)

According to the 'Chronicle of the Augustinian Canonesses of Louvain', Jane Vaughan was 'of an ancient family in Wales but her mother of the (Tudor) blood royal'. In her youth, she was said to have been a very attractive woman but 'very backward in the matter of marriage' because of her special delight in spiritual matters and prayer. The Chronicle goes on to relate how she had 'no less than thirty suitors, some whereof had seven years sought her good will, yet she could not settle her love upon any, till she yielded to her uncle, who desired her much to marry Thomas Wiseman of Braddocks (or Broad Acres), an Esquire of an ancient family in Essex'.

The Wisemans were a traditional recusant family. In their manor house at Braddocks, between Thaxted and Saffron Walden, they maintained an old Marian priest, Father Richard Jackson, and Mass was celebrated regularly for the family and for the Catholics of the district. In this atmosphere and in these surroundings Thomas and Jane Wiseman ensured the religious education of the eight children with which their marriage was blessed. It was a most extraordinary household and C.S. Durrant has described a family in which 'the daughters as well as the sons were brought up to learning of the Latin tongue and Mr. Wiseman, every Friday, would make an exhortation to his children in Latin thereby to exercise them in that language as also to give them good instruction.' (*Flemish Mystics and English Martyrs*, (1925), p. 422.)

Jane Wiseman had the comfort and consolation of seeing all her children grow and establish themselves in the Faith. Of her four daughters, Anne and Barbara became Bridgettine nuns in exile in Portugal, and Jane (frequently called Mary) and Bridget joined the Canonesses of Saint Augustine in Louvain. Two of her sons, John and Thomas, offered themselves as Jesuits but died before ordination; a third son, Robert, was a soldier who (according to Father John Gerard SJ) 'distinguished himself in battle against the heretics in the Low Countries'; and the eldest son and heir, William, described as 'a man more of heaven than this world' stayed at home to protect the family's religious and economic interests.

Thomas Wiseman died in 1585 and Jane his widow stayed on at Braddocks which her son, William, continued to maintain as a bastion of the Faith. He was in trouble with the civil authorities for hearing Mass in 1586 but he continued to maintain his chaplain and it was well known to the missionary priests that safety and hospitality always awaited them at the Wiseman home.

By 1591, William Wiseman had married Jane Huddleston and they had two small daughters Dorothy and Winifred. To this small but important family then, in the spring of that year, came Father John Gerard, the eminent Jesuit missionary, and under his influence the establishment was transformed into an even more powerful centre of recusancy.

In his *Autobiography* (1951 edition, p. 30) Father Gerard has described his first meeting with Jane Wiseman, William's mother. He writes 'This lady was such a holy soul that she felt the world had nothing more to give her. On the day I came to the house, she asked her son to bring me up to her room. As I entered, she threw herself down at my feet and begged me to let her kiss them – she said I was the first member of the Society she had seen. I refused, and she then kissed the floor where I was standing. That day she was filled with a wonderful consolation of soul that has never left her.'

Father Gerard continues,

When the family had settled down to this new life, I was able to find time for study and for some missionary journeys. My first concern, however, was to see that the whole house came to the sacraments frequently. With the exception of the widow, they had been used to coming perhaps four times a year at most: now it was every week. On feast days and usually on Sundays, I preached in the Chapel and instructed all how to examine their conscience and taught those who had the leisure for it the way to meditate. Another practice I started was that of reading ascetical books, which we did even at table, when there were no guests or visitors present. Those were the days when priests used to take their meals with the family, often in clerical dress. I had of course, a soutane and biretta with me, but Father Garnett had forbidden us to wear them except in the chapel. (*Autobiography*, p. 32.)

In 1592, Father Gerard persuaded the older Mrs Wiseman to leave Braddocks and take up residence in the dower house she possessed at Northend between Chelmsford and Great Dunmow. Here at Bullocks, she maintained her own priest and her house became 'a shelter and sure stronghold for Jesuits and all priests' so that the whole of that district could be evangelized.

Bullocks was raided by the pursuivants, John Worsley and William Newell on 26 December 1593. Jane Wiseman took refuge with a friendly neighbour, Lady Penelope Rich, at Leigh's Priory, while her chaplain, Father Brewster, another old Marian priest, was able to conceal himself in the priests' hiding hole in a chimney in one of the chambers and subsequently make his escape. Nevertheless, the pursuivants found an altar prepared for Mass and it was evident that Mrs Wiseman's behaviour at both Braddocks and Bullocks had been noted and that she was in grave danger of arrest.

In fact, she was also under suspicion on account of her visits to the captured seminary priests and Jesuits in prison at Wisbech Castle. Justice Young reported to the Lord Keeper on 2 January 1594 that Mrs Jane Wiseman 'was at Wisbech with the seminaries and Jesuits there, and she did repent that she had not gone barefooted thither, and she is a great reliever of them, and she made a rich vestment and sent it them...' And again on 14 April 1594, 'Mrs Jane Wiseman hath been also a great receiver and harbourer of Seminary priests, and other bad persons, and went to Wisbech with her two daughters, where (she saith) she was absolved and blessed by Father Edmonds, the Jesuit, and since that time her daughters are sent beyond the seas to be professed nuns, as her two other daughters were before.' (Harleian MSS, 6998.)

It is difficult to decipher the precise chronology of Jane Wiseman's activities. It would seem however that she was formally arrested on 12 January 1594, indicted at Essex Assizes and was taken up to London and imprisoned in the Gatehouse where she spent her time embroidering vestments for her beloved priests. Father John Gerard has described in his *Autobiography* (p. 52) how Mrs Wiseman was forced to appear:

before the officials who acted as judges in cases concerning Catholics. She appeared and answered very boldly, more like a free woman than a wronged and persecuted lady. She was sent back to gaol and showed very great patience and piety, attending to her own wants like a servant girl, cooking her own food, and doing her own washing. She desired this humiliating work for its own sake – she knew it was the only way to true humility – and also because it kept down her expenses. With the money she saved she supported poor Catholics.

Father Gerard goes on to explain:

while she was in prison, she always sent me half her annual income – six hundred florins. The other half she spent on the support of a priest to bring her Holy Communion on fixed days and to attend her fellow-prisoners, and also on other good works. She devoted all her time to prayer or needlework – she made vestments and other things for the altar and sent them to different people. For two whole years this was her life until God asked an even greater sacrifice of the holy lady.

Accepting that he was unable to provide sufficient evidence to have the lady condemned, Richard Topcliffe determined to trap her into a major indiscretion. He used Nicholas Blackwall, one of the minor officials at the Gatehouse to ask Mrs Wiseman to attend to the injured leg of a friend. She readily agreed to use her medical skill to alleviate the pain of the man presented to her and applied a cerecloth or poultice to his swollen limb. It was only later that she discovered that her unknown patient was in fact the Franciscan priest, Father John Jones, now Saint John Jones, one of the Forty Martyrs.

For this 'crime' Jane Wiseman was brought to court and accused of 'receiving, comforting, helping and maintaining priests'. (Catholic Record Society, vol. v, p. 363.)

As Mrs Wiseman faced her judge and jury she did not falter but she was very much aware of the powerful example of Saint Margaret Clitherow and like the Martyr of York she was not prepared to allow the members of the jury to burden their consciences with her innocent blood. Accordingly she refused to plead and under the law of the land was sentenced to death under '*peine forte et dure*'.

The wording of the sentence passed on Jane Wiseman on 30 June 1598 was very precise and she was condemned to be crushed to death in the most barbaric manner. It was ordered that she should be taken:

> to the prison of the Marshalsea of the Queen's Bench, and there naked, except for a linen cloth about the lower part of her body, be laid upon the ground lying directly on her back: and a hollow shall be made under her head and her head placed in the same; and upon her body in every part let there be placed as much of stones and iron as she can bear and more; and as long as she shall live, she shall have of the worst bread and water of the prison next her; and on the day she eats, she shall not drink, and on the day she drinks she shall not eat, so living until she die. (Catholic Record Society, vol. v, p. 367.)

It should be stressed that in refusing to plead, Jane Wiseman knew exactly what she was doing and what the consequences would be. She wished to follow Saint Margaret Clitherow and it is a measure of her love and devotion that she left the court, as Father Gerard has recounted, 'rejoicing that she had not been thought unworthy to suffer for Jesus' sake the form of death she had hoped would be hers.' (*Autobiography*, p. 53.)

It is very much to the credit of Queen Elizabeth that as soon as she heard of this cruel condemnation of a woman, she stayed the execution. 'The Chronicle of Saint Monica's Convent, Louvain' explains that 'by bribes her son got one to speak a good word unto the Queen in his mother's behalf. Who, when she understood how for so small a matter she should have been put to death, rebuked the justices of cruelty and said she should not die.'

Jane Wiseman was removed to another and worse prison and was kept for the next five years in a filthy cell, where, as Father Gerard has remarked, 'she was deprived of all she possessed except her life, which was the one thing she hoped they would take from her.'

On the accession of King James I on 24 March 1603, Mrs Wiseman received the royal pardon. She returned immediately to Bullocks where 'she continued to serve God's servants as she had done before and still kept two of ours (Jesuits) in her house.' Later she went overseas to Louvain where her daughter Mary was now Reverend Mother of the new foundation of the English Augustinians at Saint Monica's. Jane Wiseman died there, in peace, in the convent surrounds in 1610. Her last words to her confessor were, 'Father, I rejoice in God.'

ISABEL FOSTER

Isabel Foster was the daughter of Blessed Richard Langley, the Martyr. Her mother was Agnes Langley (née Hansby) of New Malton in Yorkshire and she was born on the family estate at Grimthorpe near Pocklington in the East Riding. Here her saintly father had spent much money in developing a place of rest and safety for the missionary priests and had built two houses, situated about one mile from each other, one at Grimthorpe itself and the other at Ousethorpe. Mr Joseph Gillow (1885) has quoted an ancient document which states that (Mr Langley) 'had built a very well hidden house underground, which was a great place for the priests during the persecution'.

Isabel, with her brother and three sisters formed a close family unit and were all educated in the hard school of religious persecution. They were fortunate to have several priests within their immediate family and their father's largesse and practical concern ensured that visiting priests were frequently in attendance to strengthen the Faith of the growing family and lead each child towards a special piety and holiness.

About the year 1586, Isabel Langley was married to William Foster of Earswick near York, but hardly had they set up home together than disaster struck the Langley's at Grimthorpe. A false Catholic betrayed Richard Langley to the Earl of Huntingdon, the Lord President of the Council of the North, and on 28 October 1586 a strong band of soldiers surrounded and searched the two Langley houses. The time had been well chosen: a meeting of priests was in full session. There was no time for any warning. The priests dispersed through all the secret exits which had been so cunningly contrived for just such an occasion. Some achieved their freedom but others were captured. Richard Langley could not escape. It was his house and he stood convicted of offering hospitality and harbouring the Roman Catholic priests. His guilt was deemed to be so obvious that at his trial he was condemned to death without any evidence being produced that the persons captured at his house actually were priests. He was hanged at York on 1 December 1586.

Isabel Foster had been present at Grimthorpe at the time of the raid of the priest-hunters but she was one of those who managed to escape. Subsequently, she was able to visit her father in York Castle and was moved by the piteous condition of so many of the Catholic prisoners. After her father's glorious death, she determined to do all she could to alleviate the sufferings of those Catholics who were still in prison and she paid several secret visits within the Castle walls.

In Father Christopher Grene's collection of contemporary manuscripts (Collection F) there is a document which describes graphically the way in which Isabel Foster ministered to the needs of the prisoners and gave them alms. The same document explains that in return for these works of mercy, she craved their good prayers for herself but also for her unborn baby whose birth was not far away.

It was unfortunate that a sharp-eyed prison officer, Anthony Ellis, should observe her charitable activities and recognize them as infractions of the strict laws against helping Catholics. He summoned a pursuivant who arrested her and presented her to the Dean of York, Mr Matthew Hutton. Every endeavour was made by this learned cleric to persuade Isabel to repudiate her Catholic Faith and to conform to the Church of the Establishment but all such efforts were in vain. She remained as always a loyal Catholic and did not hesitate to assure the Dean that she was proud and happy to proclaim her allegiance to the Pope. She was therefore loaded with chains and forcibly returned to the very prison from which she had just come where now she was no longer a visitor but a prisoner herself.

Isabel Foster was in good company among the Catholic prisoners in York Castle. They knew her and they remembered her father. They recalled her many acts of kindness and they tried to help her now as she prepared for the birth of her child in the unsavoury and unsanitary environments of an Elizabethan prison. The gaoler however had no such kind feelings. He knew no pity and made no allowances for her condition. He extorted as much money from her as he could but gave her nothing extra in return. The nourishment she needed was not forthcoming and the restricted space of her cell and the foul and impure air destroyed the health of the expectant mother. She was afflicted with what the chronicler calls an ague, but which was in reality a deadly form of gaol fever.

And yet even in her debilitated state she continued her prayers and devotions and repeatedly expressed her desire to receive the Sacraments. She bore all her sufferings patiently and virtuously, with joy and comfort of soul, desiring God to forgive those who were inflicting suffering upon her.

Father John A. Myerscough SJ (*Martyrs of Durham*, p. 42) has used Father Christopher Grene's contemporary document to describe her last moments and her triumphant death. He has written:

When her death was clearly drawing near, she was frequently heard to call upon her own father, the Blessed Richard Langley, desiring him either to stay with her, or to let her go with him. Those who were close by her marvelled at the words she continued to utter, just as if she was holding a conversation with someone, and repeatedly asking one and the same favour: 'Either stay with me or else let me go with you.' At last one of the women prisoners in attendance on her, bending over the dying lady said: 'I am here, what would you like me to do?'

Mrs Isabel Foster replied: 'I am not calling out to you, nor am I speaking to you; it is my own father! You must be able to see him, for he is there, standing next to you!'

The very next day she died a beautiful and peaceful death, in such a manner that it was a comfort and an encouragement to the Catholics who were present. She was buried amongst the many others who had died in prison, beneath the Castle wall. Thus did she and her child perish in the prison at York Castle on 3 December 1597.

CATHERINE SCROPE

Lady Catherine Scrope was the daughter of Henry Clifford, 1st Earl of Cumberland, and through her mother was descended from the Earls of Northumberland. She was married first to John, 8th Lord Scrope of Bolton in Wensleydale, and when he died she took for her second husband Sir Richard Cholmley of Whitby. She continued to follow the old custom of using her title from her first husband while still presiding over the household and family of her second, but was widowed for the second time in 1583.

From 1578 until 1598, Lady Catherine Scrope was in residence at the Abbey House on Whitby's east cliff and as a stalwart defender of the Catholic Faith, at least made some amends for the rather shady transactions in monastic land and property by which her husband's ancestors had established their fortune. Lady Scrope kept her own chaplain, offered hospitality to wandering priests, and extended friendship and protection to all the poor Catholics of the district. Her son, Henry, seemed only to strengthen his mother's religious position when he married Margaret Babthorpe of Babthorpe and Osgodby in the East Riding, and this lady from such a powerful Catholic family immediately formed an effective working partnership with her mother-in-law for the development of the Church and the safety of the missionary priests.

Lady Scrope's grandson, Sir Hugh Cholmley, has left an intriguing account in his Memoirs of what might have been the major religious work of both his mother and his grandmother. He has stated that until 1602, their house at Whitby was 'a receptacle to the seminary priests coming from beyond the seas, and landing frequently at that port, in so much as, I have been told, there have been in this house three or four of them together at a time, and, most coming both bare of clothes and money, have, at his lady's charge, been sent away with a great supply of both; some in scarlet and satin, with their men and horses, the better to disguise their professions.' (*Cholmley Memoirs*, p. 14.)

Now this statement is detailed and precise and the use of the word 'frequently' would seem to establish that Whitby was used as a major port of entry for the seminary priests. Sadly, historians have not found this thesis wholly convincing. Both G.W. Boddy and J.C.H. Aveling, the local specialists, have expressed their doubts, and Father David Quinlan has lamented that 'It is unfortunate that contemporary literature or records make little mention of this "frequent" landing of priests at Whitby.' (*Whitby Catholics* (1957).)

Nevertheless, Sir Hugh's statement is too detailed to be dismissed lightly and the point must be made that if Whitby were such an important port for the priests it is not likely that such dangerous information would be put into writing without very careful thought. An essential element in every enterprise of the underground Church was complete and absolute secrecy, and recusant scholars today are well aware of the problems they face as they seek to clarify pieces of information that have been deliberately hidden in the interests of security.

Some evidence is available, however, to suggest that many of Lady Scrope's guests had come from the sea. Father Hugh Sewel sailed from Normandy in the spring of 1590 with two other priests, Saint Edmund Gennings and Blessed Alexander Rawlings. Bishop Richard Challoner reports that 'They landed at Whitby, in Yorkshire, on the side of a high cliff, with great danger to their lives...' In 1597, five strangers suspected of being priests were landed at nearby Runswick Bay. When the active Puritan, Sir Thomas Posthumous Hoby, came to live at Hackness in 1596, he warned Sir Robert Cecil of the danger of priests landing along a sea coast: 'having in it sundry creeks fit to receive such persons as come for evil intent, who do ever shun great ports', but in imparting this information, the writer was merely repeating a fact that was well known to every smuggler along the coast and had been known ever since smuggling first began.

The suitability of the port of Whitby for the reception of seminary priests cannot be questioned. It was small, safe and cut off from the rest of the country by the open moors. The district was thinly populated and the local people were, by and large, very friendly to Catholics. On top of the towering east cliff, the ruins of Saint Hilda's ancient abbey were a clear signpost directing the exhausted stranger towards the Abbey House, where Lady Scrope and Lady Cholmley awaited their priests. And then later, fed, disguised, rested and properly equipped, the honoured guest was taken by boat up the River Esk to the other Cholmley property situated in the riverside ruins of Grosmont Priory. Here the tenant farmer, John Hodgson, and his wife Jane, were the custodians of a most elaborate establishment which was in reality the focal point, the rest centre and the secret headquarters for all the Catholic missionaries in the north of England.

Lady Scrope exercised power and influence throughout the district and the civil authorities found that she was a very difficult woman to control. Her house was known to be a Mass centre and from 1591 at least Father Martin Nelson was in residence at Abbey House as chaplain. She was therefore able to provide Mass for many of her friends and relations and perhaps at this time the local Catholics came together with Lady Scrope for Mass at the Abbey House rather than up the river at Grosmont where there were usually several priests.

J.C.H. Aveling has described the situation, (*Northern Catholics*, p. 182):

In 1590-1592, the Whitby House was clearly dominated by the matriarch, Lady Catherine Scrope, who was a recusant, along with her daughter-in-law, Margaret Cholmley, her daughter, Katherine Dutton, most of the Strangways family (less its head, James Strangways, Esq.)

of Sneaton and the Cholmley tenants of Fyling Hall, the Aislaby family. In 1592–1593, the full force of the High Commission was bent on Mrs. Cholmley and Mrs. Dutton, who were gaoled and conformed. Yet by 1596, Lady Scrope (untouched, no doubt because of her age and powerful connections) headed a still larger group of recusant gentry, now including her son, the head of the family, Henry Cholmley, his wife Margaret (reconciled), Mrs. Dutton (reconciled), the Fairfaxes almost entire and a heterogeneous collection of 'vagrants' mostly from the Cholmley estate in Thornton-le-Dale.

The development of this flourishing community was abruptly terminated in 1598 by the death of Lady Scrope. Even as she lay dying, she sent for Margaret Cholmley and uttered those chilling and puzzling words, 'Let the priest be put out of the house.'

Brother Henry Foley SJ has reported this incident in his 'Records of the English Province SJ' (note to vol. V, p. 768) and has drawn the conclusion that Lady Scrope had lost her Faith and that 'in her heart, she died a Protestant.' It does, however, seem most unlikely that a woman as strong and determined as Lady Scrope would spend all her long life suffering for her Faith and then surrender at the last moment when she was about to receive her eternal reward. Theologians will tell us today that such deathbed defections are always possible, but in fact are very rare and God would very seldom withdraw His grace at the last moment from someone who had spent a lifetime in His faithful service. A more suitable explanation of Lady Scrope's dying words would seem to lie in her recognition of the signs of disintegration within her own Catholic family and that she wished the priest to depart in safety before the growing power of the government agents completely conquered the weakening resistance of the Catholic community.

The old days had gone. Whitby was no longer a predominantly Catholic district, dominated by the three great Catholic families of the Cholmleys, the Salvins and the Radcliffes. The Cholmleys were losing their leader; the Salvins were weakening; the Radcliffes had already been replaced at Mulgrave Castle by the Protestant Lord Sheffield. And over and above all this was the ever-growing authority of the ambitious Sir Thomas Posthumous Hoby who was determined to destroy the Catholic Church and more particularly his old enemies the Catholic Cholmleys.

Lady Scrope could not be sure of the resilience of her family. They were disunited, torn apart by family disagreements. They were short of money and crippled by the payment of the religious fines. Her son, Henry and his wife Margaret had both been able to change their religion lightly and easily from Catholic to Protestant and then from Protestant to Catholic again. All these were signs that Lady Scrope must have observed and they could only fill her dying moments with doubts that Catholicism in her family could survive her death and that if the priest remained, he was in danger.

And so it transpired. Henry Cholmley and his wife left Whitby and the Abbey House and made their home at Roxby near Pickering. The year after Lady Scrope's death, Lord Sheffield organized a raid on Grosmont Priory. He found no priests and the Hodgsons escaped but his action served to keep the priests away and the establishment was temporarily closed. By 1603, Henry and Margaret Cholmley had both left the Church and had conformed fully to the Church of England. Their descendants played no further part in the history of the Catholic Church in England.

And yet it must be recorded that Lady Catherine Scrope's eldest son, Roger Cholmley, who had been disinherited by his father, settled at Brandsby and the Cholmleys of Brandsby make the proud claim that they are one of those few Catholic families who have endured all persecutions and never lost the Faith.

ANNE WARCOP

Anne Warcop was a Gatenby of Gatenby near Burneston, a small village between Boroughbridge and Catterick in the North Riding of Yorkshire. When she married Thomas Warcop, she moved to join him in his own house which was not far away although its exact location is not known.

Thomas Warcop was a dedicated Catholic, a loyal friend of the missionary priests and one of the most important and active organisers for the underground Church in the north of England. J.C.H. Aveling has identified him as the keeper of the rest centre for priests at a place he calls Thornton Woods, which he states 'must have been either in Richmondshire, around Bedale, or in the liberty of Ripon nearby'. But all the evidence suggests that Thornton Woods was a remote farm or leasehold and it does not seem likely that this could have been the main residence of such a powerful and distinguished family.

Father Godfrey Anstruther OP is quite certain from his study of contemporary documents that Thomas Warcop was from Winston, between Darlington and Barnard Castle on the County Durham side of the Tees but again it is not possible to associate the family with any particular house. Westholme Hall, one mile north of the village, has a secret hiding place and, according to Mr Michael Hodgetts, attics which 'suggest previous use as a chapel', but the date of construction is too late for Thomas and Anne Warcop to have lived there.

The important feature, however of the Warcop residence was not its precise location but the district in which it was situated. Thomas Warcop was both host and guide for the missionary priests, and he certainly lived in a district where he could successfully fulfill both these functions. The area was isolated and safe but it was also close to the Great North Road so that priests landing at South Shields and other north-eastern ports could easily be collected by gentlemen couriers and then started off safely on the major road to the south.

Anne Warcop was fully involved in the dangerous work of offering hospitality in her home to the priests, whom her husband protected and guided, but she seems to have moved frequently back to her old family home at Gatenby when her husband was absent on active service or when the authorities seemed to be pressing him with greater urgency. For some time she was able to avoid the consequences of her infringements of the civil law but the needs of her growing family and the burgeoning reputation of her husband subjected her to ever-increasing worries and anxieties which in so many cases she had to face on her own.

Meanwhile, Thomas Warcop was developing his talents as a locksmith and escapologist as he ranged all over Yorkshire and County Durham to help his priests and alleviate the sufferings of the Catholic prisoners. He was at home, however, in 1594 when he was caught harbouring the priest, Father Alexander Markland, and was taken as a close prisoner to York Castle. Here, he used his expertise to make his first escape from captivity but shortly afterwards he was said to have been guilty of keeping another priest called Neal, about whom very little is known except that he was a Cornishman ordained in 1579.

On Christmas Eve 1594, according to Father John A. Myerscough SJ (*Martyrs of Durham*, (1956), p. 94), the pursuivants staged a sudden raid on 'Mrs. Warcop's house, near Winsley Wood, Yorkshire'. Basing himself on information from a manuscript in Father Christopher Grene's Collection F, Father Myerscough goes on to relate how a pursuivant named 'Outlaw' met up with another pursuivant named 'Atkinson' who had come from Hull with about thirty men, obviously on the trail of Thomas Warcop, but hoping also to find a priest. The search proceeded over the whole house with much destruction of the property until at last a hiding place was discovered behind a wall and a priest, Father Alexander Rawlins emerged to give himself up.

It was a matter of good fortune for Anne Warcop that she was away at this time and therefore escaped detention but her husband, his manservant Mr Sanders and his close relative Miss Hardesty were all taken with the priest to York where, on 7 April 1595, Father Alexander Rawlins was hanged, drawn and quartered as a Martyr for the Faith.

It is perhaps of interest that Miss Hardesty (whose very title of 'Miss' suggests she was too young to be married) was a sister of the apostate priest, William Hardesty, who at least tried to help her in some way. He arranged with the authorities in York that she should be spared the horrors of imprisonment in the Blockhouses of Hull and sent instead to a certain Mr Blinkhorne's house in York, 'where she would be more comfortable and where he himself might have a better chance of inducing her to conform'. Miss Hardesty however would have none of it. She refused to listen to her brother's blandishments and announced categorically that she no longer regarded him as her brother.

Thomas Warcop was also subjected to similar persuasions. One of the Lords of the Council of the North offered to arrange for his safe journey back home to his wife and children if only he would attend the Protestant service. This Lord begged Mr Warcop to have some consideration for his wife and children but Thomas replied firmly, 'I have consideration and care for them and offer them to God but rather than offend God by going to your church and service, I will leave them all.'

Once more, Thomas Warcop made his escape from York Castle and now he developed a special partnership with Father William Andleby, who was determined to do what he could to help the poor Catholic prisoners in the Blockhouses at Hull. With great skill and daring they outwitted the ferocious custodians and in spite of 'moats and walls, gates and bars' managed to break into the prison several times to bring food, clothing and the comforts of religion to their destitute brothers and sisters.

A survey of recusants in 1595 reported that Mrs Anne Warcop and her family, recusants, were living at Gatenby while her husband 'the notorious harbourer and gaol-breaker' was in hiding. For another two years she was able to look after her family in freedom and to maintain her house as a place of refuge for the priests. In 1597, however, her house was raided for the third time and Father William Andleby was discovered in residence. On 4 May, Blessed William Andleby was hanged, drawn and quartered in York for his Priesthood and on the same day, in the same place, Blessed Thomas Warcop was hanged for harbouring the priest.

Anne Warcop was left in prison. She refused to conform to the Established Church and was still in a fetid dungeon of York Castle in 1600. Her manner of death has not been recorded.

CHRISTIANA PERSONS

In the seventeenth century, when Father Christopher Grene SJ was engaged on his great work of collecting, reading and transcribing so many historical documents about the English Martyrs, he found himself puzzled by the frequent references to 'the old woman' in the correspondence between the English Jesuit Superior, Father Henry Garnet, and Father Robert Persons SJ, the original companion of Saint Edmund Campion SJ and later, from his exile overseas, the acknowledged leader and organiser of the whole English Mission.

In time, however, the puzzle was solved and Father John Morris SJ has explained (in *Troubles of our Catholic Forefathers*, 1st series, (1872), p. 148) how it became plain to Father Grene that 'the old woman' was in fact the mother of Father Persons. At first Father Grene made a tentative note in the margin: '*videtur fuisse mater Personii*' (this seems to be the mother of Persons), but later he added: '*immo certum est*' (indeed this is certain).

That the Jesuits in England in the sixteenth century took special care of old Mrs Persons is now accepted as an established fact. Of course, Jesuit letters of that time either to or from Father Persons were written with great care lest an indiscreet or dangerous piece of information should fall into the wrong hands. Government spies were everywhere and letters were frequently intercepted. Therefore proper names were never used and special jargon was invented to disguise religious activities. Priests, for example, were referred to as workmen or shopkeepers and the metaphor was extended and understood by Catholic correspondents in Rome and Douai as well as on the English Mission.

In a letter of 20 January 1599 and in many others, Father Henry Garnet shows great concern for 'the old woman' and gives every assurance that she is well. On the other hand, in a letter of 21 April, he reports that she is 'dull'. Such close attention to personal matters in business letters about the affairs of the English Jesuits inevitably raises the question as to why Mrs Persons should receive such special treatment. Many other Jesuits in exile abroad had mothers still living in England but their personal welfare was never mentioned in these official letters. What was so special about Mrs Persons?

The answer to this question would seem to lie in her unique situation. She was the mother of the most important Jesuit of the day and if the English people of that time indulged themselves in an almost pathological hatred of all Jesuits then they reserved a particular venom and gross detestation for Father Robert Persons. He was evil personified to the English people; he was a traitor; he was in league with Spain; he was the agent of the Pope. With her son subject to such belligerent animosity and so universally disliked, Mrs Persons was exposed to greater dangers than any other Catholic woman and the Fathers of the Society would seem to have closed ranks to protect the mother of their leader.

Mrs Christiana Persons was in herself a very simple woman from Nether Stowey in Somerset. She was the wife of the village blacksmith and had reared six sons as good Protestants before she followed the example of Robert and became a Catholic. She would be about sixty years of age when Saint Edmund Campion was martyred and her son was forced to flee the country. It was then that the Jesuits came to her aid and she was 'adopted' by the Jesuit Superior. From 1587, Father Henry Garnet included her in his close circle of companions and took her with him wherever he went.

Father Godfrey Anstruther OP has described in *Vaux of Harrowden*, (p. 191) the rather motley community in which Father Garnet lived. He points out that many of the women followed the regular observance of a quasi religious house and then refers in particular to 'the old woman', and explains that she was 'Father Person's old mother'. The strength and courage required to live in such a household must have been a severe strain on Mrs Persons and it is indicative of the depth of her Faith and her fierce determination to persevere that she was able to play her full part in the religious life of the community for so many years.

A heavy burden on Mrs Persons must have been the constant travelling. For the younger members of the household a life of frequent movement was not too difficult to endure but for the older woman the life of an itinerant gipsy held no attractions and caused her much grief and pain. Father Garnet had to be ready to move on as soon as danger threatened. Sometimes very little notice could be given and each individual was obliged to pack up quickly, collect all the necessities for the next place of refuge and make sure that no incriminating evidence was left behind. And beyond all this was the ever-present fear of capture, imprisonment and possibly torture and death.

It was really no life for an old woman and it is not surprising that at times Mrs Persons was a cause of inconvenience to others and was liable to endanger lives because of her natural inability to move quickly. But the Jesuits never hesitated to keep her close to themselves and she in her turn responded as best she could despite her advancing years.

On 14 January 1600, Mrs Persons was still alive and thriving but must have been close to her eightieth birthday. In a letter of that date, Father Henry Garnet wrote, 'The old woman is very well and tomorrow we go all to her, having long absented ourselves to see how things passed. We find all well, and she hath for the most part not wanted a workman.' In other words: she has had a priest in the house with her.

But on 19 August 1601, Father Garnet wrote about her as then dead. He says that 'those who lived long with his [Father Person's] mother gave her singular commendation of honesty and gravity'. He adds that 'two gentlemen', [i.e. priests] were with her when she died, and he goes on to relate that 'when she first came to Henry [i.e. to himself] he was exceedingly comforted to have her out of danger.'

Certainly, the great Father Robert Persons must have known great relief that his mother was properly protected from the men of violence who pursued both mother and son so relentlessly and he must have experienced great joy that she was able to live and die so peacefully in the company of his Jesuit brothers.

ELEANOR HUNT

In 1599, Eleanor Hunt was an elderly widow living on her own, when a seminary priest, Father Christopher Wharton, was captured on her premises and she was therefore taken as a close prisoner with him to York Castle and there accused of harbouring a priest contrary to the provisions of the 1585 Act 'against Jesuits, seminary priests and such other like disobedient persons'.

It has been suggested that Mrs Hunt's house was Carlton Hall near Leeds but Sir Stephen Procter who actually made the arrest has stated that it took place 'at the foot of Netherdale within the park of Sir William Ingleby called Ripley Park in the said West Riding of Yorkshire'.

In Father William Richmond's manuscript of about 1610, 'The Trewe Story of the Catholicke prisoners in York Castle', there is a list of such prisoners for the year 1599. At the head of this list of fifty-four prisoners is 'Mr Christopher Wharton, Priest', and prominent among the twenty women whose names are on the list is 'Mrs. Eleanor Hunt, widow'.

Father Richmond does not include his own name among the prisoners but it is known that he suffered a long imprisonment in York from 1599 onwards and he was therefore writing as an eyewitness when he describes the conditions which Father Wharton and Mrs Hunt had to endure.

On 9 December 1599 all the Catholic prisoners were gathered together and forced to listen to a sermon from an Anglican clergyman. The Lord President of the Council of the North, the 2nd Lord Burleigh, Thomas Cecil, was present in state with members of his Council but refused to listen to the Catholic protests. A second sermon was planned for Sunday 16 December but the Catholics were better prepared for this and refused to attend. They were therefore dragged from their cells and forced to stand before the preacher. But as long as he was speaking they kept their hands over their ears. And so it went on in a most unseemly manner. The Lord President would not give in, and when the prisoners were physically prevented from putting their hands over their ears they began to shout out their protests in an attempt to drown the words of the preacher. For more than a year these sermons continued and more than fifty sermons were imposed on the reluctant prisoners, whose indignation knew no bounds but who could obtain no redress and no alleviation of conditions.

Father Wharton was brought to trial at the Lenten Assizes of 1600. He freely acknowledged that he was a priest but challenged his accusers to prove that he had been ordained after 24 June 1559 because the Act only applied to priests who had been ordained after that date. Father Wharton's life depended upon his date of ordination and Bishop Richard Challoner has made the point very clearly that the priest was more than sixty years of age at the time of his trial and might well have been ordained more than forty years.

Of course, the Court could not produce any evidence about the date or circumstances of a priest's ordination, but one of the judges, Mr Saville, affirmed that he had known Father Wharton at Oxford University some time after 1559, and 'that he was not then taken for a priest'. On this blatant supposition, the members of the jury were directed to find him guilty of the indictment and Blessed Christopher Wharton was martyred on 28 March 1600.

Once the priest had been found guilty of his priesthood then the trial of Eleanor Hunt for harbouring him could begin. She too was found guilty on the supposition of Judge Saville that she must have known Father Wharton from his Oxford days and therefore knew he was a priest within the terms of the 1585 Act. In point of fact, Mrs Hunt knew very little about Father Wharton and had only met him a few days before he was apprehended in her house.

Richard Verstegan, writing from Antwerp in 1601, and Doctor Thomas Worthington writing from Douai in the same year, were under the mistaken impression that Eleanor Hunt was brought to the scaffold as a martyr. Dr Worthington corrected himself in 1608 when in his account of Blessed Christopher Wharton, he adds, 'With him was condemned a gentlewoman for receiving him into her house, but was reprieved.' Bishop Richard Challoner makes it plain that this gentlewoman was Eleanor Hunt and adds, 'She utterly refused to save her life by going to the Protestant church, but though she was sentenced to die, and lost all her worldly substance, yet she did not suffer as was expected, but was permitted to linger away in prison, under the benefit, as it was called, of a reprieve.'

Her date of death is not known; her ultimate sufferings in prison have not been recorded; all that can be said is that she died for her Faith.

ANNE LINE

Anne Line was born about the year 1567 and was the second daughter of William and Anne Heigham of Dunmow in Essex. Her father was a strict Calvinist but as Anne grew up, she and her brother, William, found themselves more and more disenchanted by puritanism and eventually, when they were old enough, horrified their father by announcing their conversion to Catholicism. In these circumstances they were obliged to leave home and the angry father had no hesitation in disinheriting them both from the family fortunes.

At the age of eighteen, Anne Heigham met Roger Line, another staunch convert to Catholicism, and discovered that he too had been disinherited by his father for changing his religion. Anne and Roger were married probably in 1585 and despite their poverty set up house together in London and were soon actively involved in the secret Catholic life of the city. Unfortunately, at the beginning of 1586, Roger Line and William Heigham were attending a Mass celebrated by Father William Thomson in a house in Bishopsgate, when the pursuivants broke in and the whole congregation was arrested. Subsequently, Father William Thomson was martyred at Tyburn on 20 April, but Roger Line and William Heigham were first sentenced to perpetual imprisonment and fined one hundred marks. However, when it was discovered that they were unable to pay, both young men were banished from the country. William made his way to Spain and in due time became a brother in the Society of Jesus; Roger settled in Flanders, where he received a small pension from the King of Spain. For some years, he managed to share this pittance with his penniless wife, alone in London, but in 1594, when only twenty-seven years of age, he quite unexpectedly collapsed and died.

Father John Gerard SJ has described in his *Autobiography* (p. 83) how at this time he was able to help the poor, young widow by introducing her to his friends the Wisemans, who offered her accommodation at their house Braddox (Broadlands) in Essex. In Father Gerard's words, 'When her husband died in Belgium, Mistress Line was without friends in this world and was entirely dependent on God's providence. Therefore, before my imprisonment, I introduced her to the house where I was staying, and the family gave her board and lodging while I provided her with whatever else she needed.'

It was just at this time that Father Gerard was captured again and from his prison cell in the Clink he made plans to ensure that his special apostolate in London should continue even in his enforced absence. He explained that:

> many priests of my acquaintance used to come to London. As they had no place where they could lodge in safety, they put up at taverns while they were doing their business. Also, the majority of the priests coming from the seminaries over here were instructed to get in touch with me, so that I could introduce them to their Superior and give them other help they might need. My whereabouts were known and never changed and I could be found without difficulty. On the other hand, I had not always got lodgings ready for them and I could not always find a Catholic home to send them to. So I rented a house with a garden of its own in a suitable district and, with the help of my friends, I was able to get them suitable clothing and other things they needed, or find them a residence or buy them a horse so that they could visit their friends and relatives in the country. All these expenses and those of the house I paid out of the alms given to me. (*Autobiography*, pp. 81–2)

It was obvious that if this ambitious plan was to succeed while Father John Gerard was immobile in prison then an extraordinary person was required who could keep in close touch with the priest in his cell and then carry out his most complicated instructions for the safety of the missionaries and the organisation of the house of refuge. Father Gerard goes on to explain that:

> In charge of this house I put a very good and prudent widowed lady, who was later to receive the honour of martyrdom. She was from a distinguished family; her maiden name was Heigham and her husband's name Line. She and her husband were both blessed by God and had much to suffer for His sake.
>
> When I decided to establish the house I mentioned above I could think of no better person than her to put in charge of it. She was able to manage the finances, do all the housekeeping, look after the guests, and deal with the inquiries of strangers. She was full of kindness, very discreet and possessed her soul in great peace. She was however a chronic invalid – she was always suffering from one ailment or another. Often she would say to me: 'I naturally want more than anything to die for Christ, but it is too much to hope that it will be by the executioner's hand. Possibly, Our Lord will let me taken one day with a priest and be put in some cold and filthy dungeon where I won't be able to live very long in this wretched life.' So she said, and indeed her delight was in the Lord and the Lord granted the petitions of her heart. (*Autobiography*, p. 84)

Her great desire for martyrdom was also emphasized by Bishop Richard Challoner who based himself on Doctor Anthony Champney's *Annals of 1618*, when he wrote:

What was particularly remarkable in her, was the desire she had of ending her days by martyrdom: on which account she bore a holy envy to priests and others who seemed to be in a fairer way to that happy end than she, or any other of her sex, were; of which very few had suffered in this reign. However, she told her confessor, some years before her death, that Mr. Thomson [Blakeburn], a former confessor of hers, who ended his days by martyrdom in 1586, had promised her, that if God should make him worthy of that glorious end, he would pray for her, that she might obtain the like happiness.

For three years, Anne Line engaged herself in this dangerous work with great success. Just how many priests she helped cannot be known and security demanded that most of her achievements should be unrecorded. It is known however that she harboured Blessed Robert Drury for two years from 1595 and that among her guests were Father John Percy SJ who later served at Harrowden and Gayhurst, Father John Jones, the Franciscan who was martyred in 1598 and is now honoured as one of the Saints among the Forty Martyrs, and Father John Curry, who died while in residence and had to be buried within the house because it was too dangerous to bring out a body which could not be accounted for.

In October 1597, Father John Gerard effected his daring escape from the Tower and immediately returned to his own active missionary work in London. His first gesture of defiance to the Government was to organize in Mrs Line's house the Thirty Days Retreat in which he preached the Spiritual Exercises of Saint Ignatius. Unfortunately within a few months information was received that the notorious priest-catcher and spy, William Atkinson, was about to make a raid and it became necessary to close the house and disperse the inhabitants. Father John Gerard went to live in a large house he shared with the Heywoods and Mrs Line was moved to rented accommodation in another house some distance away. And here she continued her work of looking after the priests.

On Candlemas Day, 2 February 1601, a great many Catholics came together in Anne Line's house to celebrate Mass in honour of Our Lady's Purification. The size of the gathering aroused first the interests and then the suspicions of her neighbours. Urgent messages were sent to the pursuivants but when they arrived the heavy door of the Mass room was slammed in their faces and hastily locked. This gave the priest, Father Francis Page SJ, some precious moments to remove his vestments and mingle with the congregation. When the priest-hunters eventually broke in, they found everything prepared for Mass but no sign of a priest, and nobody present would acknowledge that one of their number was the officiating clergyman. While this matter was being discussed with some heat and the sheriff's men were selecting likely candidates for further examination, Father Page took advantage of the chaos to slip quietly out of the room and then rushed upstairs to the priest's hiding hole which he knew that Mrs Line maintained in a constant state of readiness.

The priest was never found; his martyrdom was delayed until a later date.

But Anne Line and most of the congregation were arrested and taken off to prison.

On 26 February 1601, Anne Line was brought to trial at the Old Bailey before Lord Chief Justice Popham and charged under the Act of 1585 with harbouring priests. Although she was still a young woman in her thirties she was so weak that she had to be carried into court on a chair and remained seated throughout the proceedings. To the preliminary question, 'Guilty or not guilty?' she made no direct reply but cried out in a loud voice so that all could hear her, 'My Lords, nothing grieves me more but that I could not receive a thousand more.' (John Gerard, *Autobiography*, p. 85.)

The evidence against her was slender but it was sufficient for the Lord Chief Justice to direct the jury to bring in a verdict of guilty and when they dutifully obliged, he then proceeded to condemn the poor widow to death. She received this sentence, Father Gerard has related, 'with manifest joy and thankfulness' and was returned to Newgate prison 'where she showed not the least commotion or change in her countenance'.

The next day, Anne Line was taken to the place of execution at Tyburn. It was a cold, frosty day but a large crowd had gathered to witness the spectacle. Among these onlookers were the usual tiresome Protestant preachers come to pester her with their persistent pleas to abandon her religion and conform to the Established Church. These she dismissed abruptly saying, 'Away with you. I have nothing in common with any of you.' Then she turned her attention to the crowd and boldly proclaimed to them all, 'I am sentenced to die for harbouring a Catholic priest; and so far am I from repenting for having so done that I wish with all my soul that where I have entertained one I could have entertained a thousand.' (Bishop Challoner from Dr Champney's manuscript, c. 1618.)

Anne Line was spared the humiliation of being hanged, drawn and quartered, but instead was degraded to the level of the lowest criminal and simply hanged in company with a number of thieves and malefactors. Many sympathetic Catholics were secretly present among the spectators and there is an eyewitness account of her death in a document preserved among the Duke of Rutland's manuscripts. This states that 'she behaved herself most meekly, patiently and virtuously to her last breath. She kissed the gallows, and after her private prayers, blessing herself, the cart was drawn away, and she then made the sign of the cross upon her, and after that never moved.'

The martyrdom of Anne Line was also witnessed by the two Martyrs who were immediately to follow her. Father Roger Filcock SJ and Dom Mark Barkworth OSB, both sentenced to be hanged, drawn and quartered, arrived at Tyburn on their hurdles just as Anne Line was being carried to the scaffold and they called on Catholics in the crowd to pray for her and to pray for them. When their turn came, Father Barkworth, 'was first taken from the sledge to follow her noble example; when he came near her, with great reverence he kissed the hem of her garment, praising her with most pious words.' (Father John Constable SJ, quoted in the 'Documents for Cause of Roger Filcock', (1741), p. 1567.) And Dr Anthony Champney quotes his very words, 'Oh, blessed Mistress Line, who hast now happily received thy reward. Thou art gone before us; but we shall quickly follow thee to bliss, if it please the Almighty.'

The quartered bodies of Father Barkworth and Father Filcock and the bodies of Mrs Line and all who died with her were unceremoniously dumped in a pit beside the public road at Tyburn, but Catholics were later able to remove the bodies of all three Martyrs for proper burial. Anne Howard, Countess of Arundel, was responsible for rescuing the body of Anne Line. She sent one of her servants to bring it to her own house and there she herself washed it reverently, and disposed it fitly, with candles burning, until it could have seemly burial.

Saint Anne Line was canonized by Pope Paul VI on Sunday, 25 October 1970 and she is now honoured as one of the Forty Martyrs of England and Wales.

MARGARET NORTON

Margaret Norton was the wife of John Norton of Ravensworth in the parish of Lamesley near Gateshead in County Durham, but very little more is known about either husband or wife until June 1600. The eminent local historian, the late Doctor Ann Forster has searched diligently for further information but has confessed herself unable to identify the family backgrounds of either John or Margaret.

According to Leonard Brackenbury in the Chalcedon Returns of 1626, John Norton was a Yorkshire gentleman and belonged to the strongly recusant family of Norton Conyers in the parish of Wath in the North Riding of Yorkshire. He was therefore a descendant of Richard Norton who took part in the Pilgrimage of Grace and who, in 1569, was accompanied by his nine sons when they joined the Earls of Westmoreland and Northumberland in the Rising of the North. Nevertheless, despite this heroic Catholic background, Doctor Forster has pointed out that the names of John and Margaret Norton do not appear anywhere in the Recusant Rolls compiled by the Government nor do they appear in any of the unofficial lists of recusants for Yorkshire and Durham. The suggestion has consequently been made, (*Recusant History*, vol. 6, No. 2, p. 62) that when Father Thomas Palaser visited the Nortons in June 1600, the purpose of his visit was to reconcile John Norton to the Church and to bring back both husband and wife to the observance of their religious duties.

Certainly when Mr Henry Sanderson, a professional priest-catcher, raided the Norton house, he found, as he expected, a priest in residence and a group of lay Catholics prepared to help him. A letter, dated 27 June 1600 from Tobias Mathew, Bishop of Durham, to Sir Robert Cecil praises Henry Sanderson and gives in fact a detailed description of what he is alleged to have achieved. The letter states:

> Finally, he did, upon Midsummer day last, enter the house of one John Norton of Lamesley in the County Palatinate of Durham, and there took Thomas Palaser, seminary priest, together with the said John Norton and Margaret his wife, Richard Sayer of Worsall in Yorkshire, gent. and John Talbot of Thornton in the Street in the same county, yeoman, and brought away all the superstitious massing stuff and prohibited books belonging to the said priest there found. At what time the said Mr. Norton followed Mr. Sanderson up and down the house with a fowling piece charged with hail shot and by him discharged at Mr. Sanderson. In the doing thereof, one of my men

112

present at that service thrust the said Norton with his rapier under the arm, whereby as God would, although he discharged the said piece, yet his aim and level failed, to the praise of God and wonderment of all that stood by, every man there looking that at the crack of the shot Mr. Sanderson had been slain.'

Father Palaser was arrested and taken to prison in Durham. With him were all the lay people present in the house. None could expect mercy. The nature of their 'crime' and the violence offered were regarded as matters of such importance that the Privy Council sent special instructions to the Bishop of Durham. In the letter of 29 July, it is stated:

Whereas there has been a certain seminary priest taken of late in those parts by the labour and industry of Mr. Sanderson, and some others apprehended also that did harbour and converse with him, because the said priest has lurked a long time in these parts, it is thought meet that some care should be taken to have both him and such others as have been apprehended very straitly examined of their behaviour and conversations, and then that such course be taken to proceed against them as shall be agreeable to the law and you shall think convenient.

The trial took place at the Summer Assizes in Durham in early August and all were found guilty as charged. In prison, awaiting execution, all were offered their lives if they would conform to the Established Church but only Richard Sayer was prepared to surrender his Faith. Blessed Thomas Palaser was hanged, drawn and quartered on 8 September 1600; Blessed John Norton and Blessed John Talbot as laymen were spared the barbarism of the priest's manner of death but each was hanged on the same day.

Mrs Margaret Norton had undergone the same sufferings in prison as the men. She too was condemned to death and she too was offered her life in return for a denial of her Faith. She remained steadfastly Catholic and refused all the blandishments of her persecutors. It was, however, discovered that she was with child and no Elizabethan official could bring himself to offer violence to a woman in that condition. She was accordingly reprieved and a petition was sent to the Privy Council seeking a Royal Pardon.

The records in the Public Record Office are clear that a pardon was granted to Margaret Norton on 5 December 1601. By this time she had languished in Durham prison for more than fifteen months and presumably her baby had been born and nursed in the filthy conditions of a damp cell.

The wording of Margaret's pardon is important because it establishes not only the offence for which she was sentenced to death but by implication demonstrates clearly that her three companions, all dying for the same cause, were undoubtedly martyrs for their Faith. The full indictment is set out in the Patent Roll (Public Record Office C66/1591) which states that 'Thomas Palliser born in England at Kirkby Wiske in Yorkshire, had been ordained and made a seminary priest by the authority of the see of Rome after the first year of the Queen's reign: and that Margaret Norton knowing him to be such had, on 24 June 1600, knowingly, voluntarily and feloniously received, comforted and maintained the same Thomas Palliser, he being then at large and not in prison.'

Mrs Margaret Norton emerged from prison as a free woman with no legal stain on her character but nothing is known of her subsequent life. Dr Ann Forster has merely recorded without comment that a woman named Margaret Norton was buried at Houghton-le-Spring, Durham in 1620, but there is no confirmation that this is the recusant who so nearly became a Martyr.

ALICE WELLS

Alice Morin of Monkton Farleigh in Wiltshire is much better known to students of recusant history as Mrs Swithin Wells. Her husband, the sixth son of Thomas Wells of Branbury near Winchester in Hampshire was an extraordinary man and an exemplary Catholic. Bishop Richard Challoner has described him as 'good-natured, pleasant in conversation, courteous, generous, courageous, and every way a gentleman in his comportment', and has pointed out that he was 'virtuously educated from his infancy, and carefully instructed in all manner of learning, fitting his age and condition'. The same bishop refers to Mrs Swithin Wells as 'a virtuous gentlewoman' and it is clear that both husband and wife worked together as equals in a powerful partnership which made their home the very centre of all Catholic activities in Wiltshire.

In his early years, Swithin Wells had travelled extensively on the Continent and on coming to Monkton Farleigh he used his experience to set himself up as a schoolmaster. In his secret Catholic school, he devoted himself to:

> training up young gentlemen in virtue and learning, with such success that his school hath been, as it were, a fruitful seminary to many worthy members of the Catholic Church; whereof one hath already gained the crown of martyrdom; others yet remain, some industrious and painful workmen in the happy harvest of souls, and some strong and immovable pillars, to support the catholic cause against so many grievous storms and tempests as are daily raised against it. (Contemporary document quoted by Bishop Challoner.)

Swithin and Alice Wells were indefatigable workers for the Catholic mission. While her husband risked his life guiding and protecting the itinerant priests in their apostolic journeys, Alice stayed at home to risk her life in offering refuge and refreshment to such other priests as could make their way to Monkton Farleigh.

It would seem that Mr and Mrs Wells were able to continue their heroic work for many years but eventually they became so well known to the pursuivants that it was deemed prudent for them to move to London where they might be able to lead a more sheltered existence. In fact, they took a house in Holborn, in Grays Inn Fields and almost immediately put their new home at the disposal of the missionary priests who regularly celebrated Mass on their premises.

Early in November 1591, a young priest, Father Edmund Gennings, lately arrived in the City, made arrangements to celebrate Mass at the house of Mr Swithin Wells. Only about ten Catholics were present when Father Gennings commenced the Mass at a very early hour in an upper room, but among them were two priests, Father Polydore Plasden and Father Eustace White, and the laymen, Mr Brian Lacey, Mr John Mason and Mr Sydney Hodgson. Mr Swithin Wells, himself was not present and therefore it was Mrs Alice Wells who made all the preparations and welcomed the priests to her house.

Bishop Richard Challoner has described how Father Gennings had just reached the Consecration of the Mass when a commotion was heard outside and the congregation realized that the priest-catchers were about to break in. 'Upon this occasion, the gentlemen before named arising from their devotions, thought proper to oppose force to force, so to prevent the profanation of the Sacred Mysteries.' As they stood shoulder to shoulder in the doorway, they realized to their horror that leading the charge of the intruders up the stairway was no less a person than Richard Topcliffe, the arch persecutor of the Church and the man responsible for the physical torture of many hundreds of Catholics. The opportunity was too good to be missed and one of the laymen seized him and 'thrust him down the stairs'.

As Topcliffe returned to the fray, his head all bleeding, Father Plasden was more concerned about the safety of the Blessed Sacrament than about his own safety and the safety of his friends. He therefore promised that all would surrender and give themselves up peaceably if only the priest was allowed to finish the Mass and consume the Sacred Species. This Topcliffe permitted but as Father Gennings said the last prayers, he was arrested just as he was, in his vestments and paraded through the streets with all his congregation, men and women, and all the 'church stuff, books etc.' to prison in Newgate.

When Swithin Wells returned home that night he found his house ransacked and his wife carried away to prison. At once he went to Mr Justice Yonge and demanded justice and the return of his wife, but the only response of the Judge was to put him in irons and commit him to prison with his wife and their friends. At his examination next day, Mr Wells maintained that he had not been present at the Mass celebrated in his house, but he wished 'that he had been present, thinking his house highly honoured, by having so divine a sacrifice offered therein'. The reply of the Judge was that 'though he was not at the feast, he should taste of the sauce'.

The trial took place on 5 December and all were condemned to death. Mrs Wells received her sentence with equanimity and rejoiced that she was to die for Christ. On 10 December she was brought out of prison with her husband and with Father Gennings and fully expected that she was on the way to execution and martyrdom, but as the two men were dragged away on the hurdle to the scaffold specially built opposite her own front door in Grays Inn Fields, Mrs Alice Wells was told that she had been reprieved and was returned to Newgate Prison to be detained indefinitely 'at the Queen's Pleasure'. Her chronicler remarks, 'That which would have afforded great joy to another, was grievously afflicting to this good lady, who lamented to see herself left behind, and not suffered to bear her husband and her ghostly father company in so glorious a death.'

Mrs Wells remained in Newgate prison for the next ten years. She exercised herself in 'fasting, watching and continual prayer'. At any moment she could have secured her own freedom by simply renouncing her Faith but this she refused to do. She endured all the sufferings and torments of prison life and was still in prison when she died in 1602. All those arrested with her in November 1591 were executed on 10 December 1591 and have been honoured by the Church. Among the Forty Martyrs are Saint Swithin Wells, Saint Edmund Gennings, Saint Eustace White and Saint Polydore Plasden, and among the other recognized Martyrs are Blessed Brian Lacey, Blessed John Mason and Blessed Sydney Hodgson. Only Mrs Swithin Wells has not been recognized.

Of course, she did not die on the scaffold as the men did but she was condemned to that death and did accept it, and surely her death in prison was caused by as deliberate an act of execution as were the others. It is difficult to see why Mrs Wells has not been honoured in the same way as her husband and her companions.

Her cause was examined in 1874 when she was among the 353 servants of God investigated by the first Westminster process. On examination of this evidence, however, the Sacred Congregation of Rites in Rome, decided that further consideration of her case should be postponed on the grounds that 'the proof of martyrdom was not sufficiently cogent'. This postponement has now lasted more than 100 years, but since her cause has never been formally introduced in Rome, Alice Wells is not even entitled to be called 'Venerable'. Is it not time that something should be done to give her the honour which is her due?

MARY TREGIAN

Mary Tregian was the eldest daughter of Charles, 7th Lord Stourton and was married about the year 1575 to Francis Tregian of Volvedon (now Golden) near Truro in Cornwall. Francis was a man of some importance in the southwest of England and had inherited extensive family estates in Devon, Somerset and Cornwall. He was therefore in a position to maintain his own chaplain and from April 1576, Father Cuthbert Mayne, the seminary priest, lived with the Tregians and under the guise of being their steward was able to ride over a wide area, saying Mass, preaching and administering the sacraments.

Unfortunately, news of these clandestine religious activities reached the newly-appointed Sheriff of Cornwall, Sir Richard Grenville and in June 1577, with a strong force of over a hundred armed men, he raided the Tregian mansion and dragged Father Mayne off to Launceston where he was martyred on 30 November 1577. Today, Father Mayne is Saint Cuthbert Mayne, one of the Forty Martyrs and is specially honoured as the Proto-Martyr of the Seminary Priests from the English College, Douai.

Arrested with Father Mayne were thirty-one Catholics from the Tregian estate and the neighbouring estate of Sir John Arundell and it is significant that not one of those who had been reconciled to the Church by the martyr-priest could ever be induced to renounce the Faith.

Francis and Mary Tregian certainly remained resolute. Francis was sent up to London and imprisoned in the Marshalsea and in Lent 1579, he was found guilty and condemned to the penalties of praemunire: life imprisonment and loss of all his goods. The Queen's friend, Sir George Carey was granted possession of all the Tregian estates and he took immediate steps to expel Mary Tregian and her children from her home. Kindly Catholics took pity on her and gave her food and shelter but she had no money and when her husband, also helpless and penniless in prison, was subjected to demands that he should pay £50 for his transport from Launceston to London, all she could do to help him was to beg, borrow and even sell some of the clothes she was wearing.

Father John Morris SJ in his *Troubles of our Catholic Forefathers*, (1872) has made use of Father Christopher Grene's document of 1593 to give a detailed account of the sufferings of Mary Tregian. He writes (p. 121):

> Mrs Tregian, being thus cruelly cast forth from a terrestrial paradise into a main ocean of ill fortune, subject unto all miseries that might happen unto man, through the poor help yet of some friends was so

furnished as shortly after, accompanied with a man and a maid, and her two little sons named before, the sweet pledges of their imprisoned father, carried her poor babes in a pair of panniers. On all sides, God knoweth, laden with woe and pain, she travelleth towards London, where Her Majesty then remained, hoping at Her Highness' hands to receive, if not full redress of her injury, yet at least some help of her misery. The whole of whose painful travel and troublesome suits taken and made in that behalf, at length, after she had most lamentably complained at Her Majesty's feet by the space of a whole year or more, obtaining no one penny for the maintaining of her life, or her poor husband, ended in this that she was rejected. But now, not finishing much more than one half of our journey, enforced to yield unto the summons of nature, amongst so many heavy and unacquainted mishaps, through the divine providence she was safely delivered of a daughter...

So Francis continued to suffer in prison.

For the space of seven or eight years together being of a strong constitution and having a very active and able body, amongst an infinite number of miseries, he yet enjoyed the benefit of health; but in the end, through cares, studies, filthy diet, most stinking air and want of exercise, he became very sickly, and so continued by the space of six or seven years; notwithstanding at this present (1593) the state of his body is much amended, and is like to recover his perfect health. (*Ibid.*, p. 137.)

It was evident that Francis and Mary suffered extremely from the pains of separation. In his early days in prison Francis wrote to his wife with love and great solicitude. Using a pin and a 'candle coal' he sent her a lengthy prayer in verse and then used the same rough and ready means to continue his verse in a most beautiful letter expressing his love for her and exhorting her to prayer, courage and holiness.

Mary Tregian, however, was not prepared to stand aside and leave her husband to suffer alone. She claimed the privilege of voluntarily sharing his cell and with him endured all the privations and torments of his incarceration. At times, she was 'extremely affrighted and deeply wounded with grief' and for a long while was 'very sickly and weak' so that 'she hardly escaped the imminent danger of death'. Nevertheless, the paper of 1593 describes how 'his wife (who liveth almost continually in prison with her husband) hath borne him eighteen children, and although through the rigour of authority they have been often separated, sometimes ten months, sometimes seven, sometimes more, she hath borne him, notwithstanding, eleven children since he was first imprisoned. Some are dead, but the most part are alive.' (*Ibid.*, p. 139.)

For twenty-eight years, Francis Tregian and Mary, his wife, suffered together in prison. Only on the death of Queen Elizabeth in 1603 was Francis released and banished from the kingdom. Now, strangely enough, his wife was unable to accompany him overseas. He went on his own to Spain where King Philip III received him with honour as a hero for the Faith and granted him a pension of sixty gold pieces a month. He was resident with the Jesuit Fathers in Lisbon when he died on 25 September 1608.

Mary Tregian lived on as a free woman in England in abject poverty. She was still alive in 1622 and still a recusant.

ANNE TESH

In December 1575, the number of known recusants in the city of York was officially recorded as only seventeen, but early in 1576, the Earl of Huntingdon, Lord President of the North intensified his pressure on the City Council and demanded a more thorough investigation which produced the surprising information of an additional sixty-seven adult recusants. It is to our purpose that of these sixty-seven new recusants, no fewer than fifty-five were women and that among them was Mrs Anne Tesh, the wife of Edward Tesh, who was described as a gentleman.

On 6 June 1576, a Royal Warrant was issued to the church wardens of the several parishes in York, commanding them to confiscate the goods of those recusants who had not paid their fines for 'not coming to church'. This warrant named among others, Edward Tesh and Anne, his wife. In November, both were summoned to appear before the Lord Mayor in order to explain themselves and to give an account of their worldly wealth in land and property but by this time Edward was in London and Anne presented herself alone. She made no secret of her persuasions and told the Lord Mayor and his entourage with blunt simplicity that 'she cometh not to church because her conscience will not serve her, for there is neither priest, altar or sacrament'.

There is no doubt that from 1576 onwards, Anne Tesh and Saint Margaret Clitherow were close friends. As Mary Claridge has said, 'Anne was clearly a kindred spirit to Margaret Clitherow' and she was certainly a member of that intrepid band of Catholic women who worked and suffered with the Saint in the Shambles. Between 1577 and 1578, Anne Tesh was in prison with Margaret Clitherow and with them were the butchers' wives, Janet Geldard and Agnes Weddell and the wives of the two poor tailors, Margaret Taylor and Isabel Porter.

The York High Commission Book for 2 August 1577, (folio 95) reports as follows, 'Edward Tesh, gentleman of Bishopfields, / "he refuseth sermons, service and the communion and his wife also", they cannot be found'. But later in the month they were found and J.C.H. Aveling has used folio 104 to produce the following information: 'Edward Teshe and wife Anne / both confessed they do not come to church and cannot "find it in their consciences as yet to come". Teshe submits to legal forfeitures. Offered lodging and conferences at Bishopthorpe in the Archbishop's house, they refused. At first committed to the Castle, eventually agreed that the wife was to go home and have conferences there, and Edward to go to the Archbishop's house.' (*Catholic Recusancy in York*, p. 178.)

It is impossible to trace all the legal ramifications of Anne Tesh's recusancy. Her appearances in the York High Commission Book are frequent and often confusing but they show the way in which she stood firm in her religion and her steadfast refusal to change in any way. On 8 April 1583 she was expected 'to yield herself prisoner to Hull today' but instead her husband took a bond so that she returned to York Castle. On 1 July she was to go to York Castle by bond, but instead she went to Bishopthorpe for more religious discussions. Later in that month, her husband asked for a recession 'hoping to conform her' but she was first committed prisoner to York Castle and then ordered to Bishopsthorpe for more conferences.

By the end of 1583 it would seem that Edward Tesh had given in and conformed or at least pretended to conform to the Established Church, but this had no effect on his wife's intransigence. She continued her close association with Margaret Clitherow and when the saint was arrested in the Shambles on 10 March 1586, Anne also was under grave suspicion for the harbouring of priests. In fact, the wretched Flemish boy in his terror gave her name to the authorities and claimed that she was one whom he had seen at Mass in the Clitherow home. Once more, Anne Tesh was arrested and found herself sharing a cell with Margaret Clitherow in York Castle. She found Margaret 'so merry and joyful of her trouble that she would say, she feared to offend God thereby' but at the same time, 'she kept great abstinence and prayer'. It was Anne Tesh's privilege to remain with Saint Margaret Clitherow until 14 March when the Martyr was taken away to her trial and eventual execution.

Anne Tesh remained in York Castle for only a short time. The authorities took firm action in their attempt to break her spirit and she was sent to that most dreaded of prisons: the Blockhouses of Hull. For the next eight years she endured the horrors of that evil place and only in June 1594 was she brought back to the less severe conditions of York Castle.

It was here that she came in contact with a certain Protestant prisoner, Reverend William Lowther, who claimed that he wished to become a Catholic and begged for information about the whereabouts of the nearest Catholic priest who could instruct him and receive him into the Church. Many of the Catholic prisoners were very suspicious of this man but he was so persuasive and seemed so genuine that eventually a small group tried to help him. With Anne Tesh in this group was her old friend Bridget Maskew and four or five Catholic men. They knew the risks they were taking but they enlisted the help of Mr Henry Abbot of Howden, who was said 'to know where all the Catholic priests were'.

Of course it was all a trap into which the Catholics were driven by their anxiety to help other people. The Reverend Mr Lowther was a rather disreputable clergyman who was under investigation by the High Commission. He had been able to prove his ordination to the satisfaction of his examiners but could not prove to them that he was what he claimed to be, the Vicar of Ledsham. In addition to this, the acting President of the Council of the North, Mr Edward Stanhope did not hesitate to express his suspicions that he was a bigamist. He describes him as 'one Lowther, a minister here, committed by my Lord Archbishop and us of the High

Commission here to the Castle, for being charged to have a wife in Suffolk and another here, but no proof to this hour come of a former wife'. (Letter of 2 December 1596 quoted by Katherine M. Longley, *Recusant History*, vol. 19, No. 1, p. 41.) And it seems more than likely now, as Katherine Longley has suggested, that Lowther was deliberately introduced among the Catholic prisoners as a spy and an agent provocateur.

Certainly he betrayed those who tried to help him. He informed the prison authorities of five men and two women whom he accused under the Act of 1581 of the capital offence of attempting to 'persuade him to popery'. All were brought to trial before the Council of the North and in his letter of 2 December, Mr Edward Stanhope could write, 'the evidence was so pregnant that they were all found guilty: and thereupon with as good exhortations as I could, I gave judgment of them: the men to be hanged, drawn and quartered, the women to be burned, which I told them was not for heresy but their due judgment for high treason.' (*Ibid*.)

On 29 November 1596, Blessed George Errington, Blessed William Knight and Blessed William Gibson were duly hanged, drawn and quartered and on 4 July 1597, Blessed Henry Abbot and Blessed Edward Fulthorpe suffered a similar fate. The execution of the women however was delayed.

The Council of the North may well have been guilty of grave injustice in reaching a verdict of guilty for Anne Tesh and Bridget Maskew but the sentence consequent on that verdict could not be faulted. It was the common law of England that women condemned for treason should suffer death by burning rather than be exposed to the indecencies of hanging and exposure on a gibbet. What troubled the members of the Council, however, was the attitude of Queen Elizabeth who was well known to have strong views on the punishment of women and who could severely punish any judges whom she deemed too harsh. And so the Council endeavoured to protect its own interests and, indeed, avoid its own responsibilities, by reprieving the women and referring the case directly to the Queen for her own decision.

The Queen's reply came in a letter from the Privy Council to the Archbishop of York and the Council of the North.

Whereas you have of late by your letters certified us of your proceedings there with divers disloyal subjects of Her Majesty that by their popish religion have been induced to treasonable practices against the State, of whom some being executed according to the law, and certain others remaining yet in prison and condemned, you desire to receive direction from us concerning these aforesaid persons whom you have foreborne to cause to be executed. Though in these cases which appertain to justice you might well enough proceed as yourselves or the Justices of the Assize shall think meet... yet since you have at this time made reference unto us, your Lordship shall understand that Her Majesty...is pleased...that the execution of the aforesaid women Tesh and Maskew shall as yet be foreborne until you shall receive further directions in that behalf. (Acts of the Privy Council, XXVII, p. 91.)

And so Anne Tesh and Bridget Maskew were returned to York Castle and left there to wait for these 'further directions' from the Queen. Of course, no further directions ever came and the women were still in prison on 24 March 1603 when Queen Elizabeth died. Their release was effected a short time afterwards by a special plea of some of their friends to the new King, James I, and Mrs Tesh and Mrs Maskew were able to spend the remaining years of their lives in the freedom of the York Catholic community where all their years of suffering in prison were accounted as their greatest glory.

BRIDGIT MASKEW

Bridgit Maskew was a sister of Blessed Robert Bickerdike who was martyred at York in August 1586. She was born at Low Hall in the parish of Farnham near Knaresborough in the West Riding of Yorkshire but moved to York, possibly in her late teens, to marry Thomas Maskew, a prosperous apothecary.

The Maskews were an important family in York. Not only was Thomas an influential merchant but his brother Robert, a grocer, had been Lord Mayor in 1574 and both continued to take an active part in civic affairs. J.C.H. Aveling has shown that Robert had some recusant connections and that Thomas, although generally a conformist, had obstinate recusants living in his house and that he himself became a Catholic for a brief period in 1590. (*Catholic Recusancy in York*, pp. 66, 69.) Of Bridget's complete and wholehearted recusancy there is no doubt.

In the early summer of 1586, Bridgit Maskew had to face the fact that her brother, Robert Bickerdike, had been condemned to death for his Faith and she rejoiced that he was about to become a Martyr. At this time she was only twenty-one years of age and was in fact six months pregnant, but at once she busied herself in preparing the beautiful white garments in which her brother could be led to the scaffold in simple dignity and seal his Faith with his blood.

A document of 1590, (probably written by Father Richard Holtby SJ and preserved in Grene's Collection E) describes the way in which this seemingly innocent act of love for her brother endangered the young wife. For her own safety, she was compelled to leave home and go into hiding as government officials threatened her on all sides. 'Despite her condition,' says the account, 'she was forced to travel hither and thither, on foot, during stormy, tempestuous nights, with the greatest danger to her health and to the possibility of a safe delivery.' Eventually, conscious of the fact that she could claim '*privilegium ventris*', the legal right of a pregnant woman to her freedom, she returned home, but her rights were ignored and pursuivants sent specially by the Archbishop of York arrested her and put her in prison.

For the next ten years Bridgit Maskew lived the life of a York recusant, but her court appearances have not been recorded. Nor is it known how much time she spent in prison. Certainly she was in York Castle in 1596, when, as has already been recorded in the account of Anne Tesh, Bridgit Maskew was one of those charitable Catholic prisoners betrayed to the authorities by the infamous clergyman, William Lowther. And so she suffered the anguish of being condemned to death and then, when reprieved, being left in prison with a sentence so indeterminate that there seemed to be no possibility of release.

Mrs Bridgit Maskew was one of the fifty-three Catholic prisoners who were dragged under protest to the hall of York Castle and there forcibly detained to hear Protestant sermons once every week in the year 1600. The best efforts of the preacher were all in vain; his unwilling congregation demonstrated their complete indifference to his words and when that failed to silence him they prayed together so loudly as to drown his voice.

There is also information that in August 1601, Bridgit Maskew was one of the fourteen Catholics in the Castle and Kidcotes who signed a testimonial in favour of Father John Mush, who was at that time suspended by the Catholic authorities for his support of the Appellants. It is perhaps significant that of the twelve men and two women who supported this petition only four men and Mrs Askew were able to write proper signatures. The others could only make their marks.

Some time after Queen Elizabeth died on 24 March 1603, Bridgit Maskew was released from prison. J.C.H. Aveling maintains that she was released before 1615 but that would seem to be a cautious estimate. It is likely that she secured her freedom very shortly after her friends petitioned King James I in 1603.

Her husband had died in 1594 but Bridget Maskew was still alive and still a recusant in 1633. The Archbishop's Visitation Book for St Mary's, Bishophill for 1615 had made reference to 'Bridgit Maskew, widow, gentlewoman, aged fifty, recusant twenty years'. It was a great if unwitting compliment to a valiant Catholic woman but it was not at all accurate. In 1615 she had been a recusant for as long as she had lived and that was fifty years, and when she died sometime after 1633, her recusancy had lasted at least sixty-eight years.

MARGARET CONSTABLE

Margaret Constable was the daughter of Sir William Dormer and his second wife, Dorothy Catesby. She was therefore subject to the powerful religious influences of these two great Catholic families and remained a staunch and active Catholic all her life. Her marriage to Henry Constable of Holderness in East Yorkshire seemed at first to present its own difficulties because the Constables had not yet declared themselves for the Old Faith. The head of the family, Sir John Constable, was officially regarded as 'doubtful or newter' in religious matters and his son, Henry, was generally accepted as a safe Protestant.

The marriage settlement was signed on 20 January 1578 and Margaret Dormer left her father's house at Ascott, alias Wing, in Buckinghamshire, and travelled north to her new life in distant Yorkshire. Her coming cannot have pleased the civil authorities and devout Protestants of the north country. Her reputation preceded her and they hated her as a Catholic and as a Dormer with many influential connections at Court and in the south. And they remembered with particular loathing that her half-sister, Lady Jane Dormer, had been one of Queen Mary Tudor's closest friends and was now living in Spain as the wife of a Spaniard, the Duke de Feria.

Many bluff Yorkshiremen felt that Sir John Constable could have chosen a more suitable wife for his son and heir but they feared the power that the lady brought with her and of course they already stood in awe of the power of the Constables in their own homeland. So Margaret Constable's Catholicism was discreetly ignored and no legal action was taken against her.

In 1587, Sir John Constable died and Henry succeeded to all the estates of Burton Constable and elsewhere. By this time, Henry was already a Justice of the Peace, High Sheriff of Yorkshire and Member of Parliament for Hedon, but now he became one of the wealthiest men in the north of England, a Baronet and the Lord Paramount of the Seigniory of Holderness. He was, in fact, too important now to be overlooked by the Archbishop and his religious affairs were subjected to close scrutiny, even though no one was prepared to tangle with him lightly.

Sir Henry's conduct in itself was above suspicion. Exteriorly he conformed fully to the Established Church and meticulously observed all the religious laws as if he were a good Protestant. But he allowed his wife full freedom to practice her Catholic religion and all his children were being educated as Catholics. He was in fact a Church Papist: in his heart a sincere Catholic but prepared to deny his Faith by pretending to be an Anglican. It was a dangerous game that he was playing but he remained resolute and determined until 1608, when it would seem that at last his conscience troubled him and he openly proclaimed himself a Catholic. He was appalled at the immediate results: the Privy Council at once seized two thirds of his estates and despite his rank and dignity he found himself in prison for an indefinite term. It was all too much for him. Once more he conformed; his lands were restored to him; he was released from prison; he returned to his old way of life content to secretly encourage and clandestinely support the Catholic activities of his wife. Only in his old age, when the authorities were no longer interested in him, did Sir Henry renounce his life of subterfuge and sincerely practice the Faith in which he had always believed.

Margaret Constable however never wavered in her fidelity to the Church. In the earlier years of her marriage, when the authorities tended to leave her unmolested, she was able to devote herself to the Catholic education of her growing family and she performed this task with great success even when in later years she was subjected to active persecution. Perhaps her greatest achievement was to ensure that the Faith she loved and cherished was passed on to her descendants. Through three of her children, Viscount Dunbar, Mrs Dorothy Lawson of Brough and Lady Fairfax of Emly, she was responsible for the continuing Catholicism of three great recusant families, and indeed it has been pointed out that among her many Catholic descendants there are not just these Constables, Lawsons and Fairfaxes, but in later generations the Swinburnes, Tempests, Withams, Traffords, Blundells, Howards of Corby, Petres, Silvertops, Stricklands, Wrights, Westons and Salvins. All in all, it is a fairly representative list of those historic Catholic families who clung to the Faith through many generations of suffering, and all were proud to acknowledge Lady Margaret Constable as their common ancestress in grace and in nature.

Lady Constable's life as a recusant was not an easy one. It was true that the authorities seemed at times to be reluctant to prosecute such an important woman but as she continued to show herself to be an active Catholic so the patience of the Church and government officials was exhausted and they took action against her. The formidable and exasperated Earl of Huntingdon, President of the Council of the North, could stand no more provocation in the early 1590s and imprisoned several Catholic ladies in Sheriff Hutton Castle. Among them, of course, as one of the leaders was Lady Constable. She seemed to thrive on adversity, organized regular Masses in prison and encouraged her companions to repeated acts of defiance. The Earl of Huntingdon was glad to order the release of these difficult ladies and return them to the custody of their husbands.

By 1592, Margaret Constable had taken up residence in a more isolated part of the Constable estates near Thirsk in the North Riding. Here the family possessed the two fourteenth-century castles of Upsall and Kirby Knowle. Separated by less than a mile and away from the main road, these castles had been accepted some time before by the Catholic Mission Superiors, Father Richard Holtby SJ and Father John Mush, as safe houses and resting places for the travelling Catholic priests, many of whom had landed on the north-east coast and were making their way south to more permanent missions. The presence of Lady Constable at Upsall and indeed of her brother-in-law, Joseph Constable and his wife at Kirby Knowle provided valuable cover for the real activities of both establishments and their many 'guests' excited little comment in the immediate neighbourhood.

Of course, great care had been taken to adapt each castle to the special needs of its visitors. Kirby Knowle had been damaged by fire in 1568 and was rebuilt by Sir Henry Constable, who used the opportunity to add 'vaults and secret passages both above and below ground'. Upsall also had a maze of vaults beneath it as a means of escape into the open countryside. It is sad that nothing now remains of these original buildings but Mr Michael Hodgetts has recorded (*Secret Hiding Places*, p. 190) that a remarkable hide survived at Kirby Knowle until the nineteenth century and he has been able to describe it as a space three feet six inches square and six feet high at the junction of two solid stone walls. The entrance was concealed by a cupboard with a false back and there was a most ingenious device which could be operated from inside the hide to admit light and air. It is from such descriptions that the nature of Lady Constable's work becomes apparent.

Unfortunately, it was not possible for any safe house to be completely safe and Lady Constable was in fact betrayed by some of those she had befriended. In 1592, a seminary priest, Father Thomas Clarke was captured and under pressure of interrogation at Canterbury lost heart, apostatized, and made a full confession of all his activities since he had landed at South Shields two years before. On 7 January 1593 he informed the authorities that Lady Constable had received him as a priest two or three times at Upsall Castle, that during his visits there he had met several other priests whom he named, and that Lady Constable kept Father Cuthbert Johnson of Richmond as her permanent chaplain at Upsall.

Lady Constable was indicted on the capital offence of harbouring priests but she cannot have stayed in prison very long. On 19 September 1593, Richard Topcliffe, the notorious priest-hunter, wrote to Lord Burleigh from Buxton in the High Peak to tell him that among the Catholics staying there with Sir Robert Dormer were 'Sir Henry Constable of Burton Constable, York, with his wife Margaret, daughter of Sir William Dormer and her "traitorous priest Johnson" '. It would seem that Lady Constable was not only free but was quite unrepentant and continuing to harbour her priests no matter what the law might say.

In 1595, Lady Constable was again in trouble with the authorities when she was accused of harbouring another priest, this time at Kirby Knowle, but once more her influential friends rose to the occasion and so showered the sheriff with letters of protest that the process against her was stayed, and shortly afterwards Queen Elizabeth herself intervened to order her acquittal in return for a very vague promise from Sir Henry that he would get her to conform.

Lady Constable of course had no intention whatsoever of conforming and within a year was being mentioned in despatches again. On 10 September 1596, one of the lesser-known but very successful priest-hunters, Anthony Atkinson of Hull, was writing to the Earl of Essex, 'There are sundry places in Yorkshire and Lincolnshire that are well known to me that harboureth Joseph Constable, and sundry traitorous priests that are kept in houses by servants and friends belonging to the Lady Constable, and all under her charges, as I am credibly informed...' (Hatfield Manuscript, quoted in Joseph Hirst, *Blockhouses of Hull*, p. 44.)

Upsall Castle was still being used as a safe house for priests in August 1607 when an officious Protestant neighbour, Sir Stephen Procter of Fountains, took it upon himself to stage a raid and discovered 'hidden in the secret vaults or caves of the Castle', three seminary priests. One of these priests, Father Cuthbert Trollope managed to make his escape. The other two priests, Father William Mush and Father Matthew Flathers were taken as prisoners to York. All this information (except that he gets Father Trollope's name wrong) is given in Sir Stephen Procter's deposition in his own trial in the Court of Star Chamber in February 1614.

More details are given by Father Richard Holtby SJ in his letter of 13 April 1608 to Father Robert Persons SJ (English Province SJ Archives 37). He refers to the three people who were condemned at York, 'viz. two priests and a gentlewoman in whose house they were taken'. He then goes on to refer to Father Flathers by name and explains that although all three were condemned to death, one priest and 'the gentlewoman' were reprieved and only Father (now Blessed) Mathew Flathers was executed.

Nowhere is the 'gentlewoman' named but it is established that the priests were captured at Upsall Castle and that at that time it was Lady Constable's house.

And there is more support for this theory in a letter which Father John Mush wrote on 27 April 1608 to Pope Paul V (Westminster Cathedral Archives, B XXIV, No. 27). He tells the Holy Father that 'at York, during Holy Week, my brother, who is a priest and another priest and the widow in whose house they were captured were condemned to death...' He goes on to relate that Father Matthew Flathers was executed in a particularly brutal manner but that his brother and the widow were reprieved and 'led back once more to the prisons'. Lady Constable was in fact a widow at that time. Her husband, Sir Henry, had died on 15 December 1607.

The evidence must not be stretched to accommodate the conclusion but there does seem to be sufficient evidence to maintain at least the hypothesis that Lady Margaret Constable was the gentlewoman who was arrested at Upsall Castle with Father Matthew Flathers and Father William Mush in August 1607 and that with them she was tried in York and sentenced to death. Just how close she came to the scaffold is not known but Father John Mush's phrase 'led back once more to the prison' would seem to imply that at least the journey to the scaffold had begun and that Margaret Constable was another of the Catholic women who almost became a Martyr.

MAGDALEN BROWNE

Magdalen Browne, the daughter of William, Lord Dacre of Gillesland, was born at Naworth Castle, Cumberland in 1538. In later life she became the second wife of Sir Anthony Browne, whose descent from the Nevilles was recognized by Queen Mary when she created him Viscount Montague in 1553. The marriage was the union of two powerful Catholic families and husband and wife worked closely together for the development and enrichment of the Recusant Church in England.

Viscount Montague had always occupied an important position in government affairs but his attachment to the Catholic Church was well known. His career prospered under the Catholic Queen Mary and he was commissioned by Queen and Parliament to accompany the Bishop of Ely to Rome to present to the Pope, England's formal request for absolution and reconciliation after the Henrician schism. When Queen Elizabeth came to the throne, Lord Montague did not renounce his Faith but even the Queen acknowledged him to be a firm Papist and a good subject. Mr Joseph Gillow has maintained that 'none of the temporal lords spoke with more freedom than Lord Montague in opposition to the Reformation, and yet he behaved himself so prudently afterwards that he never appears to have lost the Queen's favour...Lord Montague was certainly the most favoured Catholic with the Protestant party in the reign of Elizabeth.' (*Bibliographical Dictionary of English Catholics*, vol. 1, p. 328.)

Lady Montague, for her part, took full advantage of her husband's position as an honoured man of affairs and as the leading Catholic layman of the country. She built up in the two main family residences of Battle Abbey and Cowdray Park in Sussex, a Catholic organization which was for many years the equivalent of a headquarters for the whole English Mission. Both houses were ideally situated. They were close enough to London for convenience and yet far enough away for safety. Battle Abbey was in isolated country in East Sussex; Cowdray Park was even more isolated in West Sussex. In both houses, hiding places for priests could easily be constructed and many of the leaders of the English Mission took up residence and lived on the hospitality of the Montagues. Nor did Lady Montague omit to make arrangements for the devotional life of her household and all her visitors.

For many years, Father Thomas More SJ, the great grandson of the martyred Lord Chancellor, was her personal chaplain but she was also very close to Father Richard Smith DD, the future Bishop and Vicar Apostolic of England, who was her confessor and who wrote in 1609 that detailed description of her life which is the major source of information about the lady herself but which is also a most valuable account of the state and condition of Catholics in England at that time.

Father Smith has conjured up a delightful picture of a great recusant lady when he described Lady Montague as a person 'who commanded her children, encouraged her servants, and importunately exhorted others' to maintain the Catholic Faith.

At Battle Abbey Lady Montague kept three chaplains in residence, and every day it was her custom to hear at least three Masses. If visiting priests were present then it was her special delight to attend the extra Masses. Father Richard Smith has described her acts of charity:

> She gave entertainment to all that repaired to her, and very seldom dismissed any without the gift of an angel; she redeemed two out of prison at her own cost, and attempted the like for others, and gave money to other Catholics both in common and particular. Her alms, distributed every second day at her gates unto the poor, were plentiful, and such as some of the richer Protestants did calumniate that they augmented the number of beggars and nourished their idleness. When she desisted from her prayers, she accustomed (sic) to spend much time in sewing shirts or smocks for poor men and women, in which exercise she seemed to take much pleasure, sometimes also when she had leisure she visited the poor in their own houses, and sent them either medicines or meat or wood or money as she perceived their need, and when she could not perform this herself, she sent her waiting women. (Quoted from Father Philip Caraman's, *The Other Face*, p. 202.)

It was a special feature of Battle Abbey that Lady Montague concerned herself not only about the religious well-being of those in her household but also welcomed all neighbouring Catholics, to all her religious services.

> She built a chapel in her house (which in such a persecution was to be admired) and there placed a very fair altar of stone, where she made an ascent with steps and enclosed it with rails; and to have everything conformable, she built a choir for singers, and set up a pulpit for the priests, which perhaps is not to be seen in all England besides. Here almost every week was a sermon made, and on solemn feasts the sacrifice of the Mass was celebrated with singing and musical instruments, and sometimes also with deacon and subdeacon. And such was the concourse and resort of Catholics, that sometimes there were 120 together, and sixty communicants at a time had the benefit of the Blessed Sacrament. And such was the number of Catholics resident in her house, and the multitude and note of such as repaired thither, that even the heretics, to the eternal glory of the name of Lady Magdalen, gave it the title of 'Little Rome'. (*Ibid.*)

Lady Montague was discreet in the manifestations of her religion and in no circumstances would she ever parade her Catholicism flamboyantly in the presence of other people. Nevertheless she refused to cover up any of the ordinary signs of her devotion or persuasions. In many Catholic households it was customary for the more important members of the congregation to follow Mass from behind a curtain or through a peephole or through an open door or window. This was to ensure that no false brother should recognize them and betray them. Lady Montague would have no truck with such subterfuge. 'She did serve God publicly in the sight of all, that by her example she might encourage all; and when she walked abroad, by her beads or cross which she used to wear about her neck, she professed herself to be a Catholic, even to whatsoever heretical beholders, and so manifest was her religion, that scarce any in England had heard her name who knew her not also to be a Catholic.' (*Ibid.*)

Lady Montague had a particular love for Battle Abbey and indeed spent most of her time in residence there but the principal seat of the Montagues was always Cowdray Park near Midhurst and it was here in this imposing quadrangular mansion that Queen Elizabeth herself was received and entertained with suitable magnificence for seven days in 1591. The Queen was fully aware that she was living in a Catholic household but even in her old age she maintained her friendship for Viscount Montague and entrusted herself with confidence to his protection. The Montagues for their part, as loyal subjects, showed their monarch every mark of respect and honour while the various priests hidden in different parts of the property played their part by keeping well out of sight.

For the Montagues, 1592 was a sad year. Lord Montague lost his son and heir when Sir Anthony Browne died on 31 July, and then he himself died on 19 October, to be succeeded by his grandson, Anthony Maria Browne, who thus became the 2nd Viscount Montague. Battle Abbey and Cowdray Park continued as citadels of Catholicism as the new Viscount sought to emulate his grandfather as the leading lay Catholic of the kingdom. Magdalen Browne, now the Dowager Lady Montague, was allowed to retain her residence at Battle Abbey and for the next sixteen years she maintained the religious atmosphere and almost monastic rule of her house while harbouring and protecting all priests who might require her assistance. As her seventieth birthday approached she suffered much physical weakness and illness but her indomitable spirit was unaffected. She still insisted on keeping all the severe, pre-Reformation laws of the Church and her confessor, Father Richard Smith, noticed that long after she was excused, by reason of her age and infirmities, 'she did piously observe all the fasts of Lent, the Ember Days and whatsoever other were either commanded by the Church, or introduced by the pious custom of the country, to which of her own devotion she added some Wednesday.' And Professor John Bossy has added to this quotation that 'when she was dying, Smith and her doctor united, to her intense disgust, in forcing her to eat meat on Ash Wednesday, "which she never did in her life before"; even then she made them take care that the family did not catch her doing it.' (*English Catholic Community*, p. 111.)

Magdalen Browne, Dowager Viscountess Montague, died a holy death in peace at her beloved Battle Abbey on 21 January 1608, but the great Catholic work she had developed in the Montague family continued until the death of the 7th Viscount in 1787.

ELIZABETH ALLEN

Most of the information available on Mrs Elizabeth Allen is contained in a book, *In the Brave Days of Old*, written by the distinguished Catholic historian Dom Bede Camm OSB in 1899. This book seems to be a series of thrilling stories of adventure and courage, and to some people might read like fiction, but Dom Bede is insistent in his preface that what he calls these 'historical sketches' have been gathered almost exclusively from records contemporary with the events they describe, and he states quite unequivocally that 'I have refrained from embroidering the facts with imaginary details, which though they might possibly add colour and life to the narratives, would do so at the cost of fidelity to historical accuracy.'

Dom Bede Camm writes about Mrs Elizabeth Allen in his chapter entitled 'The Ladies of Rossall Hall'. She was the wife of George (Richard) Allen, the older brother of Doctor William Allen, founder of the English Colleges at Douai and Rome and by papal appointment, Cardinal Prefect of the English Mission. When her husband died in 1579, Elizabeth continued to reside in the ancient family home at Rossall Hall on the Lancashire coast in the parish of Poulton-le-Fylde and there she brought up her four children.

The Allens were, of course, well known as Catholics and made no secret of their religious loyalties. They lived therefore in constant fear of the law. Their relationship to William Allen was also well known and gave rise to further fears that all those Protestants who hated the Cardinal so much might take their vengeance on the defenceless widow and her fatherless children.

Dom Bede Camm has described Mrs Allen as 'a brave woman, worthy of her family' and certainly she was most constant in the practice and profession of her Faith. She was always ready to welcome and protect the wandering priest and with her own chaplain permanently in residence it was usual for at least two Masses to be celebrated every day in the little secret chapel in the roof of the Hall. It is possible that Father Edmund Campion SJ was received here on his northern tour of April 1581 but even if this privilege was denied to Mrs Allen, at least she and her family would be with all the local Catholics who gathered with the Worthingtons at Blainscough Hall, Standish near Wigan, where the renowned missionary certainly stayed. 'He preached daily, and for many a generation there was handed down the tradition of those wondrous sermons; and old men would tell their grandchildren how their fathers had sat in the chapel of Blainscough Hall and heard the martyred Father Campion preach his great discourse on the "Hail Mary" or "The Ten Lepers".' (Camm, *ibid.*, p. 60.)

Elizabeth Allen was a woman of great prudence. Aware of the dangers that surrounded her, she recognized in particular that two of her most powerful Protestant neighbours, Edmund Fleetwood and Edward Trafford had their greedy eyes firmly fixed on the acquisition of her property. She planned therefore to take appropriate steps to protect herself and her family. Her nineteen-year-old son had already been sent overseas for his own safety. Her daughters did not seem to be in such personal danger but to safeguard their interests in the family property she summoned a lawyer to draw up a formal deed of gift so that the three little girls became undoubtedly the legal owners of all the Allen property and assets. Then, just in case of mishap, she entrusted a sum of £500 in gold to William Anyon, her faithful steward, so that if she were to be robbed of her lands there would be at least some provision for her children.

In September 1583 the authorities referred to Mrs Allen as 'an obstinate person, refusing to come to church' and she was indicted and outlawed as a recusant. In November the dangerous and devious Mr Edward Trafford was appointed High Sheriff of Lancashire and Catholics knew that this nomination boded ill for their peace. By Christmas time there were ominous signs of danger all over the county. Armed men searched Catholic houses in Prescott and carried Catholics off to prison. The pursuivants, with the riff-raff of Manchester at their heels, had interrupted the Christmas festivities at Mosborough to ransack the house and terrify the Catholic family of Mr Lathom. The time of trial for the Allens could not be far away.

To make matters worse, Rossall Hall at that time seemed to be full of people who were especially vulnerable. Mrs Allen had her daughters with her: Helen aged about sixteen, Catherine aged about fourteen and Mary aged about thirteen. The priest, Father Bromley, was in residence for the Christmas Masses. With them also were two house guests both from notorious recusant families: Mrs Isabella Conyers, the very sister of Cardinal Allen and Miss Aloysia Haydock, whose brother, Father George Haydock, was already in prison in London for his priesthood and was soon to be martyred.

The ladies of Rossall Hall prepared themselves for the onslaught. The priest was moved to his own secret hiding place in the house. Mrs Allen and Mrs Conyers withdrew each evening to a more distant hiding place which they had prepared some time before. Miss Haydock was an invalid, incapacitated by a serious illness and she therefore relied on the compassion of the intruders and remained in the house. The three girls also remained openly at home. They were too young to be molested by the pursuivants and as the legal owners of the property it was hoped that their presence might prevent the worst excesses of vandalism and robbery.

The raid took place on 6 January 1584 and as expected the house was ransacked from top to bottom. Nothing of any great value was discovered but despite the best attentions of William Anyon the hidden gold was found at the bottom of a flour bin and several little men took their pick before the sheriff received what they had left. But much damage was inflicted on the fabric and furnishings of the house. Walls were knocked down, floorboards were ripped up, doors and windows were vandalized. Treasured possessions were removed and even the dresses and toys of the children were taken away to be redistributed to various Protestant children.

Amidst all the chaos of this orgy of destruction, Miss Haydock remained undisturbed and unperturbed but when she heard the foul language of these agents of devastation and the crude insults they were offering to the Catholic Church, she could no longer contain herself and began praying at the top of her voice for the Pope and the Church and the priests. This served only to provoke the searchers the more and, ignoring the lady's infirmities, they endeavoured to silence her by force and when this failed they carried her off to prison.

For four days, the pillage of Rossall Hall was continued and in her distant hiding place, Mrs Allen grew more and more anxious about the well-being of her daughters. In fact, she need not have worried. The young ladies were able to take good care of themselves. They eschewed the company of the intruders, maintained their own rights of ownership and refused to be intimidated. Only when they realized that their own arrest was imminent did they set themselves to escape. First, they hid the keys of the front door so that it could not be locked. Then in the early hours of the morning, they crept downstairs from their rooms, pushed back the bolts on the massive main door and slipped out into the darkness.

Their problem now was where to go. They knew the district well and they knew their friends but in those days women and indeed girls of their age did not wander the countryside without a male escort and they were obliged to indulge themselves in a nerve-wracking game of hide and seek in which the prize was their own freedom. They seem to have deliberately misled their pursuers by setting off along the sea coast to the mouth of the River Wyre where they managed to find a boat and a friendly boatman who took them across the estuary to the safe land beyond. For two weeks they wandered southwards by out-of-the-way paths until at last they reached Warrington where they were reunited with their mother in the safe house of one of their uncles.

Mrs Allen made one last attempt to protect the Allen property and her children's inheritance. She forced the sheriff, Mr Edward Trafford to lay the matter before a jury in Manchester. Unfortunately, justice was still unavailable to the poor lady. The sheriff proclaimed that the Queen's enemies had no rights and Dom Bede Camm (*Ibid.*, p. 132) has described how the packed jury of twenty-four carefully selected members 'gave the verdict previously dictated to them, which was to the effect that since the children in whose name the property was claimed had not appeared before the court, they were probably dead or else had fled beyond the seas and were therefore to be considered as dead. In this case all the property would belong to the mother; but as she was proscribed, and so outside the pale of the law, everything was forfeit to the royal exchequer.'

As soon as this decision was reached, Trafford and his deputy Worsley, the officers who had searched Rossall Hall, immediately staked their claim to all the property as one of their perquisites and a proper recompense for the time and trouble they had taken. But then two noble ladies in London also put in a claim on the grounds that the Queen had granted them all property forfeited to the Crown in the county of Lancashire. And another claimant appeared in the unsavoury person of a certain Mr Baptist, who asserted that the Queen had granted him the goods of all recusant widows and orphans 'on condition that he took charge of the young maidens and saw that they were piously and properly brought up'. In fact, all these claimants clamoured in vain because as soon as William Cecil heard of the affair he used his superior power to grab everything for himself.

So Elizabeth Allen and her daughters lost all their possessions and were reduced to such poverty that they were obliged to depend upon the charity of their friends even for the necessities of life. In these harrowing circumstances they felt they had no choice but to leave their homeland and seek a better fortune overseas with the English Catholic exiles in the Low Countries. Once more they were called upon to make a difficult and dangerous journey but this time they had their mother with them and they had to travel from Lancashire to the south coast of England. It was a journey of more than 300 miles and it took them two months but they persevered and succeeded. They spent their days hiding in thickets and woodlands and then under cover of darkness walked through the long nights. At times they recognized the homes of faithful friends and were able to relax and sleep with a roof over their heads. After much anxiety and great hardship they crossed the sea and reached Rheims on 9 September 1584, and there, writes Dom Bede Camm, 'they were received with great joy and congratulations by the illustrious princes of the House of Guise and the principal nobles and prelates of the Church of Rheims; and with even greater joy by the English exiles there, and most of all by their kinsman, Dr Allen, for whose sake they had received so great a part of their bitter cup.'

Elizabeth Allen, like many of the English exiles was granted a pension by King Philip II of Spain and on this eighty ducats a month she set up house and settled down with her family in Louvain. Very shortly after her arrival she suffered the tragic loss of her son John. He died on 24 June 1585 at the early age of twenty-one. Her youngest daughter, Mary, married Thomas Worthington of Blainscough Hall, Standish near Wigan. He also was exiled in Louvain after spending five years of his youth in prison in England for his Faith. Both Helen and Catherine became nuns as Canonesses of Saint Augustine in Saint Ursula's Convent, Louvain. Helen was professed in 1594 and died in 1603. Catherine was professed on 8 May 1595 and was one of the original band of seven English nuns who left Saint Ursula's on 10 February 1608 to found the daughter convent of Saint Monica's. She died in 1612 leaving her sister, Mary Worthington, as the sole heiress to all the estates of Rossall Hall, but Mary's claims were not legally recognized and the family never regained the property.

Mrs Elizabeth Allen never returned to England. It is certain that she ended her days in Louvain but her date of death is unknown. She was able to offer hospitality to the nuns of Saint Ursula's as they made their way to Saint Monica's in 1608, and the Convent Chronicles relate that she laid in a barrel of beer and a batch of bread to welcome the nuns to their new abode. By this time she must have been close to seventy years of age and her name is not mentioned again. Dom Bede Camm has offered her this final tribute,

'She had suffered robbery and exile, privation and danger for the faith of her fathers, and we cannot doubt that she was judged worthy of the promises of Christ.'

JANE WISEMAN (HUDDLESTON)

Jane Huddleston was the eldest of the five daughters of Sir Edmund Huddleston and his wife Dorothy Beconsall. She was born at Sawston Hall some seven miles south of Cambridge and educated there as a fervent Catholic in this strongly religious family, which had first been reported for recusancy as early as 1577. So Jane grew up in a house with its own resident priest and which was also a place of refuge and hospitality for many of the travelling priests of the district. By 1584, Sir Edmund had established two excellent hiding places for his priest-guests and later, after his death, his son, Henry, commissioned Saint Nicholas Owen to build what Granville Squiers described in 1933 as 'undoubtedly the finest hiding-place in the country'.

From this Catholic citadel at Sawston Hall, Jane moved about a dozen miles to the similar house at Braddocks near Thaxted where she married William Wiseman and became the mistress of a household which included her mother-in-law, the other Jane Wiseman and the domestic chaplain, Father Richard Jackson.

In the spring of 1591, William Wiseman met Father John Gerard SJ, the eminent missionary, and was so impressed by his words and example that he resolved to 'devote the whole of his life to furthering God's greater glory', and as a token of his determination placed his house, his family and himself at the Jesuits' disposal. Father Gerard saw clearly the advantages to his mission that would follow from residence at Braddocks but he wondered what sort of reception he might receive from Mrs Wiseman, about whom he knew very little and who might well resent the upheaval in her domestic arrangements that the presence of a Jesuit priest would demand.

William Wiseman appreciated the problem but gave Father Gerard every assurance that 'he was determined all the same, come what might, to replace his Protestant servants by carefully chosen Catholics (but in a kindly and generous way) and to win over his wife and chaplain, if he could, by gentle persuasion, and if that failed, by using his authority as master of the house.' (John Gerard, *Autobiography*, translated by Philip Caraman (1951), p. 29.)

In fact no problems presented themselves. As befitted a Huddleston, Jane Wiseman willingly accepted all the changes and as Father Gerard insisted, 'she surpassed everyone in the care she lavished on the chapel and in her attention to all my wants'. (Gerard, *ibid.*, p. 30.) The religious life of the family has already been described in the account of the older Mrs Wiseman but it has to be acknowledged that while Father Gerard established himself so carefully and prudently at Braddocks, a government spy, John

Frank, had also established himself among the servants and was supplying his real masters with a steady stream of information.

On 15 March 1594, the pursuivants raided the house in Golding Lane, Holborn, London which the spy had identified as property belonging to William Wiseman for the use of Father Gerard. By good fortune Father Gerard was not at home but several of his servants were arrested and the following day Mr Wiseman himself, unaware of any danger, called at the house and was promptly detained. All the captives stood firm and refused to talk but Mr Wiseman was put in a cell of his own and allowed neither companions nor visitors.

As soon as he heard the news about this raid, Father Gerard went at once to Braddocks to confer with Jane Wiseman. He found her surprisingly calm and together they hid away the Mass things and prepared the house for the inevitable search. 'It was really impossible for me to desert the family now,' wrote Father Gerard, (*ibid.*, p. 56), 'for they were going through such an anxious and difficult time.' So the priest stayed with Mrs Wiseman and despite the impending danger celebrated all the ceremonies and liturgy of Holy Week.

Father Gerard has left a full account of what happened on Easter Monday, 1 April 1594. He has written, (Gerard, *ibid.*, p. 58 et seq.):

...we rose earlier than usual for Mass, for we felt there was danger about. As we were preparing everything for Mass before daybreak we heard, suddenly, a great noise of galloping hooves. The next moment, to prevent any attempt at escape, the house was encircled by a whole troop of men. At once we realised what was afoot. We barred the doors: the altar was stripped, the hiding-places opened and all my books and papers thrown in. It was most important to pack me away first with all my belongings. I was for using the hiding-place near the dining room: it was farther away from the chapel (the most suspected part of the house) and it had a supply of provisions – a bottle of wine and some light sustaining biscuits and other food that would keep. Also there was more chance there of over-hearing the searchers' conversation and picking up some information that might prove helpful to us. This is why I preferred it; and it was also a well built and safe place. However, the mistress of the house (it turned out to be providential) was opposed to it. She wanted me to use the place near the chapel. I could get into it more quickly and hide all the altar things away with me. As she was very insistent, I agreed, although I knew I would have nothing to eat if the search was a long one. We hid away everything that needed hiding and I went in.

At this stage, it should be remarked that although today two thirds of Braddocks has been pulled down, the remaining wing still stands and according to Mr Michael Hodgetts contains the hide which had been built by Saint Nicholas Owen in 1592 and in which Father John Gerard took refuge in 1594. Mr Hodgetts has visited this hide, and has written in his 1989 book, *Secret Hiding Places*, (p. 57):

It is entered from the secret chapel, the usual long, low room at the top of the house. Here Owen took up the tiles from the fireplace and constructed a false hearth. Under this he burrowed down into the solid brickwork of the chimneystack. The hole adjoins the great chamber below, and is situated high up and slightly to the left of the Renaissance fireplace. It was separated from this room only by lath-and-plaster covered with panelling. The finished hole is 2 feet wide, 5 feet 2 inches long and 5 feet 6 inches tall at its highest point.

Now John Gerard was not a small man. Richard Topcliffe has said, 'he was of good stature and the Government spy, William Byrd, described him as "of stature tall".' In the restricted space of this hide, he could neither stand up straight nor lie down with ease; missionary priests had to conquer any tendencies to claustrophobia; hiding places were constructed for safety not comfort.

No sooner had Jane Wiseman tucked Father Gerard away in this tomb-like hide than the front door of the house was broken down by the pursuivants who then proceeded to ransack the house in their search for the priest. Even the tiles of the roof were lifted so that these ruthless men could examine underneath and Father Gerard has explained how 'they measured the walls with long rods and if the measurements did not tally, they pulled down the section that they could not account for. They tapped every wall and floor for hollow spots; and on sounding anything hollow they smashed it in.'

Jane Wiseman realized her own dreadful responsibility; she knew that Father Gerard would never give himself up, for to do so would imperil the lives of all his protectors. So the noble lady had just to wait with patience and conceal her anxiety. Only she knew where Father Gerard was hidden and if she were taken away then the priest's hiding place would become his tomb.

For four long days the search continued and Mrs Wiseman kept her secret but at last the intruders departed the house and she was able to rush to Father Gerard's assistance, who wrote (*Ibid.*, p. 62).

I was very wasted and weak with hunger and lack of sleep. All that time, I had been squatting in a very confined place. While the search was on, the mistress of the house had eaten nothing whatsoever, partly because she wanted to share my discomfort and find out by testing herself how long I could live without food, but chiefly to draw down God's mercy upon me and upon herself and her whole family by fasting and prayer. When I came out, I found her face so changed that she looked a different person; and had it not been for her voice and her dress, I doubt whether I would have recognised her.

Father John Gerard left Braddocks at once and made his way to London but in the great city, the traitor John Frank caught up with him and denounced him to the authorities. On 23 April 1594 the priest was imprisoned in the Counter in Poultry, which Father Henry Garnet SJ has described as 'a very evil prison and without comfort'. Here, also, Mr William Wiseman had been a prisoner for almost a month, and so in order to be near her husband and her chaplain, Jane Wiseman bought herself an adjacent house and settled in to spend all her days in caring for them both and helping them as best she could.

Father Gerard has gratefully described how Mrs Wiseman visited him frequently in the filth of his prison and supported him while seeking his 'advice and direction in all her affairs'. When William Wiseman secured his own release by means of judicious bribery, he did not leave the area but joined his wife in her new residence and they lived there together at the service of Father Gerard for as long as he was in prison.

On 4 October 1597, after three and a half years spent in prison, Father John Gerard made his escape from the Tower of London. Among those who helped him in this daring feat were Mr and Mrs Wiseman and for a short time he stayed with them in their London house in the Strand. The dangers, however, were too great for the Wisemans to continue to harbour Father Gerard and for this reason he steadfastly refused their pressing invitation to base himself once again at Braddocks.

So William and Jane Wiseman returned home on their own with a new chaplain, Father Richard Banks SJ, and for the rest of their lives maintained Braddocks as a thriving centre of Catholic resistance and a place of safety for the Seminary priests and the Jesuits.

MARGARET CLEMENT

Margaret Clement was the youngest of the eleven children of Margaret Clement (née Giggs) and her husband, Doctor John Clement. She was born in 1540 and was only seven years old when the dangers of the times obliged her father to take his whole family into exile in Flanders. Here, in 1548, Margaret and her sister Helen were sent for their education to the Dutch Augustinian convent of Saint Ursula's where their former tutor, Elizabeth Woodford, was already in residence as a nun.

In 1553 when Queen Mary ascended the throne of England, the Clement family returned to their homeland but Margaret, then aged thirteen, insisted that she wished to become a nun and she wished to stay with the Canonesses of Saint Augustine in Louvain. Her father was certainly not prepared to deny her the fulfilment of her vocation but with England now restored to the Catholic Faith he wanted her to enter the Royal Convent of the Brigettines at Sion House and in fact had already made arrangements for her cell in the renovated monastery on the banks of the Thames. On the advice of Bishop Bonner, however, he allowed her to stay in Louvain and thus spared her the pains of the suppression of Sion under Queen Elizabeth.

The story of Margaret's life was written in 1611 by Sister Elizabeth Shirley and her manuscript edition has been used by both C.S. Durrant in *A Link between the Flemish Mystics and the English Martyrs* and by Father John Morris, SJ in his *Troubles of our Catholic Forefathers*. Sister Elizabeth Shirley has written:

> In the year 1557, upon the 11th of October, our said Margaret Clement was admitted to Religious Profession after she had been five years a scholar, and one year and a half a Novice. One year of probation had been sufficient according to the constitutions of the house, but the importunity of her father to have her into England was the cause of this her so long delay. And this her long probation was the more beneficial unto her by reason that she did not one jot the less carefully apply herself to gain the perfection of a Religious life, but it was a testimony that she had gotten already what some Professed Religious do not in many years attain unto, for being proved by delay, her constancy and settled mind in God, and love to Religious life, did the more manifestly appear in her.

Margaret had been a model student and a promising novice. Now as a fully professed member of the community she was held in wide esteem.

'Sister Margaret doth chapter us all,' said one of the Sisters, meaning that by her example she corrected all the others.

Indeed, Margaret was so loved and respected by the other members of the community that in 1570, when she was only thirty years old and twelve years professed, she was elected to the office of Prioress. It was a very close election; she won by only one vote, and at once the minority party appealed to Rome on the grounds that she was one of only two Englishwomen in an otherwise Dutch community, and in any case the appointment of such a young Prioress was forbidden by Canon Law. Commissioners were sent to examine the case and according to C.S. Durrant (*op. cit.*, p. 194):

> All the nuns were given a hearing by the Visitors, and those who opposed the election, put forward, besides the objection raised as to her age, the fact that she was not of their nation and the staple accusation in such case, that she was a setter-up of novelties. But the Visitors perceiving that the opposition was motivated on nothing but her zeal in seeking to reform what had been 'slacked from want of good government, highly commended her proceedings, and gave her more full authority than before'. So Margaret was fain to submit to the yoke laid upon her shoulders, though says her biographer, 'I cannot express with what sorrow and grief she received the charge of government.'

How admirably Mother Margaret Clement succeeded, the subsequent history of her community testifies. She was a reformer who tightened up the observance of the rules and corrected laxity and abuse, but she was, wrote Sister Elizabeth Shirley, 'as careful to keep love and amity among us as the apple of her eye and so many sorts of nations, as Dutch, French, English, Spaniards, Germans, all in one house, lived in great unity and concord'.

Margaret Clements's greatest achievement, however, was to act as a beacon guiding more and more Englishwomen across the seas to the religious life in exile that she was pioneering. It was a perilous undertaking for Catholic women to escape overseas. They could not travel alone; they needed protection and every disguise demanded company. Officers of the Government were watching the roads for suspicious strangers and spies and informers infested every port. Only the courageous could make the attempt to serve God in the Louvain cloister and those postulants who came knocking on the door were familiar with the sufferings of the Martyrs and in many cases knew them as members of their own families or as close personal friends.

When Mother Margaret celebrated the Golden Jubilee of her profession in 1606, she had twenty-two English sisters in choir with her to thank God and they did not forget the other six English sisters who had died. Dom Adam Hamilton, the Editor of the Chronicle of Saint Monica's Convent, Louvain has pointed out the special relationship of these nuns with the English Martyrs. Margaret Clement, of course, through her mother, the other Margaret Clement, was closely connected to Saint Thomas More and the Martyrs of the London Charterhouse. Sister Frances Felton was the daughter of Blessed John Felton and the sister of Blessed Thomas Felton. And Dom Adam continues:

> Looking round the stalls of the Choir in 1600, one would have seen there Anne Clitheroe, the daughter of Venerable Margaret, the gentle martyr of York; Margaret and Helen Garnett, sisters to the Martyred Provincial of the English Jesuits, whose nephew was one of our venerable martyrs; Susan Laburn or Laybourne, one of whose childish reminiscences was her visit to her father, the martyred James Laybourne as he lay in chains awaiting his execution; Ann and Dorothy Rookwood, in whose saintly family fines and the dungeon were household words; Bridget and Mary Wiseman whose parents had been condemned to death for harbouring priests; Frances Burrows, who at eleven years of age, though threatened with instant death, had saved a hunted priest from pursuivants; Helen and Catherine Allen, nieces to the great Cardinal, whose mother had barely escaped with life from the persecutors... There are few nobler pictures in the Annals of religious Communities than that of those brave old days of this illustrious English House of cloistered religious. (C.S. Durrant, *A Link between Flemish Mystics and English Martyrs*, (1924), p. 215.)

By 1609, it seemed to many that the time had come for the English Sisters to branch out and found their own convent, and two of the sisters, Sister Catherine Allen and Sister Elizabeth Shirley broached the subject officially with their Superiors. Old Mother Mary Clement was now blind and had been obliged to retire from being Prioress at the time of her Golden Jubilee celebrations in 1606. Now she was consulted by virtue of her seniority and joyfully supported the proposal. Her successor as Prioress, Mother Winifred de Castro gave her formal consent and promised to give whatever assistance she could. The neighbouring Benedictine Abbot of Vlierbeke offered them a suitable house, not far from Saint Ursula's and the Archbishop himself, Matthias van den Hove, drew up a canonical deed by which he released the English Sisters from their obedience to the Prioress of Saint Ursula's and appointed the feast of Saint Scholastica, 10 February 1609 as the date on which the change was to be implemented.

This new house of Saint Monica's was begun in great poverty. The sisters had to beg from the sisters who remained at Saint Ursula's; they had to beg from the townsfolk of Louvain; and they had to beg from their families in England. But the Convent succeeded and twenty years later had so many English sisters that a new foundation was made at Bruges.

Mother Margaret Clement, the great pioneer and the foundress of this extraordinary spiritual movement could play little part in the development of Saint Monica's, but suffered the burden of her years and her blindness as a member of the new community. She was seventy-two years of age when she died in 1612 and had been a nun for fifty-five years and Prioress of Saint Ursula's for thirty-six years. 'The Old Mother' had lived in exile from England

146

since she was seven years of age but through her daughters in religion she made a major contribution to the growth of the Church in her native land through all those terrible days of persecution even to our own day.

KATHERINE RADCLIFFE

Katherine Radcliffe was the daughter of Sir Roger Radcliffe, who in 1550 married the wealthy Bigod heiress and thereby took possession of the extensive estates of Mulgrave Castle near Whitby in the North Riding of Yorkshire.

Sir Roger was a man of some influence in the county and was commonly accounted to be a Protestant. By 1564, he was a Justice of the Peace and Thomas Young, Archbishop of York described him as a 'favourer of religion', but in point of fact there were many signs that he was a secret Catholic. He enjoyed a close friendship with Robert Pursglove, former Prior of Guisborough and deprived suffragan Bishop of Hull, but now, since 1561, a formal recusant who was included in an official list of 'stiff papists' and forbidden to travel more than twelve miles from his residence at Ugthorpe. Such friendships were dangerous and Roger Radcliffe had too many Catholic friends for safety's sake. Richard Salvin, the deprived priest from Hinderwell, was believed to be living on the Radcliffe estate at Borrowby. In 1576, hospitality was extended for three months to Robert Norton, a notorious recusant, and in 1577 several Catholic refugees from County Durham were kindly received and supported. It is difficult to escape the conclusion that Sir Roger Radcliffe was a Church Papist who masqueraded as a Protestant in order to save his estates while his wife and daughter were able to practice more openly as Catholics.

In 1564-5, Roger Radcliffe bought Ugthorpe Manor from Robert Pursglove and Katherine Radcliffe took up residence in Ugthorpe Old Hall. Here in the isolation of the Moors and surrounded by stalwart Catholic friends she devoted herself to the Catholic cause and became well known in the district as the leading recusant.

When Dom Bede Camm OSB, the noted Catholic historian visited Ugthorpe in the early 1900s, he inspected Katherine Radcliffe's Old Hall and found much of Catholic interest, although he lamented that the house had 'fallen from its ancient dignity' and was now a farmhouse. He observed that 'in an out-building to the left of the Hall, which is now used as a cow-byre, there is a curious priests' hiding-place made in a chimney,' and that 'Another cow-byre close to the Old Hall (on the right as you face the front door) was once a Catholic Chapel.' And Dom Bede continues:

> People still living remember their parents speaking of the time when they used to hear Mass regularly in this humble sanctuary. There is little enough now to tell of its former sacred character, though there

148

still can be seen what is called a holy-water stoup, but which is perhaps more probably an aumbry. It is sad to see this building, which once witnessed the Sacred Mysteries, now the home of the beasts of the field. But after all, it was in such company that the Saviour of the world was born. (Dom Bede Camm, *Forgotten Shrines*, p. 290.)

As long as her father was alive, Katherine Radcliffe seems to have been unmolested by the civil authorities, but when he died in 1588 she was at once exposed to the harsh realities of a man's world. She was a defenceless woman on her own and it is a matter of some speculation as to why she never married. She had sufficient wealth for a marriage settlement; she was from a good family with powerful friends; she was known and respected throughout Yorkshire and even had connections at Court in London. And yet, quite contrary to the universal custom of the times, she never married and one is left with the impression that she was in fact practicing voluntary celibacy as an unofficial nun on the pattern later developed by Mary Ward and her first disciples at Osgodby.

Katherine Radcliffe never owned Mulgrave Castle. It was left in her father's will to her half-brother, William, but he seems to have been beset by difficulties and played little part in public life. Katherine was commonly regarded as the head of the family and as soon as she received her own inheritance of Ugthorpe she endeavoured to demonstrate her patriotism and loyalty to the Crown by making, on 14 May 1588, an ex gratia payment of £25 to subsidize defence arrangements against the Armada. Her generosity unfortunately served little purpose. Within three years, the whole Mulgrave estate was taken from the family and granted by Queen Elizabeth to one of her sea captains, Lord Sheffield, for his services against the Armada, and despite his Catholic wife and his own earlier leanings towards Catholicism, the noble lord set himself up as the leading Protestant in the predominantly Catholic area and eventually secured his further prize for subservience when he was appointed Lord President of the Council of the North.

J.C.H. Aveling has pointed out that 'the Radcliffes of Mulgrave and the Babthorpes of Osgodby in the East Riding were, by tradition, the two most striking cases of Catholic gentry who lost their all as a result of recusancy fines,' (*Northern Catholics*, p. 130) and certainly the loss of Mulgrave was a decisive blow to the Radcliffes from which they never really recovered.

Another Catholic of those days, Thomas Meynell, has maintained that the Radcliffe 'lands were lost by reason of pretended Concealment as many think for want of management' but there is ample evidence that Roger Radcliffe managed his estate with care and skill. It seems much more likely that the lands were lost because the astute and grasping Lord Sheffield spotted and exploited a legal weakness in the Radcliffe title to Mulgrave. After all, the whole estate had been confiscated by King Henry VIII when the owner, Sir Francis Bigod, was executed as a traitor after the Pilgrimage of Grace and the restoration to his son Sir John Bigod may well have been legally flawed.

Katherine Radcliffe continued to live at Ugthorpe Old Hall but she knew no peace from the pursuivants and informers and her activities were such that she was forced to pay heavy fines and subject herself to frequent imprisonments in York. The details of her life can be pieced together mainly from her 'criminal' record, but it is difficult to ascertain the precise times when she was in prison and when she was in Ugthorpe.

Her first conviction was in 1590 and at this time her estate was seized for the rest of her life and two-thirds forcibly let for a mean rent of just over £70 a year.

In *The Blockhouses of Hull*, Mr Joseph Hirst has quoted the following statement from the Acts of the Ecclesiastical Commissioners of the North (p. 111):

> Tuesday, 30th. May, 1592, the Archbishop presiding, the Commissioners did set down and decree that Mrs. Katherine Radcliffe and Mrs. Margaret Cholomley (sic) should be sent to the Keeper of Rotherham Castle to be kept prisoners there for their recusancy, in case the Keeper come within seven days now next coming to enter bond for their safe keeping etc.; but if he do not come, that the said Mrs. Radcliffe shall be presently after the expiration of these seven days sent to Hull...

And it should perhaps be added that only the most determined and difficult Catholic prisoners were sent to the Blockhouses in Hull, where the prison arrangements were much more cruel than they were in York. To be sent to Hull was a clear sign of the importance that the Government attached to Katherine Radcliffe and a clear sign of the leading role she was playing in Catholic affairs.

She was free again for part of 1592 and it was reported to the civil authorities by Thomas Clarke, an apostate priest, that Father Cuthbert Crawfurth was her chaplain at Ugthorpe at that time and in his confessions this same Thomas Clarke acknowledged that in the past, he himself had said Mass 'at Mrs Katherine Radcliffe's manor house at Ugthorpe'.

Katherine Radcliffe was in prison again in 1593, and J.C.H. Aveling has noted that despite her obstinate refusal to obey the law, she was 'not without sympathy and even Court patronage', and he goes on to explain that 'the Privy Council noted that suit was made for her release on compassionate grounds by some "persons here of good account at Court".' (Aveling, *op. cit.*, p. 130.) Whether this influence achieved her release or not is not known but Catholic life in Ugthorpe continued unabated.

The Pipe Office Rolls for 1592-3 give a list of the names of those recusants owing large sums of money to the Exchequer and in this list Katherine's name appears twice. The Cecil Papers for 1592 (reference 22/26) state that among the seminary priests in Yorkshire 'yet untaken' is Mr David Englebe (sic) 'often at Ugthorpe'.

In 1596 the authorities once more suspected the presence of a priest at Ugthorpe and later that year they managed to name him as Richard Parker. There would seem to be no doubt that priests were regularly in residence at Ugthorpe but only some were brought to the attention of the authorities.

And all this time, Katherine Radcliffe remained constant and accepted whatever the law might impose on her. Father John Knaresborough in his manuscript the 'Suffering of the Catholics' has given a list of fifty-three Catholic prisoners who were in York Castle in 1599. It is interesting that twenty of these prisoners were women and of course among them was 'Mrs Katherine Radcliffe of Ugthorpe, gentlewoman'.

This was perhaps her last visit to prison. The final years of Queen Elizabeth's reign and the early years of the reign of King James I ushered in a quieter period for Catholics when the laws against them were not enforced with such rigour. Katherine still had to pay her fines and endure the loss of her property but the local civil authorities must have lost heart and realized that a woman with such strength and determination could not be defeated and the more prudent officials were content to leave her well alone.

Her role as the leading Catholic in a thriving Catholic community was also emphasized in 1599, when violence broke out at Dunsley on the Mulgrave estates. James Sisson and John Cornforth as sheriff's deputies attempted to seize the cattle of Henry Fairfax because as a Catholic he had not paid his recusancy fines. Their efforts were forcibly resisted by a group of some eighteen to twenty Catholic men, who were said to be 'weaponed with staves, pitchforks, bows and arrows' and who were soon reinforced by another party of twenty horsemen and ten footmen who were armed with 'bows, halberds, fowling-pieces, callivers, javelins, staves, swords and daggers'. In the ensuing conflict some of Sisson's men were wounded but all were disarmed and were then taken to the house of 'Mistress Katherine Radcliffe at Ugthorpe' for examination.

It was a sign of Katherine Radcliffe's stature in the community that she should be the one to scrutinize the warrants of these intrusive officials and then, having satisfied herself that they were authentic, she took it upon herself to order them to leave the district. Despite the humiliations of her imprisonments, Katherine Radcliffe demonstrated very clearly that she was still a very powerful woman among her own people.

But the Catholics living in the Ugthorpe area were not just the country folk who had been born and bred on the moors. Katherine Radcliffe attracted to herself and offered warm hospitality to a large collection of Catholic men and women who came to her from afar to seek the safety of her protection and the services of her priests. In 1590, among her refugee guests at Ugthorpe, Egton and Whitby were Lady Anne Neville and two members of the Fulthorpe family as well as the Readmans, the Hardings, and Henry Thorney, gentleman. In 1597, J.C.H. Aveling reports that the Readmans of Mulgrave sold their lands and joined 'Katherine Radcliffe's sizable collection of poor relations and pensioners'. (Aveling. *op. cit.*, p. 180.) By 1603, this lady of the manor had settled a small group of Catholic farmers as sub-tenants on her lands at Goathland and by 1621 Aveling maintains that Katherine Radcliffe's house 'was almost an Osgodby or Saint Anthony's, Newcastle, sheltering a round dozen of vagrant Catholic gentry relations', including now, in addition to the Readmans, the Hardings and the Fulthorpes the more recent arrivals of the Ridleys from the north, the Salvins from Egton and Lady Anne Ingilby. (Aveling, *op. cit.*, p. 269.)

Katherine Radcliffe would seem to have died in 1621, triumphant in her cause, but impoverished. Shortly after her death, Roger Radcliffe, her nephew and her heir was described by Thomas Meynell as 'now a poor gentleman, destitute of all means to live'. Perhaps he moved away; he is never mentioned in the local recusant rolls. By 1636, the remaining Radcliffes had sold the manor of Ugthorpe, their last major possession in the district, but many of them continued to live in the neighbourhood as poor recusants.

In the Catholic folklore of the moors, Katherine Radcliffe is remembered even today as a great Catholic lady in her own right. Historically, it is not unrealistic to credit her with a major share in the preservation of the Faith in that part of Yorkshire. She must have known the boy, Nicholas Postgate of Egton Bridge, and she may well have helped him on his way to Douai. She died just as the future Martyr began his studies for the priesthood but she had prepared the way for him so well that when he returned to the moors as a priest some forty years later, there were still many Catholic people to welcome him and the debt they all owed to Katherine Radcliffe has never been forgotten.

ANNE CLITHEROW

Anne Clitherow was the second child and eldest daughter of Saint Margaret Clitherow. She was born about the year 1574 and would therefore be about twelve years of age when her mother was martyred in 1586.

At that time, Anne was one of the oldest children in the secret school which Saint Margaret had set up for her own children and some of their Catholic friends in the family home in the Shambles at York. Her older brother Henry had already escaped to Rheims in France in order to study for the priesthood and Anne was well aware of the dangerous times in which she was living and her responsibility to protect the priests whom she knew were frequently in residence in the hidden room.

Perhaps the children knew too much. Perhaps the schoolmaster, Mr Brian Stapleton, trusted them too much. They had the run of the house and they knew where the secret door was and even how to open it. Father John Mush did not hesitate to express his disquiet that so much was known by so many very young people.

The good priest's fears were justified on 10 March 1586 when the sheriffs of York came to the house, seeking the priest and hoping to incriminate Margaret Clitherow as a harbourer of priests. At first, their search was fruitless. The escape routes were so well planned that the priest and the schoolmaster made rapid and successful exits. All the searchers could find was a diligent housewife busily engaged on her domestic duties and a group of small schoolchildren bereft of their teacher. The ensuing scene is not difficult to picture: the harsh words of the men, the threats against the children, the blows, the nips, the humiliations, the growing terror of the children until the weakest could stand no more and gave away the information that resulted in the discovery of the Mass room and the arrest and martyrdom of the lady of the house.

It is noteworthy that the one who cracked was not Anne Clitherow, the 'weak' girl, but the Flemish boy who was at least the same age as Anne and possibly older. There is no evidence that Anne said anything but the terrified boy said more than enough.

Margaret Clitherow was immediately separated from her children; in fact she never saw them again. She was taken to the Manor and then to the Castle. Father Mush says explicitly that 'the children and the servants were all sent to divers prisons'. Perhaps Anne was allowed to stay with her younger sister and brother, who were aged respectively ten and five years old. Perhaps the separation was even more drastic than that and they were kept apart from each other.

Just before her death, Margaret Clitherow, from her prison, sent to her daughter in her prison a very special and symbolic present. All this great woman had to give were the stockings and shoes she had worn to prison. Now she sent them to Anne with all her love, but 'signifying' as Father Mush has pointed out, 'that she should serve God and follow her steps of virtue'.

Anne Clitherow and her brother and sister were released from prison after the death of their mother. They returned to their father's house in the Shambles, and shortly afterwards he married again. The name of this, his third wife, is not known, but Anne was certainly not happy with her new stepmother. She ran away from home about the year 1589 when she was but fifteen years of age, and Katherine Longley suggests that she did this in order to avoid an arranged marriage. It would seem that even at that very early age when it is most unlikely that she had ever seen a nun in her life, she was already contemplating a religious vocation.

The position of such an ardent Catholic in John Clitherow's Protestant household cannot have been an easy one and there is no information as to when Anne returned home. By 12 July 1593 she was a prisoner again, this time in Lancaster Gaol, 'for causes ecclesiastical'. John Clitherow went to the Earl of Derby with a letter from the Lord Mayor of York in an effort to obtain his daughter's release. He promised to pay a bond for her 'to be conferred withal by some learned and godly preachers' and 'if she cannot be conformed, then to make her appearance before the High Commission'. (York House Book, xxxi, f 20.)

Anne Clitherow had come of age by 1596 and as soon as possible she made the hazardous journey across the seas to Louvain where she entered Saint Ursula's Convent. She made her profession as a Canoness of Saint Augustine in 1598. The Convent Annals state that 'she followed well her holy mother's virtuous steps, for she was a very good religious, and one that set herself very seriously to the way of perfection...She laboured well in the overcoming of her nature and the practice of solid virtue. She also by her own industry got the Latin tongue so well as to understand it perfectly.'

In common with the other English nuns in a predominately Flemish community, Anne Clitherow 'assisted much in the erection of Saint Monica's Convent, Louvain' to which most of the English sisters moved on 10 February 1609 (Convent Annals). Anne herself was not able to make the move because 'she wanted friends to allow her means'. In other words, she lacked the wealthy friends who could have given her the necessary financial assistance and her Protestant father was not likely to help her. And so she remained at Saint Ursula's as one of the four English nuns who 'lived happily amidst their Flemish Sisters'. (Convent Annals.)

C.S. Durrant has described in *A Link between the Flemish Mystics and the English Martyrs* (p. 221) how these four English nuns lived in Saint Ursula's and helped the foundation of Saint Monica's. 'They furthered the foundation by every means in their power; Sister Anne Clitherow was especially zealous, and by her counsel and assistance greatly encouraged Sister Shirley (foundress of the new convent). A sisterly intercourse was kept up between the two convents, and when any were admitted to Saint

Monica's, they were sent before receiving the religious habit to visit Saint Ursula's.'

When these four English Sisters died, the Annals of Saint Ursula's record that 'they left behind them in that cloister much edification of virtue and a note of sanctity.' Anne Clitherow was probably just forty-eight years of age when she died on 3 August 1622, but she had been a nun for twenty-six years.

The nuns of Saint Monica's were driven out of their home by the French revolutionaries in 1798 and came back to England, first to Amesbury in Wiltshire and then in 1861 to Newton Abbot in South Devon. With them they brought a treasured possession: it was a unique copy of the Abstract of Father John Mush's *A True Report of the Life and Martyrdom of Mrs. Margaret Clitherow* published in 1619. The book is dedicated to 'the Virtuous and Devout Religious Sister Anne Clitherow, of the Order of Louvain'.

SISTER DOROTHEA

The mysterious Sister Dorothea was one of the first of Mary Ward's English nuns to actively engage herself in the dangerous apostolate of the English Mission. Like all her fellow-workers she had to seek safety in secrecy but over and above the ordinary demands of security, Sister Dorothea pursued obscurity and anonymity as expressions of her religious virtue and humility. She had entered the Institute of the Blessed Virgin Mary as a simple lay sister but from what is known of her it is evident that she was a highly educated woman, a lady by birth and indeed of some position in the polite society of her day. None of her Sisters in religion knew her surname or the name of her family and it has been suggested by Mother Catherine Chambers IBVM (*Life of Mary Ward*, vol 2, p. 28), 'that she must have obtained from Mary Ward the permission that this ignorance should last on even after her death. The old French Necrology, which states the day of her death, though not the year, gives her no other nomenclature.'

All that is known about Sister Dorothea is preserved in a report which she made to her Superior, Mother Frances Brookesby, in 1622 and which is kept in the Nymphenburg Archives of her Institute. The report is headed, 'A relation of one of ours, a lay-sister, one of those that live in villages in England', and the narrative begins,

> According to your command I intend in the best and briefest manner I can to relate my proceedings and manner of living: which is in the house of a poor woman, pretending to be her kinswoman. And by the means of my worthy lady H.H., who only knoweth who I am, I have sometimes means of frequenting the sacraments for myself and others: the want of which is indeed very great, and the greatest suffering I have; all the rest is nothing, neither is this much considering for Whose sake it is.

Sister Dorothea's 'worthy lady' is known to be Lady Timperley who lived at Hintlesham Hall near Ipswich in Suffolk. Mary Ward was well acquainted with the people of Suffolk and Lady Timperley was a daughter of Sir John Shelley of Sussex and a near relation of one of the Sisters of the Institute. Sister Dorothea's assignment to Hintlesham is therefore probably due to this connection.

In England at that time some of Mary Ward's nuns were living in secret in a quasi-community in London but most were established in isolated villages and country houses from which bases they ventured forth to evangelize all classes of society in the surrounding district. Like Sister Dorothea they wore lay dress and used every endeavour to allay Protestant suspicions by keeping out of the public eye. Sister Dorothea's story is important in its own right as a detailed account of her life and work but it is also important in its reflection of the life and work of so many other intrepid woman who lived and worked for the Faith as she did.

In her report Sister Dorothea describes her work: 'I dare not keep schools publicly as we do beyond the seas, especially at my first coming, because it was before Easter when presentments are accustomed to be, and all sorts of people looked into, but I teach or instruct children in the houses of parents, which I find to be a very good way, and by that occasion I get acquaintance, and so gaining first the affection, after with more facility their souls are converted to God.'

Sister Dorothea continues:

> Besides teaching of children, I endeavour to instruct the simple and vulgar sort. I teach them their Pater, Ave, Creed, Commandments etc. Those who in respect of the fear of persecution, loss of goods and the like, I cannot at the first bring to resolve to be living members of the Catholic Church, I endeavour at least so to dispose them that understanding and believing the way to salvation, they seldom or unwillingly go to heretical churches, abhor the receiving of their profane Communion, leave to offend God in any great matter, or more seldom to sin, and by little and little I endeavour to root out the custom of swearing, drinking etc.
>
> I tend and serve poor people in their sickness. I make salves to cure their sores and endeavour to make peace between those at variance. In these works of charity I spend my time, not in one place but in many, where I see there is best means of honouring God. But it is much to be lamented, that when poor souls are come to that pass that they desire nothing more than to save their souls, by means of the sacraments, it is incredible to say how hard a thing it is to get a priest to reconcile them; partly through the scarcity of priests and partly through the fear of those with whom they live. I had at once three in great distress for the space of half a year. I could by no means get one, although I went many miles to procure: neither could my lady help me.

Just before Easter, 1622, Sister Dorothea walked twelve miles to find a priest and eventually succeeded in persuading a secular priest to return with her and reconcile some of her group. Not long afterwards she found a Benedictine who reconciled another three for her. Unfortunately news of these activities was passed on from mouth to mouth and soon became public knowledge. The local Anglican clergyman was instructed to denounce her formally from his pulpit but finding only the single name 'Dorothea' on her deed of excommunication, he feared a trick and refused to do anything about it.

At Lady Timperley's request, Sister Dorothea went to live for three weeks with a neighbouring Catholic gentlewoman who was in great distress because all her family were non-Catholics and her sick husband was close to death. By her presence, her words and her example, Sister Dorothea comforted the dying man and then at his request secured the services of a Jesuit priest who prepared him sacramentally for an edifying death. When Lady Timperley and her Benedictine chaplain, Father William Palmer, visited the house shortly afterwards, they were impressed to find a 'neat chapel' and a thriving Catholic community for all members of the household had followed the example of the father of the family and joined the Catholic Church. Sister Dorothea goes on to report that 'The Jesuit Father and the Benedictine, as my lady told me, fell into talk of me, both of them commended me much: the Father wished there were a thousand such as I in England. I was fearful lest they should suspect who I was, but the lady did assure me they had not the least suspicion of me, for if they had, she was assured they would not have so much commended me, for neither of these did approve but much oppose against Mrs Mary Ward and her company.'

These conversions to Catholicism did not go unnoticed by the local people and Sister Dorothea was summoned before the Justice of the Peace to explain herself. She was urged to conform herself to the laws of the realm and threatened with imprisonment if she would not yield. In her own words, Sister Dorothea recounts how the Magistrate:

> would needs have a reason why I would not go to their churches. 'My reason is,' says I, 'because I am a Roman Catholic, therefore will go to no other church but our own.'
>
> 'This answer is not conformable to the laws of God, the King and the realm,' said the Justice.
>
> I answered that it was conformable to the laws of God and that was sufficient for me.
>
> 'Well,' said the Justice, 'I see you are resolute. Therefore, as a friend, I wish you for your own good not to meddle with others, to keep to yourself what you know.' And then he added, 'I will do more than I can well justify' and dismissed the case.

Sister Dorothea returned to Lady Timperley and then accompanied her to London where to her great joy she met many of her old friends from the days before she entered the religious state. None of them recognized her in her new role and she was able to help many with their religious difficulties and confirm them in their Faith. In fact, she could humbly boast that Father Palmer 'likes so well my endeavours in converting of souls and instructing the ignorant, that he was desirous that Mrs. Arrendall (sic) and others should do the like'. And so for two days Sister Dorothea was commissioned to stay with Lady Arundell and her ladies and instruct them in her techniques and religious approaches which were proving so successful in her own apostolate.

Towards the end of her report, Sister Dorothea tells Mother Frances Brookesby of the repeated attacks that were being made by otherwise devout Catholics on Mary Ward and her sisters. Ill-informed gossip and misunderstandings had made the sisters very unpopular in England and Sister Dorothea heard many people 'speak bitterly against our Mother and the Company'. And yet the people who were attacking these devoted and exemplary sisters were in fact the very same people who were praising Sister Dorothea without realizing that she was indeed one of them and proud to have that honour. Only Lady Timperley knew this secret and because she was known to be a friend of the sisters there was a widespread fear that she would influence Sister Dorothea to join them. 'Sometimes,' wrote Sister Dorothea, 'my lady is merry to see how fearful they are lest she should persuade me to be what already she knoweth I am.'

Sister Dorothea lived on her own in obscurity and she died in obscurity. So little is known about her but the heroism of her life and the magnitude of her apostolate is clearly discernible and the few details which are available establish her honoured position as one of the first of the new nuns to work on the English Mission. Of course, in time, many others followed her example but Sister Dorothea was one of the great pioneer nuns of seventeenth-century England, and deserves recognition in her own right as well as recognition as an ardent disciple of Mary Ward.

ANNE VAUX

Anne Vaux was born at Irthlingborough in Northamptonshire and was baptized there on 9 July 1562. Both her parents were Catholics. Her father was William, the third Baron Vaux, and her mother was Elizabeth, the daughter of Sir John Beaumont of Grace Dieu in Leicestershire. Unfortunately, her mother died within a month of Anne's birth and her father was left with the family of four small children. Following the customs of the times, Lord Vaux remarried almost immediately and chose for his second wife Mary, the daughter of another dedicated Catholic, John Tresham of Rushton. In due time this marriage was also blessed with children and all in all there were nine very young children in the nurseries of Harrowden Hall in 1568, when Edmund Campion took up his appointment as tutor for them all.

The teaching and influence of this most renowned of Oxford scholars had a most profound effect on all the children. All reached a high academic standard but more importantly all were confirmed in their attachment to the Catholic Church and never wavered in their Faith.

Henry Vaux, the eldest son and heir, was twenty-one when Father Edmund Campion returned secretly to England as one of the first Jesuit missionaries on 5 June 1580. At once, Henry rushed to the assistance of his old teacher and shared with him the common danger as both engaged themselves in the active apostolate of the Mission. Indeed so close was their attachment that when Saint Edmund Campion was martyred on 1 December 1583, Henry Vaux determined that he himself would replace his friend as a Jesuit priest and he crossed the seas to study for the priesthood.

In July 1586 another two Jesuits slipped quietly into England. One was Father Robert Southwell, a relative of Lord Vaux; the other was Father Henry Garnet. Within a few days of their arrival, however, Father Garnet found himself most unexpectedly in charge of the Mission for the whole country. At once, he moved out of London to seek the assistance of the Vaux family, who had been so highly recommended to him by Robert Southwell and by Edmund Campion. In fact, none of the male members of the Vaux family were in any position to help and it was therefore Lord Vaux's daughters who undertook what Father Godfrey Anstruther has called, 'the most hazardous task that could fall to the lot of two young women: the task of harbouring public Enemy No 1, the Jesuit superior.'

At this time Anne Vaux was unmarried and no more than about twenty-four years of age. Her sister, Eleanor, would be about twenty-six and was the widow of Edward Brookesby. Both sisters devoted the rest of their lives to the protection and maintenance of the priests. Their real names seldom appear in official reports to Rome but they are frequently mentioned as the widow and the virgin.

In a formal letter of March 1593, for example, Father Garnet gave an account of a special meeting of all the Jesuits in England.'We chose for this meeting,' he wrote, 'the house which we had hitherto almost always used for this purpose, belonging to the two sisters, the widow and the virgin, illustrious by birth, fidelity and holiness of life, whom I sometimes in my thoughts liken to the two women who used to lodge Our Lord, or those holy matrons, sisters also, who continually honour and succour your whole family, especially in Rome.'

Father Garnet goes on to relate how this meeting was interrupted by the pursuivants and priest-hunters who:

> unexpectedly arrived and hammered on the doors, which had been slammed in their faces. Doors were bolted, everyone warned, books collected. Pictures, Rosaries, chalices, vestments and all other signs of our religion were thrown into the culvert, together with the men. The mistress of the house was stowed away in a separate hiding-place of her own, both to prevent her being torn from her children and carried off to prison, and also because she is rather timid and finds it difficult to cope with the threats and evil looks of the searchers. On this occasion, as often before, when this same pursuivant paid us a visit, her younger sister (the aforementioned virgin) posed as the mistress of the house.
>
> At length everything was disposed of with such despatch that not a sound could be heard through the whole house. Then a pursuivant and a companion were admitted... Then they set about searching the whole house. Everything was turned upside down; everything was closely examined, storerooms, chests and even the very beds were carefully ransacked, on the off chance of finding Rosaries or pictures or books or Agnus Dei hidden in them... The pursuivants soon grew tired of their fruitless search and were invited to breakfast... After breakfast, the whole house was searched again, but when they saw that they had no hopes of success, they accepted a bribe for the lady herself and for the man who fled and they departed.

In this same letter Father Garnet paid his own tribute to Anne Vaux. He wrote,

> I've no idea with what patience, ladies in Italy would put up with this. Here we have been sold into slavery and have become hardened to this sort of barbarity. But on top of all this are the endless altercations with these most persistent fellows. The virgin always conducts these arguments with such skill and discretion that she usually counteracts their persistence and their interminable chatter. For though she has all a maiden's modesty and even shyness, yet in God's cause, and in the protection of His servants, virgo becomes virago. I've often seen her so

exhausted by the chronic weakness that she nearly always labours under, that she found it painful to speak two or three words, yet on the arrival of the pursuivants she suddenly rallies to such an extent that she has been known to spend as much as three or four hours arguing with him. If there is no priest in the house, she is full of apprehension but the very presence of one so heartens her that she is convinced that the Devil can have no power in her house. (Stonyhurst MSS, Anglia I, No. 73.)

It was of course too dangerous for the Vaux sisters and their honoured guests to stay in any one place for any length of time. Fortunately, they were wealthy women owning several houses and the Jesuit headquarters could be moved from one to the other. Their Protestant friends helped them, knowingly or unknowingly, by renting extra houses to them. Secrecy of course was essential and Anne's presence by Father Garnet's side often served as a means of allaying suspicion that he might be a priest. Even when he was called further afield on his religious duties, Anne would invariably accompany him. Inevitably this caused some comment and a letter of complaint has been preserved in the archives of the Inner Temple (Petyt MSS 538, fol. 415). It was written in 1598 and suggested that Father Garnet 'should be asked how he can justify carrying a gentlewoman up and down the country with him and thereby give such bad example to his subjects'. Such petty and ungenerous complaints serve only to enhance the reputations of the persons complained about.

Anne Vaux was in reality a most saintly woman. Father Godfrey Anstruther OP made a most scholarly examination of her life and did not hesitate to assert that Anne 'had taken the vows of religion privately and was to all intents and purposes a nun. Her small property belonged to the community and her life was directed by Father Garnet.' (*Vaux of Harrowden*, p. 191.)

For almost twenty-five years, Anne Vaux and Father Garnet worked closely together in this way. She was his housekeeper, his secretary, his guide, and his security officer; he was her chaplain and spiritual director. Together they made a good team and enjoyed an excellent working partnership. All might have been well had not the discovery of the alleged Gunpowder Plot provoked a more severe drive by the Government against the Catholic priests.

By September 1605, Anne was aware that a violent plot of some sort against the King and Government was being developed and she warned Father Garnet that some of his closest friends were under deep suspicion. When the Plot was 'discovered', Father Garnet and his company moved discreetly to Hindlip Castle, ten miles from Worcester, the seat of Thomas Abingdon. This was a huge, rambling house in which the Jesuit brother, Saint Nicholas Owen, had done much work and thanks to his particular genius, the old mansion was well provided with secret and very secure hiding holes.

For some six weeks the Catholic community was undisturbed but in early January 1606 the place was raided. Father Garnet and his companion Father Edward Oldcorn took immediate refuge in one of the priest's hiding places, and he later related, (State Papers, 14/19, No. 11) that 'After we had been in the hole seven days and seven nights and some odd hours, everyman may well think we were well wearied, and indeed so it was, for we generally sat, save that some times we could half stretch ourselves, the place being not high enough, and we had our legs so straightened that we could not sitting find place for them, so that we both were in continual pain of our legs, and both our legs, especially mine, were much swollen.'

While the priests suffered like this, Anne Vaux and Mrs Dorothy Abingdon, the lady of the house, busied themselves by trying every trick they knew to keep the searchers away from the hiding places. It was also their responsibility to surreptitiously provide food and drink for the entrapped priests. The official report to the Government later made mention of 'the marmalade and other sweetmeats' which were found when the priests were eventually obliged to give themselves up, and this report goes on to emphasize that 'their better maintenance had been by a quill or reed through a little hole in the chimney that backed another chimney into the gentlewoman's chamber, and by that passage candles, broths and warm drinks had been conveyed in unto them.'

Father Garnet was taken to London as a close prisoner and Anne Vaux voluntarily followed him at a safe distance. She took up residence near the Tower where the priest was incarcerated and did what she could to help him. Communication was difficult; it could only be achieved by smuggled letters written with orange juice as invisible ink. But the authorities became aware of Anne's involvement and on 11 March 1606 she too was arrested and became a prisoner in the Tower. She managed to catch a brief glimpse of Father Garnet on 3 May 1606 when he crossed the courtyard to the hurdle on which he was to be dragged to his place of execution and martyrdom but she was not allowed to speak to him.

Anne Vaux was kept in prison for another three months but her health was not good and her eyesight was deteriorating. In a letter of 17 August the new Jesuit Superior, Father Richard Blount, announced her release when he wrote, 'Mistress Anne is at liberty, but much discontented that she is not with Mr. Ducket [i.e. martyred with Father Garnet], but we have put her in good hands again and I believe the customers and she will live together, but I fear not long.' (Stonyhurst MSS, Anglia III, No. 64.)

In fact, Anne's health was much better than reports had indicated and as soon as she left prison she once more joined up with her sister, Eleanor; together they befriended another Jesuit, Father William Wright and for the next thirty years they looked after him and kept him in safety.

At first, they all lived in the Brookesby house at Shoby in Leicestershire where they seem to have achieved a certain peace and quiet without any interference from the authorities. It was only in 1623 that the name, Anne Vaux, appeared on the list of recusants in the neighbouring parish of Saxelby, when she was accused of owing £240 in religious fines.

In 1625, both Anne and Eleanor were convicted at Leicester Castle of recusancy and both were stated to be owing £240 in fines but there is no record that they ever paid.

The date and circumstances of Anne Vaux's death are not known. She may have been still alive in 1637 but the retiring life of her old age was in stark contrast to the heroic activities of her youth. She died as she had lived, a dedicated Catholic and a fearless protector of the priests.

ELEANOR BROOKESBY

Eleanor Brookesby was the eldest daughter of William, the third Baron Vaux and was born about the year 1560. Like her brother Henry and her sisters Elizabeth and Anne she was much influenced by the family tutor, Saint Edmund Campion, and she remained a staunch and active Catholic all her life.

About the year 1577, Eleanor was married to another determined Catholic recusant, Edward Brookesby, who had already distinguished himself by his services to the Catholic cause but her married life lasted for less than four years. Before June 1581 her husband was dead and she was left with two small children, William and Mary.

Even before her husband's death, Eleanor had proved her worth as a Catholic hostess. It was to the Brookesby house at Green Street, East Ham that Father Robert Persons and Father Edmund Campion were conducted immediately on their arrival and it was in that house that Father Campion set up his secret printing press for the first time.

As a widow Eleanor moved her residence to the manor house of Great Ashby in Leicestershire. This was Brookesby property which had been given to her as part of her marriage settlement and was well situated in the south-western corner of the county, only six miles from the boundary with Warwickshire. It was always an advantage for a recusant to live close to a county or diocesan boundary for the crossing of such a boundary could render pursuivants powerless and in some cases invalidated their warrants. Eleanor soon bought a second house in Warwickshire which she kept as a place of refuge, but it was to Great Ashby that Father Garnet came in the autumn of 1586 and it was in Great Ashby that Eleanor and her sister Anne, the 'widow and the virgin' lived together in close harmony while applying themselves full-time to the needs of the Church and the safety of their priests.

Father Garnet has acknowledged in a letter of March 1593 to the Jesuit General in Rome (Stonyhurst, Anglia, vol. I, p. 73) that Eleanor was 'a little timid and finds it difficult to cope with the threats and evil looks of the searchers', but this should not be allowed to detract from the courage and dedication she showed in harbouring so many priests in so many different places.

The Vaux sisters presided over a very unusual community which was in itself a plausible cover for the presence of Father Garnet. Besides Eleanor's two children there was her adopted daughter, Frances Burroughs. There was also a nephew of Father Robert Persons SJ and an old woman who was always called simply the 'old woman' but who has been positively identified as the elderly mother of Father Persons. And another permanent member of the household was Father Garnet's personal servant, a very small cockney carpenter who had a twisted leg and walked with a limp and who was known to all his friends as 'Little John'. In fact, his true name was Nicholas Owen and he had an extraordinary gift for constructing those intricate hiding places which saved the lives of so many priests. In later life Nicholas Owen became a Jesuit brother; he was martyred in 1606 and canonized as a saint in 1970 as one of the Forty Martyrs.

This was the community which moved from house to house in an almost continual procession to safeguard the secrecy of the Jesuit activities. Father Godfrey Anstruther has described how they were living in 1594. For two years they had remained in London, apparently unmolested.

Their life was as near conventual as the troubled times would allow. There would be the regular round of prayer and spiritual exercises, but punctuated by the constant coming and going of Jesuits to consult their Superior, the bi-annual meetings, the arrival of mysterious messengers with letters from the Jesuit General and Father Persons, and the despatch of Father Garnet's long letters full of news of the brethren, written with equal facility in English, Latin or Italian; letters which seldom miscarried, in spite of the growing industry of the secret service and false brethren. Yet life was lived at a tension difficult for us to imagine, with the constant news of arrests and executions to remind them of their danger: the ever-present shadow of the Tower, the torture chamber and the awful death at Tyburn, which was the penalty for being a priest or for harbouring one. (Anstruther, *Vaux of Harrowden*, p. 195.)

In 1600, Father Garnet and his community moved to a house called White Webbs on Enfield Chase in Middlesex. It was a large house suitable for fourteen Jesuits to meet at any one time and set in its own grounds. It was rented in the names of Mrs Perkins (Anne Vaux) and Mrs Brookesby who lived there very quietly as was their custom. Before the end of the year the house was receiving priests in large numbers and Father Garnet acknowledges gratefully that 'the charges of housekeeping being great', the costs were shared between the Jesuits and the sisters.

By Easter 1605, Father Garnet suspected that White Webbs had been discovered by the Government and it was decided to spend less time there. Once more the Vaux sisters helped with finance and the manor house of Erith (Kent), on the banks of the Thames, was rented, but by midsummer this house also was under surveillance. On 21 June, Father Garnet wrote to a nun at Louvain:

Besides the general affliction we find ourselves now betrayed in both our places and are forced to wander up and down until we get a fit place... We kept Corpus Christi Day (30 May) with great solemnity and music and the day of the octave (6 June) made a solemn procession about a great garden, the house being watched, which we knew not till the next day when we departed twenty five in the sight of all, in several parties, leaving half a dozen servants behind and all is well. (Foley, vol. IV, p. 141.)

On 30 August 1605, Father Garnet and all his household made their way to the ancient shrine of Saint Winefred's Well at Holywell on a most extraordinary pilgrimage. It was an exercise in audacity as well as devotion. As the pilgrims made progress through the Midlands their purpose was recognized by other Catholics who did not hesitate to join them in their pious project, By the time they reached the holy well they were a party of thirty people and it is significant that it was the women who walked the last stage of the journey bare-footed.

It was the lull before the storm, a pleasant interlude before a return to the grim realities of religious persecution. Eleanor was aware that some sort of plot was afoot. She recognized the signs of a conspiracy and with Anne she deplored them. Many of her friends seemed deeply involved and she feared the consequences especially when the news of the Gunpowder Plot spread like wildfire throughout the country on 2 November. As expected, White Webbs was one of the first Catholic houses to be raided but all the Catholic residents had escaped. In fact, Eleanor Brookesby managed to hide herself so well that her whereabouts have never become known.

The sad events of Father Garnet's execution and Anne Vaux's imprisonment have already been related but as soon as Anne was released on 11 May 1608 she made all haste to join Eleanor. Once more the sisters applied themselves to the harbouring of priests and gave an immediate welcome to Father William Wright SJ. At first they all lived at Ashby in Leicestershire but they moved to Shoby in 1615 when Eleanor inherited the manor house there from her father-in-law, Robert Brookesby.

Here, Eleanor lived a quiet and private life devoting herself not only to the well-being and safety of Father Wright but also to the religious education of her grandson, Edward Thimelby, who in due time became a seminary priest and was even suggested as a possible President for the English College at Douai. (Dodd, vol. III, p. 392.)

And it was here in Shoby, according to her grandson Father Thimelby, that Eleanor Brookesby died in 1626. She was about sixty years of age and had spent all her adult life in harbouring and protecting priests.

FRANCES BURROUGHS

Frances Burroughs was another member of the Vaux family to distinguish herself in the defence of the Church. Her mother, Maud, was a sister of William, the third Baron Vaux and her father was Anthony Burroughs of Burrow-on-the-Hill in Leicestershire. She was born about the year 1576 as one of the younger members of a very large family, but her mother died when Frances was only five years of age and the small girl was adopted by her first cousin, Mrs Eleanor Brookesby, who brought her fully into her own family and ensured her Catholic education.

By the time she was eleven, Frances was playing her full part with Eleanor Brookesby and Anne Vaux in harbouring the priests, and the Louvain chronicler has recorded (Chronicle of Saint Monica's, vol. II, p. 165) that:

> She showed great courage when the pursuivants and other officers came to the house to search for priests, church stuff or Catholic books, which was there often to do, (sic) the rest hiding them in secret places made in the house for that purpose. But she was always let out to go up and down to answer the officers, because her courage was such that she never seemed to be daunted or feared of anything.

The Chronicle goes on:

> It happened when she was but eleven years of age, a priest being at Mass in the chamber above, and another priest present, a great noise was heard in the house below; and fearing it to be as indeed it was, the priest desired the gentlewoman of the house to go down, and the girl with her, to see what the matter was. They went, and in the hall found, through the negligence of the doorkeeper, the pursuivants and constables entered with many swords drawn. Which the child seeing, cried out, 'Oh! put up your swords, or else my mother will die, for she cannot endure to see a naked sword.' The officers perceiving the gentlewoman's countenance to change, believed her, and put up their swords. But Frances runneth back again, pretending to fetch some wine for her mother, shut the doors, gave warning to the priests, helped to hide them, and then came back again to the pursuivants, having frustrated them in their expectation for they could find no priest.

The Louvain Chronicle also describes how, on another occasion, Frances was threatened by one of the pursuivants, who held a naked dagger to her throat and told her he would stab her unless she betrayed the hiding places of the priests. The little girl replied, 'If thou dost, it shall be the hottest blood that ever thou sheddest in thy life.' Her baffled assailant could only express his admiration by saying that 'it was a pity that a maid of her courage should be spoiled with papistry.'

When she was seventeen years of age, Frances decided that she wished to give herself completely to God as a nun, and the Jesuit provincial, Father Henry Garnet, arranged for her to be smuggled across the seas to Louvain where a group of English ladies was already established under Mother Margaret Clement as Canonesses of Saint Augustine at Saint Ursula's monastery.

The development of her vocation has been described by Frances herself through the pages of the Louvain Chronicle:

> Being now come to years of discretion and some ripeness of judgement, conversing daily with priests and hearing many good things (and sometimes her cousin talked of a sister of hers, called Elizabeth, who was a nun at Rouen in France of Saint Clare's Order), she got thereupon a great love unto that kind of life, although she could not imagine what it was to be a nun. Being ashamed to ask, she contented herself that surely it was a fine thing, but wavering in her mind, sometimes she would be a nun, sometimes not; thus she continued working with her mind some ten years.

Eventually Frances made up her mind and spent one year as a scholar in Saint Ursula's and a second year as a novice before she took her solemn vows on 13 July 1597. For twelve years, she fulfilled her vocation faithfully in this convent but on 9 November 1609 she was transferred to join the other English ladies in the new foundation of Saint Monica's Convent, which was situated in the same town and not very far from Saint Ursula's.

Here the twenty-five English nuns prepared themselves for the day when they could return to their homeland but as year succeeded year and the persecution showed no signs of abating they were forced to resign themselves to permanent exile.

It is perhaps difficult to recognize in the staid contemplative nun the vivacious eleven-year-old girl who defied the pursuivants, but Frances persevered in her vocation. Most of the time she suffered from sickness and her health was never robust but her strength of character was such that she gave much edification with her patience, humility and obedience.

Sister Frances Burroughs died as a Canoness of Saint Augustine on 3 March 1637. She was fifty-nine years of age and had been a nun for forty years. But she is remembered as the courageous young woman who risked her life to protect her priests.

ELIZABETH VAUX

Elizabeth Vaux was born Elizabeth Roper and she was a great-niece of Margaret Roper, the favourite daughter of Saint Thomas More. In 1585 she fell in love with George Vaux who was in fact the son and heir of William, the third Baron Vaux, by his second marriage to Mary Tresham. To marry for love was quite unusual in those days and both George and Elizabeth were obliged to defy their parents who were making arrangements for different matches. The young couple were married at Harrowden on 25 July 1585 when George at least was under age and his father at once disinherited him.

George was reinstated as the heir to Harrowden and the barony before his death in 1594, but Elizabeth was left with six small children and the legal complications of disputed property.

The situation at Harrowden has been described by Father John Gerard SJ who was appointed chaplain to the family in 1598. (Gerard, Life, chapter XXIII):

> I visited a noble family, by whom I had long been invited and often expected, but I had never yet been able to visit them on account of my pressing occupations. Here I found the lady of the house, a widow, very pious and devout, but at this present overwhelmed with grief at the loss of her husband. She had indeed been so affected by this loss that for a whole year she scarce stirred out of her chamber, and for the next three years that had intervened before my visit had never brought herself to go to that part of the mansion in which her husband died.
>
> To this grief and trouble were added certain anxieties about the bringing up of her son, who was yet a child under his mother's care. He was one of the first barons of the realm; but his parents had suffered so much for the faith, and had mortgaged so much of their property to meet the constant exactments of an heretical government, that the remaining income was scarcely sufficient for their proper maintenance.

Father Gerard goes on to describe the way in which he 'weaned her mind from that excessive grief' and 'gradually brought her to change that old style of grief for a more worthy one'. Indeed, with Father Gerard, Elizabeth Vaux began a new life and her close partnership with the priest was very similar to that of her sisters-in-law, Anne Vaux and Eleanor Brooksby, with Father Garnet.

Again we have Father Gerard's own description of how Elizabeth developed her own spiritual life:

170

In the first place therefore, she resolved to lead an unmarried life; secondly to aim at poverty in this sense, that all her actual fortune, and all that she might ever have, should be devoted to the service of God and His ministers, while she herself should be but their servant to provide them with what was necessary; lastly, she gave herself above all to obedience, and determined to reduce her love to practice no less perfectly than if she had taken a vow; nay it was her only trouble that it was forbidden to priests of our Society to receive vows ...(quoted by Anstruther, *Vaux of Harrowden*, p.239.)

Having placed her resources completely at the service of the Mission, Elizabeth Vaux made several attempts to rent near London suitable properties as safe houses for the priests but the dangers were too great and she was eventually obliged to make use of the old family home of Harrowden. Here she built a new wing of three storeys close to the chapel and Nicholas Owen was commissioned to build a priest's hiding hole as part of the original building. Two Jesuits, Father John Percy and Father John Gerard, took up residence as chaplains and each devoted himself to his own particular work.

Father Gerard used Harrowden as his centre of operations and spent much of his time visiting the local gentry of Northamptonshire and the Midlands beyond the county boundaries. He made many converts to the Catholic Faith and was able to set up many Mass centres. But Harrowden was much more than the Mission Headquarters for a large area of central England; it was also a Jesuit College, founded and developed at the height of the persecution.

Elizabeth Vaux was obliged to keep the Privy Council informed as to how her son was being educated, and to fulfill this obligation she thought it politic to make sure that the tutor she employed should be a Protestant. Thomas Smith, an Oxford graduate, held the post for a time but he was so impressed by the religious atmosphere of the house that he became a Catholic and in due time a Jesuit. Nevertheless the existence of this Protestant 'school' was sufficient cover for the young Lord Vaux and his companions to be educated properly as Catholics.

And so Harrowden flourished as a house of religion and a place of refuge. Elizabeth Vaux preserved the Mass in her own chapel and took every precaution to maintain the freedom of her priests. She became very well known in Catholic circles as a religious hostess and close friend of Father Gerard but despite every effort to keep her activities secret it was inevitable that the Government should look on her with suspicion and classify her as an obstinate papist.

Lord Vaux was sixteen in the spring of 1605 and his education was almost completed when his mother, Elizabeth, committed a grave indiscretion. Concerned that negotiations for her son's marriage were being unduly prolonged she complained in a letter to her friend, Agnes Lady Wenman, that the delay was due to the fact that both she and her son were 'obstinate papists' and then asked Agnes to pray because soon 'Tottenham would turn French'. This was an old saying, meaning that something extraordinary was going to happen, and when the letter miscarried and fell in the wrong hands it was presumed that Elizabeth was making reference to a Catholic rebellion and was therefore guilty of high treason.

When, therefore, the Gunpowder Plot was 'discovered' in London on 5 November 1605, Elizabeth Vaux realized that she and her friends at Harrowden were in grave danger and immediately steps were taken to hide away all the incriminating evidence of Catholic practices. At this time she was harbouring three priests, Father John Gerard SJ, Father Richard Singleton and Father Thomas Strange and as soon as these priests had removed the Blessed Sacrament and closed the chapel they set out to join Father Henry Garnet at Coughton. Unfortunately, the country was once more enduring a storm of anti-Catholicism and the priests and their companions were recognized as they approached Warwick and arrested at Kenilworth on the evening of 7 November. The consequent interrogation gave the Government more information about the seditious proceedings at Harrowden and it was therefore no surprise to Elizabeth Vaux that on 12 November a large government search party arrived to investigate her home.

Father John Gerard described the events as follows:

> The house was beset with at least a hundred men and those well appointed. The young Lord made no resistance, as having no cause to fear, but brought the Commissioners presently into his mother, who delivered unto them all the keys of her house, and willed them to use their pleasure. They searched for two or three days continually, and searched with candles in cellars and several dark corners. They searched every cabinet and box in her own closet for letters, in hope to find some little scroll that might show Father Gerard had been an actor in this treason, or that she or her son had received some knowledge of it. But they found not with all this diligence the least tittle of advantage in the matter, insomuch that the chief man in commission for this search (though an earnest Puritan) yet sent a very full information unto the Council that he had found the house most clear, the young Lord and his mother very submissive unto authority, admitting any kind of search or inquiry that he could desire, and yet very confident in their own innocency: and that he found not any preparation in the house for war, or any show at all that they had the least knowledge of any such attempt intended. (Gerard, *Autobiography*, p. 138.)

Despite this official report of Elizabeth Vaux's innocence she was summoned to London by the Privy Council on 18 November 1605 and was confined with the wives and kinswomen of nine of the alleged conspirators in the Gunpowder Plot. When she was examined by the whole Council, 'she did clear herself fully,' wrote Father Gerard, 'from all cause of suspicion in that treason, and affirmed constantly, that although she were a firm Catholic, and so would live and die by the grace of God yet that fact (the Gunpowder Plot) she did as much mislike and condemn as themselves; and that so she had been taught by those who had care of her soul.'

Father Gerard goes on to describe how,

They urged her that she knew Father Gerard and had received him many times in her house. She answered she hoped none could justly accuse her that she had received him or any other priest, and that she would not accuse herself, the same being a penal law. They insisted she was bound to tell of him, for that he was known to be a traitor and a chief plotter of this action. She answered with serious protestation that she had never the least cause to think so of him (if she did know him as they presupposed); and said that she had heard so much good of the man (though she did not know him) that she would pawn her whole estate, yea, and her life also, that he was not guilty of that Plot, nor justly to be touched with it.

The Council were plainly not going to be forestalled by the courage of this woman and they reminded her that 'she was now in the King's mercy to live or die' but that 'she should have her life and lose nothing of her estate, if she would tell where Gerard the Jesuit was to be found. She answered, she knew not; but if she did know she would not tell it to save her life and many Lives.

"Why then," said they, "Lady, you must die."

"Why then, I will die, my Lords," said she, "for I will never do the other."'
(Gerard, *Autobiography*, p. 140.)

It would seem that the Council were bluffing when they threatened her with immediate death but she had no means of knowing this and to Elizabeth Vaux and her friends the prospect of martyrdom seemed very close. In fact, she was committed, not to prison but to the house of a certain gentleman in the city, 'where she was well respected and yet kept so close that not her own son might come to see her'. Of course, in all these dealings with the Privy Council it has to be appreciated that Elizabeth Vaux was one of the great ladies of the land and the Councillors accordingly felt themselves obliged to treat her with the respect due to her as a woman and especially as a woman of power and wealth. She was therefore able to secure her own freedom later in that month of November when she appealed to the soft heart of Lord Salisbury and begged forgiveness without compromising her principles. He secured her release on the bond of Mr Lewis Pickering but laid down the condition that she should remain in London.

Encouraged by the success of her first letter to Lord Salisbury, Elizabeth Vaux tried again five months later and again she succeeded. On 17 April 1606 she was allowed to return home to Harrowden where she took up once again her old life of piety and religion by harbouring two Jesuits, Father John Percy and Father Nicholas Hart.

In October 1609, Lord Vaux achieved his majority and Elizabeth was able to hand over to her son such of his patrimony as remained after the crippling government fines had been paid. She continued to live on at Harrowden with her chaplains but Father John Gerard was no longer with her; his superiors had withdrawn him from the English Mission in 1606 and he was destined to spend the rest of his life on the Continent.

English spies on the Continent kept a watchful eye open for Father Gerard and there were many reports that he had been sighted but by the end of 1609 all trace of him seemed to have disappeared. Nevertheless official investigations continued and at Christmas 1610 there was a strong rumour that he had slipped back into England. The rumour had no foundation; Father Gerard was in Rome at that time; but Lord Salisbury thought he knew his man and drew the conclusion that if Father Gerard was in England he would be at Harrowden, and accordingly gave orders for a surprise search of the house to be organized.

The task was entrusted to Gilbert Pickering, a Justice of the Peace from Titchmarsh and he certainly did not allow himself to be impeded by any finer feelings of courtesy or compassion. His arrival at Harrowden Hall on 31 October 1611 took all the residents by surprise.

> Accompanied by a numerous posse, (he) scaled the walls at midnight, and broke into the Fathers' rooms before they could receive the least warning. Not content with this, he broke into the chapel close at hand, and in the King's name, seized the rich altar furniture, plate and vestments. Mrs Vaux was sent to London to appear before the Council, and, after examination, was cast into the Fleet prison. The Fathers (Percy and Hart) were for some days kept in Pickering's house. (Foley, Records of the English Province SJ, vol VII, p. 1028.)

Father Henry More, the Jesuit historian (1586-1661) states (quoted in Foley, *ibid.*, vol. I, p. 170) that Elizabeth Vaux was also kept for a time in the house of Pickering, who 'then conducted them, with the sacred furniture, surrounded by javelin-men, in a sort of triumph to London. Arriving at the Palace, London they were taken to the Gatehouse prison, Westminster. Lord Salisbury looking out from a window of the Palace, said, on seeing the cavalcade arrive: these are not the ones I sought for.' His heart was obviously set on capturing Father Gerard before all others but his raid on Harrowden had succeeded in capturing two Jesuits and the lady who was harbouring them.

Father Godfrey Anstruther OP has described the sad situation: 'The great citadel had fallen. The house that had sheltered so many hunted priests through more than thirty years was now empty and desolate. The magnificent chapel that Father Gerard had described in his autobiography written only two years before was now stripped and desecrated. Elizabeth Vaux was in the Fleet and her two chaplains in the Gatehouse.'(*Vaux of Harrowden*, p. 393.)

On 19 February 1612, Elizabeth Vaux was arraigned at the Old Bailey before the Lord Mayor of London and the Anglican Bishop of London, and 'was required to take and pronounce on the holy Gospel of God a certain oath contained and specified (in 3 Jac. ch. 1) ... entitled An Act for the better discovering and repressing of popish recusants, and that the same Elizabeth Vaux obstinately ... refused to take that oath as it was proferred to her.' This oath was not the Oath of Supremacy of 1559 but the new Oath of Allegiance which had been framed just after the Gunpowder Plot but condemned by the Pope in 1607. Elizabeth 'offered to have sworn all loyalty to the King, yea, though the Pope should excommunicate him' but she persisted in her refusal to take the Oath of Allegiance as prepared by Parliament.

Elizabeth's case is fully documented in the Catholic Record Society's volume XXXIV, pp. 65 and 66, and her sentence is still on record in the dread words, 'Therefore it is decreed by the same Court, that all the lands, tenements, goods and chattels of the aforesaid Elizabeth Vaux shall be forfeited to the said Lord the King, and that she, Elizabeth Vaux shall suffer the imprisonment of her body during the good pleasure of the said Lord the King, according to the form of the statute in a case of this kind made and provided.'

By this time, Elizabeth Vaux was approaching her fiftieth birthday and in the conditions of those days was already an old woman. Nevertheless, she was obliged to endure the rigours of imprisonment in Newgate where Father Almond affirmed from the scaffold 'the keepers are corrupt and the prisoners continually ill-treated.' It is then no surprise that on 3 July 1613 Elizabeth was so ill that she was released from prison for eight months in order to recover her health. In fact, such was the inefficiency of legal proceedings, the eight months became five years, and she was still unofficially free when on 1 March 1618 her brother, Sir Christopher Roper, and Sir Thomas Brudenell entered into bonds of £1,000 each to enable her to remain out of prison but in their care and charge.

But by this time Elizabeth had left Harrowden, never to return. Perhaps the memories were too sad; perhaps she had no money for repairs and refurbishment; perhaps she was too tired to continue the struggle. Whatever the reason, in 1616 she had moved her residence to Boughton just outside Northampton. It was a very quiet time for Catholics. The persecution was reduced to a constant attack on the recusant's purse. Between 1616 and 1628 only one priest was put to death. Father Godfrey Anstruther has described how 'the dwindling Catholic gentry were no longer feared but were treated with contempt. They were debarred from all public offices and lived a life of obscurity and retirement. The more adventurous sought service in foreign lands and in foreign armies; the others entrenched themselves in their embarrassed estates, farmed their lands and practiced their religion in secret. It was a quiet life.' (*Vaux of Harrowden*, p. 430.)

In this quiet life, Elizabeth Vaux slipped into obscurity. She was still alive in 1627 when she is mentioned as a beneficiary in the will of Mary, Lady Fermor, but this is the last recorded reference to her. She died privately; her date of death is not known; her place of burial has been forgotten; but Elizabeth Vaux is an important person in the Catholic history of England.

Catherine Fairfax

Catherine Fairfax was the eldest daughter of Sir Henry Constable of Burton Constable in Holderness. Her mother was Margaret Dormer and she was therefore possessed of all the Catholic advantages of those two powerful families. She was born in the later 1570s and as a growing child was a frequent visitor with her family to the great Fairfax estates of Walton and Gilling Castle. It was therefore no surprise when in 1594, despite her tender years, she was married to Thomas Fairfax, son and heir to Sir William Fairfax.

Her husband does not seem to have been educated as a Catholic and in later life was a very determined Protestant. His father, in fact, has been praised by the Earl of Huntingdon as 'free from suspicion in matters of religion' and the religious conformity and reliability of his household did much to impress the civil authorities. Thomas was therefore able to take the religious tests of Cambridge University and was a fellow commoner of Gonville and Caius College from 1590 until 1594. By 1599 he was a member of the Council of the North and in 1603 he was knighted by King James I during his royal visit to York. In 1608, Lord Sheffield made him his Deputy as Vice-President of the Council of the North. It was indeed a signal honour and mark of respect and quite extraordinary for a man with a Catholic wife to be so honoured. In his letter of appointment, Lord Sheffield emphasized that 'although it is not usual for any to supply this place whose wives are recusants, yet my good opinion of yourself and the hope that I have of your own freedom from that sect will not suffer me to admit of that bar to your employment'. In 1629, Sir Thomas Fairfax achieved a long-standing ambition when he was created 1st Viscount Fairfax of Emly in the Irish Peerage although he never seems to have ventured across the Irish Sea.

The fact that her husband was deemed so Protestant in religious affairs served only to assist Catherine Fairfax in the practice of her own Catholic religion. She had inherited the Dormer taste for piety, spent most of her day at her devotions and encouraged her family and household to join her in frequent prayer. Indeed, such was her reputation for sanctity that it was said that God used to entertain her with musical instruments and many people are said to have heard the sound of what they took to be a lute, when they could find no physical evidence that such an instrument was in the house.

At Walton and Gilling Castle, Catherine Fairfax entertained and protected her priests. She resolutely refused to attend the services of the Church of England and generously provided her friends and relations with the Mass for which they all yearned. Her husband must have known what she was doing and must have been prepared to shut his eyes to her many legal offences. He seems to have allowed her full freedom to practice her religion as she wished and was content that she should shelter behind his official position. J.C.H. Aveling has commented on 'her remarkable immunity from fines and bother for her open recusancy'. (Biographical Studies, vol. 3, No. 2, p. 88.)

Aveling goes on to explain that, 'Lady Fairfax had Catholic maids who accompanied her everywhere. But whereas, there are many cases of lesser men, conforming husbands of Catholic wives like Thomas Allanson, being prosecuted for harbouring Catholic servants at that period, Sir Thomas Fairfax was never presented for this offence.' It was also a statutory offence to send one's children abroad to be educated in Catholic schools. Yet Lady Fairfax seems to have persuaded her husband to allow his eldest son to go to Brussels, a younger son to go to the English College at Douai and perhaps a third (in this case with a limited permit from Secretary Calvert) to go abroad, actually to Rome.

Indeed so Catholic were Lady Fairfax's children that her second son, Henry, offered himself for the English Mission as a Jesuit and served for some time until eventually he abandoned his vocation and joined his father in working for the Protestant cause within the family.

Lady Fairfax and her children were well known as Catholics and never hesitated to proclaim their Faith. It was inevitable that she should be noticed by the Government and although there is no record that she was ever punished, she is possessed of a long and honourable list of prosecutions and convictions. The York Diocesan Records named her as a non-communicant in 1600, 1604 and 1605 but apparently no action was taken. The North Riding Quarter Session Records show that she was convicted of recusancy in 1612, 1613 and 1614 but give no further detail. In 1615, the York Diocesan Records state that she was brought to trial for sixteen years of recusancy and that charged with her at the same time were her friends Mrs Thomasina Dakins and Mrs Frances Rose. Between 1616 and 1623, she made many appearances before the bench and was convicted in 1616, 1619 and 1623, but in none of these cases is there any information as to possible fines or imprisonments. The lady seems to have braved her accusers and defied them to take action. They, for their part, with one eye on the formidable Viscount Fairfax, were content to make their point simply by having her present in court before them and disregarding the relevance or importance of any sentence.

In 1624, Catherine Fairfax was delighted when her eldest son, Thomas Fairfax returned home from his schooling in Brussels and showed himself to be a devout and dedicated Catholic. The young man's father was not so pleased. He was prepared to ignore his wife's recusancy but a recusant son was quite a different matter. Sons inherited property; sons were fully subject to the Law. A recusant son could lose the entire estate for which the 1st Viscount Fairfax had laboured so strenuously and so successfully. He was not prepared to allow his Catholic son to risk the future of the family and the future of the estates for purely religious reasons.

Accordingly, the younger Thomas was exiled from home by his father and forced to live far to the north in Northumberland and Cumberland as a

Catholic vagrant. At the same time the Viscount took legal steps to ensure that a Protestant Trust was set up to prevent his son from ever owning his inheritance.

Catherine Fairfax never wavered in her religious beliefs and when she died in 1626 she bequeathed to her son a Catholic Faith which flourished through succeeding generations of the family so that the Fairfaxes of Walton and Gilling were able to play a very important role in the developing story of English Catholicism.

ANNE ARUNDEL

Anne, Countess of Arundel was the eldest daughter and eventual co-heiress of Lord Dacre of Gilsland. After her father's death, her mother became the third wife of the 4th Duke of Norfolk and to further his grandiose dynastic plans the Duke made immediate plans for the betrothal of Anne to Philip Howard, his own son from his first marriage to Lady Mary Fitzalan. The marriage contract was finalized in 1569 when bride and bridegroom were each twelve years of age and the marriage itself took place in 1571.

The following year, the youthful husband went up to Cambridge University, where he acquired a love for 'polite literature', but unfortunately also acquired a love for wild living. He gave little thought to his wife and when he went to Court in 1575 allowed himself to degenerate into a dissolute, immoral spendthrift. Of course wives were not welcome at Queen Elizabeth's Court but Philip seems to have gone to great lengths to pretend that he was an unattached gentleman devoted only to the Queen. Very seldom did he come home and Anne suffered all the pains of a rejected wife.

In 1580, Philip inherited the Earldom of Arundel from his Fitzalan grandfather and this seems to have calmed him down a little from the riotous life he was leading; but according to his biographer, the 14th Duke of Norfolk, Philip experienced a much deeper conversion. He was present at the religious disputation in the Tower between the suffering Jesuit, Father Edmund Campion, and the Anglican scholars, and this disputation enabled him to perceive 'on which side the truth and true religion was'. Philip Howard reformed himself and was received back into the Church by Father William Weston SJ. Penitent, he returned to his wife only to discover that she too, in his absence, had become a Catholic and for the first time in their lives they were able to live together as husband and wife in love and harmony.

Such changes of course could not go unnoticed. The Queen herself became aware that Philip was leading a very different life and that he was no longer the irresponsible courtier that she had known and admired in the past. She suspected a religious conversion had taken place and paid a state visit to Arundel House to find out for herself. John Martin Robinson, in his history of the Dukes of Norfolk, has explained how 'Philip provided a sumptuous banquet, at the end of which the Queen declared her satisfaction, gave him many thanks for her entertainment there and informed him that he was imprisoned in his own house.' (M.A. Tierney, *History and Antiquities of Arundel*, (1833), p. 376.) The next day he was interrogated by the Privy Council on the matter of his religious beliefs 'whereto in all things he answered so wisely and warily that he was released'.

Philip Howard was well aware of the dangers that threatened him. His own father, the Duke of Norfolk, had been executed for treason just a few years before. Now be realized that Queen Elizabeth still feared the power of his name and his family and that she had a personal hatred for him and his wife. He therefore made plans to escape to the Continent and secretly boarded a ship at his own port of Littlehampton at the mouth of the Arun. He might well have got away and lived safely ever after had he not been betrayed by his chaplain, 'Father' Grately, alias Bridges, who was in fact no priest but a government spy.

Philip was committed to the Tower on 25 April 1585 and twelve months later was called to the Star Chamber and found guilty of breaking the 1581 statute 'by being reconciled to the Church of Rome'. He was not sentenced to death but was fined £10,000 and imprisoned during the 'Queen's pleasure', which was but another name for a life sentence.

In prison the Earl was badly treated. He was strictly confined in his small cell and allowed very little exercise. He wrote about his gaoler that 'His injuries to me both by himself and his trusty Roger are intolerable, infinite, daily multiplied, and to those who know them not, incredible: and the most that you can imagine, will be far inferior, I think, to the truth when you shall hear it.' John Martin Robinson has written (*Dukes of Norfolk*, p. 74):

> All this together with his own austerities made him physically ill, but as he wrote in Latin on the wall of his cell: 'the more suffering for Christ in this world, so much the more glory with Christ in the next'. He retained his sanity by a regular routine of prayer and contemplation, as if he were a priest, reciting the appointed offices of the day from a breviary which his wife had smuggled to him; such was the intensity of his concentration that his knees became black and misshapen from kneeling on the flagstones of the floor.

For ten years, Philip endured these conditions and during all that time he was not allowed to see his wife or children. Anne wrote to him continually and supplied his needs as best she could but even when he was dying from dysentery (some said he was dying from poison) the cruel Queen would allow him no visit from his wife. He died at twelve noon on Sunday 19 October 1595.

During all these years, Anne knew the pains of separation from her beloved husband and she knew the frustrations of not being able to help him as she would have wished. She herself, although known to be a Catholic,was never imprisoned but was continually harassed by the Queen's emissaries. John Martin Robinson has provided some of the details (*Dukes of Norfolk*, p. 78):

> Lady Arundel was treated throughout with unnecessary callousness. On her husband's attainder the royal agents descended on Arundel

House stripping it bare, taking her jewels, her carriage, and all the furniture except some of the beds. She was allowed to stay as a lodger of the Crown in the empty rooms with a pittance on which to live, but whenever the Court came to Somerset House (next door in the Strand) she was ordered to the country lest the nearness of her presence might disturb the Queen. It is even recorded that Queen Elizabeth, on visiting Arundel House in the absence of Lady Arundel and finding an inscription in a window on the theme of the sadness of life in this world and hopes for a better in the future, scratched an unpleasant message underneath 'expressing much passion and disdain ... on purpose to grieve and afflict the poor lady'.

And yet through all these years of anxiety, suffering and loneliness Anne did not hesitate to involve herself fully in the dangerous work of the Church. Although she could not visit her own husband in the Tower, she managed to disguise herself and visit Father William Weston SJ, the priest to whom they owed so much, and who was in prison in the Clink in 1585. She offered him sufficient money to bribe his captors and effect his escape but according to Father Henry More's *History of the Jesuit Mission*, written in 1660, Weston replied, 'Not at all. My capture had nothing to do with money. For my part I will not be saved by money. If God wants it so, He will move the hearts of those who shut me up to restore me to liberty.' (Trans. Francis Edwards SJ, p.184.)

Just before Christmas 1586 Anne was living alone in Arundel House, when her visiting priest, Father Martin Array was either captured or died. In seeking a temporary replacement she was presented with Father Robert Southwell SJ who misunderstood his invitation and installed himself as a permanent chaplain.

The Countess only realised what had happened a few days later when Southwell 'began upon occasion to speak of procuring some secret convenience to be made in some part of the house, wherein himself and his few books, together with the Church stuff, might be hidden in case any sudden search should happen to be made, as it was usual in most Catholic houses where any priest had residence'. So Southwell stayed at Arundel House until his arrest in the summer of 1592, and it was not until some years after his arrival that the Countess told him with some amusement that he had originally been an unintended lodger. (Michael Hodgetts, *Secret Hiding Places*, (1989), p. 14.)

For those six years from 1586 until 1592 Anne and Father Southwell formed a most effective religious partnership. She risked her life to give him protection and hospitality. She bought him a printing press which she installed in her own house. She provided the funds that he and the other Jesuits needed so badly for all their good works and indeed Father John Gerard has paid tribute to her in his *Autobiography* when he points out that Father Southwell alone had a great benefactress.

Anne, Countess of Arundel played a very prominent part before God in the mission of Father Robert Southwell but it was a partnership from which she herself derived much spiritual benefit. As she grieved for her imprisoned husband, it was Southwell's task, wrote Father Henry More SJ 'to soothe her with every healing balm he could think and he explains in great detail (*History of the English Mission*, trans. Father Francis Edwards SJ; p. 237):

> Through spoken word and written exhortation, he taught the Countess of Arundel not only to bear her bereavement (i.e. separation from her husband) but also to accept it for the love of her sublimer spouse, Christ Himself; also by pouring out her prayer more frequently to God she could show that more abundant obedience which she could not give her husband while he was absent from her. For her assistance, Southwell drew up a rule of life which was subsequently printed, and so helped even more people. He also wrote her a more diffuse letter of consolation. In the event, that likewise proved most useful in easing the smart of Catholics generally. Southwell also brought solace to the Countess by his very understanding letters. Among them are those he sent after Arundel's condemnation to death. In this way, Southwell was able to strengthen a noble mind already braced to surrender the ultimate forfeit of life itself.

When Father Robert Southwell was arrested in 1592, he was first tortured by Topcliffe but he refused to give away any information about his friends and supporters. Thankful for thus escaping arrest herself, Anne was courageous enough to send him clean linen, a bible and a copy of the works of Saint Bernard.

Anne also involved herself particularly in the protection of Father John Gerard SJ. In 1594, according to his *Autobiography*, the priest went to London and 'stayed with a person of high rank and was completely safe. It was at this house that Father Southwell had lived before he was captured and imprisoned in the Tower of London.' The 'person of high rank' was undoubtedly Anne, Countess of Arundel.

Again it was the same lady who played some part at least in Father Gerard's escape from the Tower on 4 October 1597. The Countess of Arundel and her daughter, both suitably disguised, had managed to visit the priest in his cell in the Salt Tower and were able to carry secret messages back and forth so that arrangements could be made for a boat to be waiting for the prisoner as he descended by rope from the high walls and the roofs of the prison buildings to safety and freedom.

After the death of her husband, Anne never married again but devoted the remaining thirty-five years of her life to prayer and good works. She showed a most enthusiastic devotion to the Fathers of the Society of Jesus and was honoured by them as the foundress and chief benefactor of their house at Ghent.

In her old age, in 1624, she successfully petitioned King James I for possession of her husband's body, which had been unceremoniously buried in what was now the Anglican chapel of Saint Peter ad Vincula in the Tower of London. With all the dignity and respect of the Roman liturgy, the Earl of Arundel was reburied in the Fitzalan Chapel at Arundel.

Anne Howard, Countess of Arundel died at Shifnal in Shropshire in 1630 when she was seventy-four years of age. Her last wishes were respected and she was buried beside her husband at Arundel, but an event she had not been able to foresee was to separate husband and wife. In 1970, Philip Howard, Earl of Arundel, was canonized as a saint and a martyr by Holy Mother Church and his bones were taken from their resting place beside his wife and solemnly enshrined in the Cathedral of the new diocese of Arundel and Brighton, where he is now honoured by so many people as their Patron Saint.

DOROTHY LAWSON

Dorothy Lawson was born in 1580 at Wenge, the ancestral home of the Dormers in Buckinghamshire and was the second daughter of Sir Henry Constable of Burton Constable in the East Riding of Yorkshire and his wife, Margaret Dormer. She was therefore sister to Henry Constable, the first Viscount Dunbar and sister also to Catherine Constable, whose husband became the first Viscount Fairfax of Gilling and Emly. Dorothy herself was married on 10 March 1597 and the husband chosen for her was Roger Lawson, the eldest son of Sir Ralph Lawson of Byker in Northumberland and his wife, Elizabeth Burgh, in whose right he had inherited Brough Hall in Richmondshire.

The wedding ceremony was given great importance and was celebrated at Wenge with no little pomp and circumstance. Afterwards, the young couple and their entourage made a stately progress across country to Dorothy's home at Burton Constable Hall, where as Father Palmes reported, 'all Holderness came to congratulate them, some as friends and allies others as servants and vassals'. Next day, bride and bridegroom moved on their triumphant way towards Brough Hall but six miles short of the end of the journey, Sir Roger Lawson with a hundred horsemen was waiting to welcome his new daughter-in-law to his home. He lifted her from her horse and put her on

> a snow white steed he had brought for her, caparisoned with crimson velvet, embroidered with swans and martins of pearls; these the arms of Lawson, those of Brough ... After the performance of those sweet mutual addresses, (Sir Ralph Lawson) applied himself to her father, of whom yet he had so much as taken notice, and the rest of her honourable train with the highest rhetoric of civil respect, that the sharpness of his wit, improved by the best breeding of England could advance ... Between the two knights, her own father on the right hand, her father-in-law on the left, she rode more like Esther or princess than a subject or esquire's spouse until arriving at a fair green before Brough Hall, she met with a second encounter or volley of ceremonies given by her mother-in-law, the Lady Lawson, who greeted her with the salutation of the most welcome guest that ever her house had received. (Father William Palmes SJ, *The Life of Mrs Dorothy Lawson*, (1646), p. 12.)

After such adulation, it is noteworthy and quite typical of Dorothy Lawson that 'she stole the time before she reposed, for evensong and examen of conscience, which since she was capable, she never as much as once in her whole life omitted.'

And so Dorothy Lawson set up house at Brough Hall under the tutelage of Lady Lawson, who was herself a formidable Catholic and in fact had been one of the Catholic ladies put in prison at Sheriff Hutton Castle in 1592. Neither Sir Ralph Lawson nor Roger wished to be known as Catholics and both, at this time, seem to have been Church Papists, but courteously and diplomatically they spent much time in London on business so that their wives were free to make all the religious arrangements for their joint household.

Before the arrival of Dorothy Lawson, Lady Lawson had been accustomed to journey forth every month in search of Mass. Dorothy however made different arrangements. Knowing that the Jesuit Superior, Father Richard Holtby lived only four miles away and that he was the brother of Sir Ralph Lawson's steward, Mr Anthony Holtby, an immediate message was sent demanding his presence. As a result of that meeting, Father Holtby agreed to come to Brough and lead Mrs Lawson in the Spiritual Exercises of Saint Ignatius and he agreed also to send a priest every month for Mass. From these beginnings Brough developed as a recusant Mass centre with its own chapel, its own priest's hiding hole and its own resident priest for over three hundred years.

In this Catholic atmosphere Dorothy Lawson reared her children. But by 1605 the house at Brough Park was too small for the growing family and it was necessary to move back to Northumberland where the Lawsons had originated, and where Sir Ralph Lawson was in possession of an old manor house at Heaton near Byker on the north bank of the River Tyne. In this house, Dorothy Lawson and her children took up residence but the father of the family continued to spend much time in London at his legal work in the Inner Temple.

It was here, in late 1613 or early 1614, that Roger was taken seriously ill and an urgent messenger was despatched northwards to summon his wife. Despite the fact that she was at the time well advanced with another child, Dorothy set out at once on the difficult journey to the south. She arrived in time to comfort her husband and at her entreaty he called for a priest to hear his confession and reconcile him to the Catholic Church. He died, fortified by all the rites of the Church and with his wife by his side.

In seventeenth century England, the speedy remarriage of a widow was expected as a matter of course, especially if that widow were an heiress and endowed with many children. Dorothy was certainly not short of money. Her husband had made ample provision for her in his will and her father and her father-in-law were ready to offer generous help. Of course, she needed much help. Heaton was a large establishment and she had many children. Her biographer says she had twelve; Sir William Lawson maintained in 1855 that 'she seems to have had fifteen children in all, though the family pedigree says nineteen.' All in all, a second marriage seemed inevitable. But to the surprise of her family and friends, Dorothy

Lawson refused to contemplate such a step and insisted that she wished to lead a single life in the service of the Gospel.

That her motives for this determination were strictly religious has been confirmed by her chaplain and biographer, Father Palmes. He refers to her vow 'to pass the remainder of her days in angelic chastity', (p. 24) and he explains also how 'she intended to expend the rest of her life like a solitary sparrow in the holes of a rock, or mourning turtle, that never had mate but one, and vowed never to know another.' (p. 23.)

Dorothy Lawson returned home at once to apply herself to the needs of her children. Now for the first time in her life she was completely in charge of her own household and could make all her own decisions without reference to any man. She obtained the services of a resident Jesuit priest and what had formerly been designated as the 'children's prayer room', now became the chapel where the priest was able to celebrate daily Mass. The religious education of the children was entrusted to the priest and in due time all these children, with the exception of the heir, were sent to colleges and religious houses overseas in the hope that religious and ecclesiastical vocations would be nurtured.

Mrs Lawson's first personal chaplain was a Father Legard SJ, about whom very little is known but the influences of this obviously holy priest were profound and he took his duties as spiritual director very seriously indeed. The Records of the English Province of the Society of Jesus pay tribute to them both when they note that by his 'continual advice and assistance, she daily improved not only in her own perfection but became visibly more active towards her children and neighbours. When she first arrived at Heaton there was but one Catholic family in the parish or circuit. At her death there was not one heretic family and six altars were erected for divine service.' (vol. V, p. 717.)

Mrs Lawson relied heavily on her priests. Professor John Bossy relates with some amusement how at times she over-emphasized this reliance and he quotes the manner in which 'she insisted on taking advice on agricultural problems from her priest, William Palmes, who knew nothing whatever about them and had hastily to consult others.' (*English Catholic Community*, p. 258.) What a contrast to Charlotte Jerningham who expressed her regret that 'these good priests cannot confine themselves to spiritual matters.'

But Mrs Lawson was always concerned about spiritual matters and consulted not only her own chaplain but also her great friend, Father Richard Holtby SJ, who made his more permanent residence with her and absented himself only to attend to his wider duties as the Jesuit Superior for the north of England. It was Father Holtby who provided Dorothy Lawson with her chaplains and it was Father Holtby who organized the religious affairs of the district so well that his network of secret altars and hiding places has never been discovered.

Heaton Hall, however, was not intended to be a permanent Catholic centre. At the request of her father-in-law, Sir Ralph, the Hall was sold and steps were taken to build a new house for Dorothy and her extended family not far away on the banks of the Tyne at a place called St Anthony's. The

Records of the English Province relate that 'her reasons for choosing that locality were: first, because the place was holy, dedicated in Catholic times to Saint Anthony, his picture being decently placed in a tree near the River Tyne for the comfort of seamen; secondly, for that it was more private than Heaton and free to frequent her chapel.'

In planning and building this new house, Dorothy Lawson was fortunate to have Father Richard Holtby at her side because the Jesuit Superior had much experience in devising such buildings and was himself a very skilled craftsman with a reputation second only to that of Saint Nicholas Owen, the Jesuit brother as an ingenious and successful designer of hiding holes for priests.

The house was large. It was intended to be a family home for many children as well as a Mass Centre, a Jesuit Headquarters and a resting place for itinerant priests. Father Holtby was invited to bless the first stone and in the Biography of Dorothy Lawson it is recorded (p. 30) that:

> at the end of the house, opposite to the water, she caused to be made the Sacred Name of Jesus, large in proportion and accurate for art, that it might serve the mariners instead of Saint Anthony's picture: and when the fabric was ended, she dedicated the whole to Saint Michael and Saint Anthony, and each room, (the chapel excepted which was consecrated to the Mother of God) was nominated and publicly known by the name of some particular saint.

Shortly after the construction of this magnificent house, Dorothy Lawson lost her chaplain. Father Legard had served her with devotion and distinction for several years but died in either 1623 or 1624. His place was taken by Father Henry Morse, then a Jesuit novice but later to achieve heroic stature as the priest of the Plague and one of the Forty English Martyrs. Within twelve months, Father Morse was arrested in Newcastle upon Tyne and after some little time in prison there was transported to London. Father Holtby then appointed Father John Robinson SJ to be the Lawson chaplain but he was captured on his ship in the river before he had even set foot on shore. And so Father William Palmes (or possibly Palmer) was appointed chaplain and he stayed with Dorothy Lawson until her death.

It is this Father Palmes who has left for posterity the detailed biography of Dorothy Lawson which is the major source of information about her life and works. He stayed with her about seven years and knew her intimately as priest, friend and spiritual director. He does not hesitate to profess his belief in the extraordinary sanctity of his spiritual child and he endeavours to explain her heroic attachment to the Gospel and her unceasing efforts to proclaim the Catholic Faith to the people of the district. At first the burden on Father Palmes was very heavy. Mrs Lawson expressed to him her desire to become a recluse in her own house but after consultation with Father Holby it was decided that this would not be conducive to the greater service and glory of God and permission was refused. Mrs Lawson accepted the decision humbly and willingly and applied herself to a more active religious life which was centred on her own house but spread outwards to help all who lived in the vicinity. This work was much more congenial to Father Palmes and he worked with great zeal to further all the spiritual projects of his mistress.

Father Palmes has described the household of Dorothy Lawson as if it were a religious house or convent. He has stated that:

> her chapel was neat and rich; the altar vested with various habiliments according to the fashion in Catholic countries. Mass in the morning; Evensong in the afternoon about four of the clock with the Litany of Loreto to recommend to the Sacred Virgin's custody the safety of her house and a De Profundis for the faithful departed; between eight and nine at night, the Litany of the Saints at which all her servants were present. On Festival days they also heard Mass and Evensong, and when there was not a sermon in the morning, there was usually a catechism in the afternoon, to which the children of her neighbours were called with her own household, and herself never absent, delighting much to hear them examined and distributing medals and Agnus Deis to those that answered best. (Biography, p. 43.)

Father Palmes goes on to explain how Dorothy Lawson celebrated the full liturgy of Easter and Christmas and how at such times she entertained many Catholics from the surrounding countryside with food and drink. She was well known as a gracious hostess but she was also well known as a lady who cared for all who suffered and she frequently ventured forth to assist the needy.

> When any fell into trouble or sickness, no occasion of business, weather or time, were it night or day detained her; yea she often went sick and returned sound, in so much that it passed as a proverb amongst us... To women in childbirth she never went without comfort of both sorts: relics for the soul and if they were poor, cordials for the body. For these offices, she gained so much on the opinion of neighbours, that they would generally say, they feared not if Mrs Lawson were with them. (*Ibid.*, p. 45.)

'Her liberality did bountifully extend to the poor, both by vow and necessity; these she hourly relieved, feeding the hungry, clothing the naked, and because she was a widow herself, she kept a purse of twopences for widows.' Father Palmes delivers himself of the powerful statement that 'as long as I lived with her, which, alas was but seven years, ... none of her parish, man or woman departed this life without help, or infant without baptism'. (*Ibid.*, p. 46.)

Dorothy Lawson's charity towards the Jesuits is also worthy of record. When her chaplains, Father Henry Morse and Father John Robinson were in prison for the Faith in Newcastle, 'she furnished them with church stuff, washed their linen, provided them with all the necessaries for clothes and victuals, and though Mr Morse was known to belong to her, nevertheless preferring his convenience before her own safety, she adventured to visit him in gaol and petitioned the magistrate he might enjoy the liberty of the town for his health'. (*Ibid.*, p. 46)

And Father Palmes goes on to explain how well she provided for him as her chaplain.

> To her ghostly father nothing was wanting fit for the condition of a religious man. He was accommodated with a good chamber and library, with all things belonging to himself in a genteel and plentiful way; and according to the custom of the colleges, she gave him a viaticum when he went abroad, the remainder of which he restored when he returned home. I dare avouch, that for the space of seven years, I neither knew what was in my purse when I took journey, nor she what I expended out of it, when I gave it to her at my return. (*Ibid.*, pp. 46-7.)

To the Rector of the Society, she gave each year a sum of £10 and also the tithes of the salmon fishing on the estate and each year she financed the Jesuit retreat when half a dozen of the Society would live with her at her expense for eight days.

For such acts of charity Mrs Lawson was widely known and respected by Catholics and non-Catholics alike. She openly professed her Faith but she made no religious distinction among those she served, and all, irrespective of their theological viewpoint could recognize the holiness of the woman and the multiple good works which she achieved. There was therefore considerable anxiety over a large area in 1631 when news came from St Anthony's that a serious illness had beset her. For six months she lingered on as a chronic invalid, in great pain, confined to her bed, 'with a consumption or cough of the lungs'. She suffered in patience and equanimity but she was aware that the time was fast approaching when she must meet her Maker and for that joyous event she prepared herself confidently. She died on 26 March 1632 at the age of fifty-two.

Many tributes and compliments had been paid to Dorothy Lawson during her lifetime but the news of her death produced grief and sadness over a very wide area and the manner of her funeral was the most remarkable tribute and the greatest compliment that had ever been paid to her.

Her Requiem Mass was celebrated in her own chapel at St Anthony's at eleven o'clock on the very night she died and even at that short notice more than a hundred Catholics were present. Next day, her eldest son, Henry Lawson was the chief mourner and:

> all the gentry thereabouts were invited and a dinner prepared for them. The poor of that and the bordering parishes were served that day with meat; the next with money. Divers boats full of people came in the afternoon from Newcastle, all plentifully entertained with a banquet; and when these civil respects were ended, we carried the body in the evening to Newcastle in her own boat, accompanied by at least twenty other boats and barges, and above twice as many horses, planting them on both sides of the shore till their arrival at the city.

They found the streets shining with tapers, as light as if it had been noon. The magistrates and aldermen with the whole glory of the town, which for state is second only to London, attended at the landing place to wait on the coffin, which they received covered with a fine black velvet cloth and a white satin cross, and carried it but to the church door ... (*Ibid.*, p. 60.)

At this point, perhaps, a reminder is necessary that the year is 1632 and that the Penal Laws are still in full force against the Catholics so that every Catholic taking part in that funeral procession was dicing with death. In these circumstances, what happens next is almost unbelievable were it not for the word of the eyewitness, Father William Palmes SJ.

At the foot of Pilgrim Street, where once stood the old church of All Hallows, a small group of Protestant dignitaries awaited the funeral cortège of the recusant Dorothy Lawson. The Church of England clergyman, the Reverend Samuel Barker was there; so was the Mayor, Sir Lionel Maddison; so was the sheriff, Francis Bowes. The Catholics could only hope that these stern upholders of the Law would shut their eyes to the presence of so many Catholics and would allow the vicar to conduct the Anglican Service, which was always required for Catholic burials. In fact, the vicar had other ideas. He knew that many Catholic priests were present among the mourners and now, with great charity and remarkable courage, he defied the Penal Laws and invited any such priest to come forward and preside in his place at the funeral ceremonies. Father Palmes felt himself to be unworthy of this honour, so it was another priest, unnamed, who took over the service and with Catholic rites laid Mrs Lawson's body to rest in her grave in the Protestant church while the Protestant ministers and the Protestant mourners stood around in love, sympathy and respect. It was a most unusual funeral for a most unusual lady and an extraordinary tribute to the sheer goodness of a holy woman, whose virtue transcended all denominational barriers.

GRACE BABTHORPE

Grace Babthorpe was the daughter of William Byrnand, later to be Recorder of York. Her mother was a daughter of Sir William Ingleby of Ripley Castle but she died in giving birth and Grace, an only child and therefore sole heiress was brought up by her formidable grandmother, Lady Ingleby of Ripley.

In 1578, when she was fifteen years of age, Grace was married to Ralph, the eldest son of Sir William Babthorpe of Babthorpe and Osgodby in the East Riding of Yorkshire. After their marriage, both being very young, Ralph was sent to London to study law at the Inns of Court and for some years, in order to avoid trouble, he reluctantly conformed to the Church of England. Meanwhile, Grace stayed at home at Osgodby Hall and remained a staunch and enthusiastic Catholic.

Father John Morris SJ in his *Troubles of our Catholic Forefathers,* (Series 1, p. 228) uses a seventeenth century manuscript then preserved at Saint Augustine's Priory, Abbotsleigh to describe Grace Babthorpe's first clash with the Earl of Huntingdon, Lord President of the Council of the North. An edict had been published calling on all gentlemen with Catholic wives to present themselves to the authorities for more questioning. Grace Babthorpe presented herself with the others but was taken to one side by the Lord President, who asked her when did she go to the Anglican Church.

> She answered him, 'Never'. He demanded then how many Masses she had heard. She said, so many that she could not reckon them. At this, he began to stamp. He lastly, seeing her remain so constant, made her the next day to appear before the whole Council Table at York, where himself and their bishop were chief, and seeing her to stand firm, they thought to try all means possible; wherefore first she was committed unto a lawyer's house in York, a most hot Puritan; and others also in divers houses, where they brought almost daily ministers and others to persuade her, as also even at table eating with them she could not be quiet from hearing their blasphemies against the Catholic Faith. And having endured this for a fortnight, and seeing they prevailed nothing, the Lord president committed six of the best sort to prison in an old castle of the Queen's, where they were not permitted to come together nor converse with each other...

Among the six ladies who were thus incarcerated in Sheriff Hutton Castle were Lady Constable of Holderness, Mrs Ingleby of Ripley, Mrs Metham of

Metham, Mrs Lawson of Brough and Mrs Babthorpe of Babthorpe and Osgodby. It was said that 'the President intended never to have released them unless they yielded' but these spirited ladies refused to give in and maintained themselves at all times with dignity and not a little humour. When Anglican ministers were sent into the castle to 'confer' with the prisoners, they were told very plainly by these women that they had not come into prison in order to dispute about their Faith but that they had come in order to profess their Faith. When the keeper told them that he had bound himself for £400 to keep them apart from each other and even to prevent them speaking with each other, Lady Grace Babthorpe told him that 'he was very simple to bind himself in such manner for a man hath enough to do to keep one woman and would you undertake to keep and rule six women?'

For two years these ladies were supposed to be in solitary confinement, but their enterprise and ingenuity enabled them to lead a very different life. Lady Babthorpe managed to get in touch with a priest who came to the bars of the window at night and heard confessions and brought Holy Communion without alerting the guard. But not content with this, the ladies wished for Mass and so Lady Babthorpe, 'taking a chisel and a hammer, and getting some to play at shuttlecock, that they might not hear her at such times as she cut the freestone of the window on the inside, where bars of the grate went in, so long time till she could take in the whole window and let in the priest; and when he was gone, put up the grate again, and nothing was seen on the outside ...'

Eventually, the Lord President acknowledged that he had met his match in these ladies and they were returned to their husbands. Lady Grace Babthorpe was kept a little longer partly because she was clearly the leader but also because she had her small daughter in prison with her and she refused to allow the child to attend the Protestant services.

In due time, the Babthorpe family were reunited in freedom at Osgodby and indeed, Sir Ralph himself, at his wife's behest became a good Catholic and suffered persecution even as she did.

The spiritual rule of life at Osgodby has been described by one of the priests who served there:

Our house I might count rather as a religious house than otherwise, for though there lived there together in it three knights and their ladies with their families, yet we had all our servants Catholic. On the Sundays, we locked the doors and all came to Mass, had our sermons, catechisms and spiritual lessons every Sunday and holiday. On the work days we had for the most part two Masses, and of them the one for the servants at six o'clock in the morning at which the gentlemen every one of them without fail and the ladies if they were not sick, would even, in the midst of winter, of their own accord be present; and the other we had at eight o'clock for those who were absent from the first. In the afternoon, at four o'clock, we had Evensong, and after that, Matins, at which all the knights and ladies, except extraordinary occasions did hinder them, would be present, and stay at their prayers all the time the priests were at Evensong and Matins. The most of them used daily some meditation and mental prayer and all, at the least every fourteen days and great feasts, did confess and communicate; and after supper, every night at nine o'clock, we had altogether litanies, and so immediately to bed.

In her Recollections, Lady Grace Babthorpe described the same situation in rather broader terms when she wrote, 'Yet it pleased God to be as much served in our house as in any other place, for we were never without the comfort of His priests, and as often three or four at a time as one; and whosoever wanted a place till they were provided, our house was their stay, so good a man was my husband.'

Lady Grace Babthorpe was a woman of great strength and she built up at Osgodby a religious centre which was a place of refuge for the priests and a centre of inspiration for the poor Catholics of the district. She wrote:

For the poor Catholics in our parish of Hemingborough the persecution has been greater than I can relate, for no Catholic could keep any goods, no, not the poor folks keep a cow to give their children milk, but it was taken from them; and of late years they forced them to pay twelve pence every Sunday. And of such as had not money, they take their goods, and of the poor that had not great goods, they took such things as they found in their houses, as their vessels, of some their porridge pots, and of others clothes off their beds, and if they had more coats than that on their backs, they took them, and of one that had, with her work in the summer, got a piece of cloth to clothe her children with, they took it from her; and those they could get nothing of, they sent to prison.

The strain of living in such circumstances of persecution and the continual harassment by pursuivants became too much for Sir Ralph's failing health, and he felt obliged to leave Osgodby to his son Sir William, while he and Lady Grace settled in safer surrounds in London where they were not so well known. Even here, they had a Priest in their lodgings when there was a sudden pursuivant raid. The priest was captured and was being taken to prison when Sir Ralph sent one of his trusted servants after the party to effect a rescue. The servant carefully played one of the oldest tricks known to mankind. He took the pursuivants to the tavern, filled them with strong drink and enabled the priest to make his escape.

This was really the end of the road for Sir Ralph. He could endure no more. He obtained on the recommendation of his doctors, a Government licence to travel overseas to take the beneficial waters of a spa. Unfortunately, he never achieved the peace and quiet he so desperately needed. He died at Louvain in 1617 on the very day he had completed the Spiritual Exercises of Saint Ignatius.

Lady Grace Babthorpe determined at once that being a widow she would not marry again but would offer herself to God as a Canoness of Saint Augustine in Saint Monica's Convent in Louvain. She made her profession in 1621, when she was almost sixty years of age and she never left the Convent again. The Annals of the Canonesses relate that:

> She lived in religion devoutly and gave special example of humility, nothing regarding what she had been before, but submitting herself willingly to all religious discipline, and honoured the nuns, though much younger than herself in years ... (She lived) not only with edification to others, but also with great contentment to herself, taking much pains in the reading of her Great Office, for by reason of her years she was dispensed from reading and singing with the Choir. Therefore she kneeled by, and performed the divine service by herself, being bound to her Breviary in respect that she was a veiled nun. So much reading apart was very painful to her aged sight, which notwithstanding she performed with great care and diligence for the love of God. As also she bore patiently such things as happened to her contrary to her nature and former breeding, not complaining thereof, though she felt it sometimes hard.

For thirteen years, Lady Grace Babthorpe lived in the cloister as Sister Grace Babthorpe and fulfilled her vocation in every way. She died suddenly but not unexpectedly in 1635 when she was seventy-two years of age.

Lady Grace Babthorpe demonstrated in her life at Osgodby, in her life in prison and in her life at Saint Monica's Convent all those qualities of faith, devotion and determination which were required from all the Catholic women of her day but her teaching and example was so powerful that even after her death her work for the Church was continued and developed by her children and their descendants. Of her nine children, Robert became a Benedictine monk and two of his brothers Jesuits. Their sister, Barbara tried her vocation with the Benedictine nuns of Brussels, but then joined her cousin, Mary Ward, (who had also been subjected to the Babthorpe influence at Osgodby from 1598 to 1605) and became in time the Superior General of the Institute of the Blessed Virgin Mary.

In succeeding years, the family gave so many sons and daughters to the Church as priests and nuns that their generosity inevitably sowed the seeds of family extinction. When Lady Grace's great-granddaughter, Sister Mary Anne Barbara Babthorpe, died in 1711 as the second Babthorpe to be Superior General of the Institute of the Blessed Virgin Mary, she was succeeded in that high office by her sister, Sister Mary Agnes Babthorpe. But by that time the whole Babthorpe family consisted of one priest and two nuns. Then Sister Ursula Babthorpe died as a Canoness of Saint Augustine in Bruges on 1 November 1719 and Sister Mary Agnes Babthorpe died in Munich on 20 February 1720. For almost eight weeks, Father Albert Babthorpe SJ had the honour of being the sole survivor of this ancient and devoted family but when he died on 13 April 1720 the family was no more.

ELIZABETH COTTARD

Very little is known about the personal life of Elizabeth Cottard but she was certainly one of the Catholic prisoners in York Castle in 1635 and her struggles and sufferings there have been carefully recorded by a contemporary writer, whose original manuscript is now in the Public Record Office at Brussels. A copy of this document has been used by Brother Henry Foley SJ in his 'Records of the English Province SJ', vol. V, series XII, p. 764.

Elizabeth Cottard's 'crime' was that she was guilty of harbouring a priest. The name of the priest is not known but he had been captured in Elizabeth's house in 1625 and both priest and harbourer had been committed to York Castle. After five years of suffering the priest had died but Elizabeth had lingered on and in 1635 had completed ten years in captivity with no prospect of release. She was classified as a 'poor prisoner' and with her were four other 'poor prisoners':

> Henry Routh, a poor tailor, of sixty-four years of age, who hath remained a prisoner there for his conscience and for no other cause, twenty-eight years. Henry Baneston, a poor weaver, hath remained there a prisoner for the same and no other cause, about eleven years. Michael Whitfield, a poor lame man, of fifty-six years, hath remained a prisoner for fourteen years for the same cause. James Wallis, a poor man of sixty-eight years of age was committed for having beads and crosses found about him, which they accused him for desiring to give Catholics, and for that he hath remained there in prison twenty years. (*Ibid.*, p. 764.)

Elizabeth Cottard was in good company. Her companions were all long-term prisoners and despite their advanced years were all as resolute and determined as she was. All endured great hardship because they shared the burden of poverty and were unable to meet the demands of the prison officials who required payment for ordinary food and lodging and expected frequent 'sweeteners' if not blatant bribes if the harsh conditions of life were to be at all alleviated. Prisoners needed money to obtain the most basic necessities and they needed money for any little comfort the grasping guards might offer them. Wealthy prisoners prospered; the poor had to rely on the charity of their friends.

Local Catholics tried to help their brothers and sisters who were in prison. Sums of money were set apart 'for the poor prisoners'; there were frequent collections among the community; but all such efforts were only of limited value. As the manuscript points out: 'It is to be less wondered at that they are sometimes in such plights, because the country (i.e. the district) is very poor and many of their benefactors are dead, and therefore men live out of sight, and consequently out of mind, and the time of their suffering hath been so long that men have grown dull in relieving them.' (*Ibid.*, p. 765.)

The document then goes on to give more detail about the sufferings of the poor prisoners and quotes the powerful evidence of a certain AB, whose identity is not disclosed but who is described as 'a gentleman of a good house, and his elder brother now a knight, and a very virtuous Catholic, and hath been a long time prisoner with them'. These credentials are strengthened still more by the insistence that he writes as 'an eye-witness' and makes his statement 'with a safe conscience'. It is therefore from his own experience that AB can relate that the poor prisoners were able to have but one meal a day and that this meal consisted of 'a mess of pottage, made of oatmeal and water. They had rye bread and ale at a penny a gallon to drink. Upon Sundays, a gallon of milk was mixed with six gallons of water, which could not make their pottage so much as white but only grey.' On this meagre diet, Elizabeth Cottard and her companions subsisted for the many years of their captivity.

AB's statements have been fully supported and indeed enlarged by the unlikely authority of Dr James Raines, the Anglican Canon Residentiary in York in the latter years of the nineteenth century. In his Preface to 'York Castle Depositions', Canon Raines has described the condition of the prisoners and the state of York Castle in the seventeenth century and has written as follows:

> It is impossible to speak in terms of too strong retrobation of the state of the northern prisons and of the conduct of their keepers. They were dens of iniquity and horror in which men and women were herded together indiscriminately. The dungeons of the Inquisition were scarcely worse. Some of them had no light and no ventilation; several were partly under water when there was a flood. The number of prisoners who died in gaol during this century is positively startling. And how could they live in such places, where they were treated worse than savages themselves? The ordinary conveniences and necessaries of life were denied to them. They were at the mercy of the gaolers for their food and for everything they possessed. They had the meanest fare at the most exorbitant price. If they resisted, there were irons and screws that compelled them to be silent...These are painful pictures, but happily they represent scenes which are no longer to be witnessed. (*Ibid.*, p. 766.)

Canon Raines had no axe to grind for Catholics and indeed is writing with the cool detachment of the honourable historian on more general matters. His concern is the condition of prisoners in general, but he is, in fact, describing very accurately the manner of life of Elizabeth Cottard and her companions during their long sojourn in York Castle, and indirectly at least, is paying tribute to the courage and constancy of the Catholic prisoners who were prepared to suffer so much for the sake of their religion.

Great efforts were made by their friends to relieve the prisoners as best they could and the valiant AB did not hesitate to go to London to make representations at Court on behalf of Elizabeth Cottard and her companions. King Charles I was known to be favourably inclined towards Catholics; his wife, Queen Henriatta Maria was a most devout Catholic who practiced her religion openly. A humble petition was therefore presented to the Queen asking her to intercede with her husband the King and secure freedom for the poor Catholic prisoners who had spent so long in York Castle. The Queen's heart was touched; she readily accepted their plea and made her personal request to the King. The King listened with sympathy and compassion and granted his wife's petition. He gave orders to the York Circuit Judge, Judge Strawley, that on his next Assize visit to that city, he should free all those prisoners who had been convicted on religious grounds. Unfortunately, the Judge managed to misunderstand the royal instructions and before freeing the Catholic prisoners, he demanded that each of them should take the Oath of Allegiance, which, of course, in conscience no Catholic could accept and they therefore remained where they were in prison.

There was some indignation in official circles that the King's will should be thwarted in this way by a mere judge and the matter was referred back to the Queen by outraged courtiers. Again the Queen spoke to the King and again the King gave orders for the Catholic prisoners to be freed. But this time, in giving his instructions, the King himself demanded (unthinkingly, it would seem) that the Oath of Allegiance should be required as the first step to freedom and to this the Catholic prisoners would not and could not agree and so were unable to avail themselves of the royal clemency.

In such circumstances, Elizabeth Cottard and her friends lost heart and withdrew their petition. There is an air of finality about the chronicler's statement, 'So they are where they are and there are likely to remain.' They did however receive some small assistance because, 'towards the relief of their misery and great want, a course was taken to move the Queen's almoner to bestow the Queen's alms upon them, and so he did very christianly and courteously; and delivered five pounds for them to their solicitor, and purposed to send them some little things besides at four several times of the year, if they continued still in prison.' (*Ibid.*, p. 764.)

AB, however, was not prepared to give up and continued his efforts on behalf of the prisoners throughout 1635. He sought now to enlist the aid of Signor Gregory Panzani, the mysterious Papal Envoy who was living in London. Panzani was the official representative of Pope Urban VIII but was accredited directly to Queen Henrietta Maria rather than to King Charles I. Much of his work was secret but he was a faithful if devious servant of the Pope and if his assessment of the affairs of Bishop Richard Smith led to the virtual suppression of the episcopate in England for the next fifty years then at least he disabused his Master of the belief that the conversion of the King was imminent. Panzani was recognized in royal circles in London and reluctantly allowed some influence but of course, in Catholic circles the full power of the Vatican was behind him. He could have done much to have helped the poor prisoners in York but he was too much of a diplomat to commit himself. He dismissed AB by telling him that 'he knew not what to do therein for the present, but that he would speak with Father Phillipps about it, and wished the said AB to meet him there, which he did.'

Perhaps by this time, a more experienced man of affairs than AB might have realized that he was getting too involved in dangerous political affairs and delicate matters of ecclesiastical policy. Father Robert Phillipps was in fact a Jesuit, (although not of the English Province) and a special confessor to the Queen. He certainly had no wish to imperil his mission by concerning himself with the plight of poor Catholics in prison and although he expressed his desire to help, 'he did not see how it could be done' and absolved himself from any responsibility.

AB returned to Gregory Panzani and as a last resort humiliated himself as a beggar and asked outright for money for the relief of the prisoners. 'Whereupon, he did with much courtesy, but yet professing the straitness of his own means, give twenty shillings for their relief, and wished it had been much more.' (*Ibid.*, p. 766.)

And that is all that is known at this moment about Elizabeth Cottard and her companions. Perhaps they spent the rest of their days in prison; perhaps they managed eventually to secure their own release. But, whatever their fate, they were ready for martyrdom and Elizabeth Cottard deserves to be included among the great Catholic heroines of seventeenth-century England.

ELIZABETH FALKLAND

Elizabeth Falkland was born in 1585 and was brought up as a Protestant. Her father, Sir Lawrence Tanfield of Burford Priory in Oxfordshire occupied a high position in Queen Elizabeth's Government as Lord Chief Baron of the Exchequer and was determined to maintain his office by his firm attachment to the Church of England.

From her earliest childhood, Elizabeth was passionately devoted to study and her intelligence and application was such that she was always far ahead of the other girls of her age and as she grew older she made such progress in her literary and scholastic work as to earn the respect and admiration of her family and friends. Flora Fraser has claimed in her book, *The English Gentlewoman* (1987) that Elizabeth Tanfield taught herself Latin and Hebrew at home; Joseph Gillow (1885) says that she also taught herself French, Spanish and Italian and that she even dabbled in what he was pleased to call Transylvanian.

According to the custom of the time, this precocious child was given in marriage at the age of fifteen to another good Protestant, Sir Henry Cary of Aldenham and Berkhampstead in Hertfordshire. It was of course a business arrangement. Sir Henry was Master of the Queen's Jewel House and could recognize a wealthy heiress when he saw one; the Tanfields for their part could recognize a promising government official with great ambitions.

According to Flora Fraser, the early days of the marriage were not particularly happy. The child-bride 'enraged her mother-in-law by refusing to humour her conceit. Lady Cary then locked Elizabeth in her chamber, which she little cared for but entertained herself with reading. Enraged, Lady Cary took away all her books, with command to have no more brought to her. Even this punishment was vain. Elizabeth set herself to make verses.' (*English Gentlewoman*, p. 66.)

Within five years of her marriage, Elizabeth became a Catholic. Professor John Bossy has quoted a contemporary opinion that she was 'a woman of most masculine understanding, allied with the passions and infirmities of her sex', but he maintains also that she was 'one of the very few among the sixteenth century crop of learned women, if not the only one, to convince herself by reading of the truth of the Catholic Faith.' (*English Catholic Community*, p. 159.)

Doctor David Lunn in his History of the English Benedictines, however, has referred to Elizabeth as 'saintly, erudite and eccentric' and has made the suggestion that some monks of Saint Benedict were involved in her conversion. He refers specifically to Father Benedict Price and Father Leander Jones but details are lacking.

The remarkable feature about Elizabeth's conversion, according to Professor Bossy, is that for twenty years she kept this secret to herself and only in 1624 did her husband discover to his horror that he was in fact married to a Catholic. It was a great blow to him; he felt humiliated and betrayed; and especially he feared that his government career was endangered. He had made much progress since leaving the Jewel House. In 1618 he was the Comptroller of the Royal Household of King James I; in 1620 he had been raised to the Scottish Peerage as Viscount Falkland; and since 1622 he had exercised real power as Lord Deputy of Ireland. A Catholic wife would expose him to grave suspicions of disloyalty and could seriously affect his future prospects.

Lord Falkland decided to make it plain to the world that he abhorred his wife's Catholicism. He separated himself from her and sent her back to London in disgrace. As far as he was concerned his wife was dead. And so he made no provision for her accommodation or support. Her seven children were taken away from her and lodged, according to the strict letter of the law, in good Protestant households and far from their mother's influence.

King James I was grossly displeased at Elizabeth Falkland's conversion and gave orders that she was to be confined indefinitely to her house in London. Joseph Gillow has described her sufferings:

> For six weeks she was thus a prisoner in her rooms, her household being wholly Protestant, and no Catholic venturing to come near her. Dr Cozens, one of the King's chaplains was sent to her, but was unable to make any impression on her faith. After this she was treated with great harshness and an attempt was made by her husband to starve her into submission, but after some time she was set at liberty. Lord Falkland would allow her nothing, and she was obliged to live on the charity of her friends, both Catholic and Protestant; her mother turned her out of her house in London, where she had lived since her return from Ireland; and both her husband and her mother bitterly reproached her for her change of religion, and told her that her misfortunes were owing to herself, and that she deserved all she suffered. (Bibliographical Dictionary of English Catholic, vol. ii, p. x.)

Embarrassed by her poverty and unwilling to impose any longer on the generosity of her friends, Elizabeth Falkland found a dilapidated cottage on the banks of the Thames and settled there with her devoted Catholic maidservant for some months until she managed to find rented accommodation in the city. For three years she experienced the pains of extreme poverty and then in 1628, the Privy Council of King Charles I took notice of her plight and provided her with a residence at Cote in Oxfordshire and then forced her husband to pay her an allowance of £500 a year. But by law she was still deprived of her children.

During these years of suffering, Lady Falkland resumed her scholarly studies. She translated into English Cardinal Perron's reply to the theological treatise of King James I, but all copies of her work were seized by the Archbishop of Canterbury and solemnly burned as dangerous books. Later, Lady Falkland translated all the controversial writings of Cardinal Perron and offered them to her fellow Catholics for instruction and devotion. She also produced original biographies of Saint Mary Magdalen, Saint Agnes the Martyr and Saint Elizabeth of Portugal.

In 1629, Lady Falkland took part in that extraordinary pilgrimage to Saint Winefred's Well at Holywell in Clwyd where, with an amazing bravado, more than 1,400 lay persons and at least 150 priests defied the penal laws to celebrate just as in pre-Reformation days the feast of the saint on 3 November.

In May 1630, Lord Falkland was recalled from Ireland. His wife's conversion had hardened him in his attitude to Irish Catholics and they in their turn disliked him intensely. A Protestant friend expressed his situation succinctly when he said, 'by the clamour of the Irish and the prevailing power of his popish enemies, he was removed in disgrace'.

Lord Falkland returned to England in humbling circumstances and blamed his wife for all his troubles. In London, he refused even to see her and once more reduced her to a state of chronic poverty. At this point, Queen Henrietta Maria intervened in the Falkland affairs and by her compassion and sympathy was able to bring about a complete reconciliation between husband and wife. From this time onwards Lord Falkland was a changed man. He became a good and loving husband, deeply concerned about his wife and children. He grew to appreciate more and more the values of the Catholic religion and it is believed that when he died in 1633, he died as a Catholic.

As Elizabeth Falkland commenced her widowhood, she was heartened to be told that her four daughters had all been received into the Catholic Church, but to her distress her eldest son, Lucius, now the 2nd Viscount refused to have anything to do with his mother and spoke out with vehemence against the Catholic Church. Every effort was made by Lucius to destroy the Faith of his sisters but he was thwarted by their courage and determination. He also tried to ensure the Protestant upbringing of his younger brothers by appointing a notorious bad character, William Chillingworth, as their tutor. The two little boys, Patrick aged nine and Henry aged eight were thus subjected to the harmful influence of a man who has been described as a 'doubt ridden, ex-Catholic chaplain'.

The boys and their tutor were taken to the Viscount's home at Great Trew where he had gathered together most of the best wits and scholars in England. The atmosphere of the place was certainly anti-Catholic and from the dangerous theories of pure reason and methodical doubt, Lucius led his distinguished followers to the extreme Protestant sect of the Socinians, which denies the existence of the Trinity and the Divinity of Our Lord.

Elizabeth Falkland was horrified that her sons should be exposed to such evil and with the help of her daughters, she determined to get them away by kidnapping if necessary. The opportunity presented itself during the general chaos of a family reunion in London. The boys escaped from the house at night, ran for a mile in the dark, and then tiptoed through the sleeping city until they reached the banks of the Thames where the hired boatmen were tipsy but still able to row them downstream to safety. Then the waiting Benedictine Fathers smuggled them out of the country to their monastery in Paris.

In 1636, Elizabeth was obliged to leave London because of the plague, but at this time she was reconciled to her son, Lord Falkland, who gave her a better house and more generous financial support. In these more comfortable and peaceful circumstances she could apply herself more readily to her literary pursuits and charitable exertions, and she enjoyed three happy, carefree years before she died in October 1639. She was fifty-four years of age. By special permission of Queen Henrietta Maria, Elizabeth Cary, Dowager Viscountess Falkland was buried in the Royal Chapel and her funeral Mass was sung by the Capuchin Fathers.

It remains to record that Patrick and Henry, when they finished their schooling in Paris, tried their monastic vocations and lived for a time as Benedictine monks, but neither persevered. The four girls all became Benedictine nuns in the Abbey of Our Lady of Consolation at Cambrai and died in the peace of their communities. Lucius, the eldest son, the 2nd Viscount Falkland, never became a Catholic. He was thirty-four years of age when he died with honour serving his King on the battlefield of Newbury on 20 September 1643.

MARY PERCY

Lady Mary Percy belonged to the ancient and noble House of Percy, which for so many centuries was the most powerful and popular family in the north of England. Her grandfather, Sir Thomas Percy, was one of the leaders of the Pilgrimage of Grace and gave his life for his Faith in 1537. Her father, Blessed Thomas Percy, the Seventh Earl of Northumberland followed his father's example and played his part in the Rising of the Northern Earls but his execution at York in 1572 has been recognized by the Church as a true martyrdom.

Mary was born in Old Aberdeen in Scotland on 11 June 1570 when her father and mother were fleeing from the wrath of Queen Elizabeth and she was only three months old when her mother carried her beyond the seas to the greater safety of Flanders. She never saw her father again but as she grew up she remained very close to her mother who spent all her days trying to restore the fortune and fame of her husband the martyred Earl. Mother and daughter lived in various convents in the Low Countries, but by 1591 Mary had returned to England and was in residence with her married sister, Elizabeth Woodroff, at Wooley, Royston in the West Riding of Yorkshire.

Father John Gerard SJ in his *Autobiography*, (Fontana, p. 56) has described how he used to make journeys into the north country in order 'to visit and encourage certain persons who gave great support to our common cause'. He is always most careful not to incriminate people by mentioning names but there is no doubt about the identities of the two sisters whom he frequently visited. He writes, 'They were the daughters of one of the oldest earls in the country who had died a Martyr for the Faith. At the time the two ladies lived in the same house and they wanted to have me to stay with them altogether, and not merely visit them occasionally. This was impossible, but they placed themselves under my direction in spiritual matters.'

Father Gerard goes on to pay tribute to the Lady Elizabeth, whom he calls the older sister and who was:

> the mother of a family and became, as it were, a pillar supporting the afflicted Church in those parts. She kept two Priests in her house and received with great kindness any others who happened to be passing (and there were many for that part of the country was well provided with priests and the Catholics were numerous, though they belonged mostly to the lower classes). Actually I was hardly ever in her house without meeting six or seven priests before I left.

Living in such a house with its ascetical atmosphere, Mary (or Maria, as she was more commonly called) had every opportunity to grow in holiness and to practice that special unofficial form of religious life which was such a distinctive feature of such households. Father John Gerard could describe her in this way: 'The other sister God kept for Himself. She was unmarried, self-effacing and modest, with a disposition well suited to higher things. Much of her time she gave to prayer, and the world seemed to lose its lustre and heaven to dazzle her. Later I sent her over to Father Holt in Belgium and he wrote to me about her in these words, "No person who has ever come here from our country has given more edification or done more to raise the good name of England."'

In Brussels, Mary met several other English Catholic ladies who like her, had been practising their religious life informally in England and who now wished to commit themselves to public vows and community life. Some of these ladies had already entered foreign convents and with this end in view, Lady Mary Percy first stayed at the Augustinian convent of Saint Ursula's in Louvain where several English ladies had made profession.

In 1596, Lady Mary made her decision to become a nun, but she was not attracted to the Dutch practices of the Augustinians at Saint Ursula's and the only English convent then in existence was that of the Bridgettines at Lisbon in Portugal. Mary wanted somewhere closer to England and decided to set up her own convent at Brussels.

She and her friends were of course in close touch with Father William Holt SJ and it was on his advice that they resolved that their new convent should be a Benedictine foundation. The Annals of this Brussels Convent for 1597 state that the reason for their choice of Saint Benedict was that the Order of Saint Benedict had flourished more than any other Order in times past in England and they hoped to be able in their own persons to help to restore Benedictine monasticism to their own country.

Lady Mary Percy was able to use her own money to buy suitable premises for her convent in 1598 but for the legalities of her foundation she depended very much upon Father Holt. The Convent Annals make it clear that it was Father Holt who secured the necessary briefs and permissions from Pope Clement VIII as well as obtaining the approbation of the local Bishop and the civil authorities. On 15 August of that same year, Father Holt said the first Mass in the great hall designed to be the Benedictine Church of the English Ladies in Brussels.

It was, of course, necessary for these new nuns to be trained and accordingly a request for assistance was made to the great monastery of St Peter's in the city of Rheims in France, and Lady Jean Bartley was sent from that house to ensure the canonical establishment of the new convent.

The Convent Annals for 1599 state:

On 14 November my Lady Jean Bartley was blessed Abbess by my lord Archbishop of Mechlin, and eight young English ladies offered themselves to be her subjects. On the 21 November, the same month and year, being the feast of the Presentation of the ever glorious Virgin Mary, these eight ladies, of which number my Lady Mary Percy was the first and chief, received the holy habit at the hands of my lord Mathias Hovius, Archbishop of Mechlin, in the presence of their highnesses the Archduke Albertus and his Duchess, the Lady Isabella Clara Eugenia, the Infanta of Spain, and all the chiefs of the town of Brussels.

It is difficult to overestimate the importance of this religious foundation for the future development of the struggling Church in England. Of course Lady Mary Percy and her friends were not the first Catholic ladies to graduate from the country house convent to authentic religious life. Several English women had already joined established foreign convents, but Lady Mary Percy ushered in a new era of English Convents abroad for English nuns and the education of Catholic girls.

In the first half of the seventeenth century, no fewer than twelve English convents were founded on the Continent of Europe and by the end of that century the total was twenty-one. No explanation has yet done justice to such an extraordinary outburst of religious activity in such unlikely circumstances. All these brave women had had to endure the torments of persecution in their own land and then as nuns giving up the world they had condemned themselves to perpetual exile.

Each convent was important in its own right but Lady Mary Percy's foundation at Brussels had special importance as the spring and origin of many other Benedictine foundations. In direct line of descent from Brussels were the convents of Ghent (1624) and from Ghent came Boulogne (1652), Dunkirk (1662) and Ypres (1665). Even Cambrai (founded independently in 1623) and its daughter house at Paris (1651) could claim spiritual descent from Brussels. These are the convents and the nuns who persisted on the Continent until the French Revolution when they were driven from their exile back home to England and became the foundation stones of the new religious life and vitality which graced the emerging Church of nineteenth-century England.

Of course, Lady Mary Percy's convent was contemplative and her nuns strictly enclosed according to the understandings of her times. Their spirituality was much influenced by the heroism of the Martyrs. Most of them had had practical experience of conditions in England and many had blood relations who had given their lives for their Faith. They received many visitors fresh from England and their chaplains were frequently priests who had been tortured and imprisoned on the English Mission. Nevertheless, they applied themselves to the modern devotions of their day and were much influenced by the spiritual writings and traditions of the sixteenth-century Flemish mystics.

By 1604, the Brussels convent of the English ladies had a reputation for being strictly reformed. In that year, for example, Florence de Werguignoel sought the assistance of the sisters in her project of founding a reformed religious house at Douai and they obliged by lending her a copy of their as yet unpublished constitutions.

Lady Mary Percy had always been firmly pro-Jesuit. She knew how much she owed to the Jesuit Fathers who had encouraged her in her vocation and helped her to found her convent. But as early as 1609, Lady Mary Lovel, then a postulant, left the community because she felt the other sisters were losing their attachment to the Jesuit way of life. Perhaps it is not surprising that this should be so; it was after all a Benedictine convent. The pity was, however, that instead of a natural progress from Jesuit influence to Benedictine, the sisters were subjected to the effects of the unfortunate controversies that were raging in England between the Jesuits, the Benedictines and the Seminary priests.

In 1616, when Lady Mary Percy was elected Abbess, the Jesuit-Benedictine controversy within the convent was a major problem. In 1624, the pro-Jesuit sisters moved to Ghent to make a new foundation and there was more serious trouble in 1628. Despite all these defections and the consequent strain on the Abbess, Lady Mary Percy continued to preside over some fifty nuns, all of whom in good time were prepared to exercise their Benedictine loyalties and obedience.

Lady Mary Percy died in 1642. She was seventy-four years of age and had been a Benedictine nun for forty-two years and the Abbess for twenty-nine years. Like her martyred father, it was possible for her to say at the end, 'Remember that I die in the communion of the Catholic Church and that in life and in death I am a Percy.'

MARY WARD

Mary Ward belongs by birth and right to England's Martyr Community within which she lived and worked for almost thirty years but she belongs also in a special way to the Universal Church, which she enriched and strengthened by her new vital concept of religious life and by the foundation of her Institute of the Blessed Virgin Mary.

Three centuries after her death, Cardinal Francis Bourne, Archbishop of Westminster; paid tribute in 1921 to Mary's pioneering work of genius and her fundamental position in the development of religious life for women. He wrote:

> It is a duty of gratitude to recall continually to the Catholics of England, and indeed of the whole United Kingdom as well as to the Teaching Orders of religious women throughout the world, that the existence of modern educational and charitable Congregations, such as we know them, in their almost countless multiplicity, was made possible by the supernatural foresight, the heroic perseverance and sufferings of Mary Ward. She waged the battle to the point of apparent defeat, of which they are now reaping the victory.

Mary Ward was born at Mulwith near Ripon in Yorkshire on 23 January 1585. Her father was Marmaduke Ward; her mother had formerly been Ursula Wright. The child was thereby related to most of the important Catholic families of Yorkshire. Reputedly the first word she spoke was 'Jesus', but Mary herself has acknowledged in her Autobiography that she was 'not then addicted to any one virtue. When my grandmother commanded me to pray I sat in the place but spent my time in sports.'

From 1590 until 1595, Mary was with her grandmother, Ursula Wright, at Ploughlands in Holderness and she was much influenced by the venerable old lady who had spent fourteen years in prison for her Faith and who was 'so great a pray-er that I do not remember in that whole five years that I ever saw her sleep, nor did I ever awake when I perceived her not to be at her prayers.'

By the year 1600, Mary was living with her cousins Sir Ralph and Lady Grace Babthorpe in their quasi-religious house at Osgodby in East Yorkshire. Here she enjoyed the privilege of at least one Mass every day and the constant presence of priests and devoted lay Catholics. And here amid the constraints and dangers suffered by all members of the Martyr Community, the young girl recognized her call to the religious life. She had no doubts and no reservations. She would write later, 'This grace of vocation, by the mercy of God, has been so continuous that not for one moment have I thought of embracing a contrary state.'

As the strength of her sense of vocation grew, Mary became increasingly aware of the limits of her experience. There had been no convents in England for seventy years and it is unlikely that she had ever seen a nun in her habit. She had heard old stories from aged people about the happy days when English nuns flourished in English convents and perhaps more realistically she had heard the more recent accounts of the displaced, expelled nuns living in loyal obedience to their Rule in the secrecy and privacy of their old family homes, but very few of these courageous ladies were still alive. Catholic women who wished to be nuns had to disguise themselves and then engage in all manner of subterfuge to escape the country and settle overseas in one of the contemplative convents. And such women could never return home to tell others about their experiences.

So when in 1606, Mary Ward crossed the seas to St Omer to enter the noviceship of the Poor Clares she had no practical experience of the accepted forms of religious life as it was understood at that time, but she did have other experiences which in due time would serve her well. At Osgodby, she had recognized the enormous value of the unmarried ladies who lived there in a sort of lay community and who spent their time in prayer, religious observance and the teaching of religion to the children. She had recognized also, from her regular visiting of the poor Catholics in prison in York, that many of the women so incarcerated had formed themselves into praying communities, centred on the celebration of Mass whenever possible, but communities so intense and so concerned about the salvation of souls that prayer overflowed into good works. This mixed life of contemplative prayer and apostolic activity, in the understanding of the people of those days, was suitable only for the laity, and as a true child of her times, Mary Ward gave no immediate consideration to the possibility that some day religious sisters might be able to combine the contemplative and the active ways of life within their religious communities. Certain of God's call that marriage was out of the question for her and that He wished her to become a nun, Mary had no option but to join a contemplative community in exile.

For eighteen months Mary Ward endured the noviceship of the Poor Clares but she was not happy and gradually came to realize that that way of life, excellent though it might be for others, was not for her, and she left the noviceship to return home. She was convinced that God was still calling her to the religious life but her call seemed to be to a new way of religious life and at first she was not at all clear what it was. In poor, suffering England her thoughts became clearer. She saw the opportunity 'to do all the little I could for God and for the good of those there'. She saw how necessary it was for the struggling Church in England to develop an educated laity and in particular she realized that women as mothers and first educators of their children in the Faith had a vital role to play. Why was it not possible for women to live their religious lives to the full and yet undertake those works of education and charity which were such marked features of the lives of the young women teaching in the country houses and of the lives of the older women working for the Church within and without the prison walls?

Back in England as a laywoman, Mary Ward returned to the apostolic life which meant so much to her. Her friend and biographer, Winefrid Wigmore, has described how she once more took her life in her hands and braved the pursuivants and informers as she laboured for the salvation of souls among rich and poor. She moved to London, took lodgings in the Strand and mixed in high society. She presented herself as a beautiful lady of fashion but beneath her satins and velvets she had a hair shirt eating into her flesh. She prayed and she fasted and she visited the poor and the sick and especially the emaciated Catholic prisoners in their vile dungeons; '...in her wonted, mild sweet manner', she reclaimed the lapsed and strengthened the weak and brought many wandering souls back to the safety of the Church. 'As far as I can judge,' said Mary herself, 'I did not spend that time ill.'

Inevitably other young women were attracted to join her. Soon she had a spiritual posse of seven active apostles: Mary Poyntz, Jane Browne, Catherine Smith, Winefrid Wigmore, Susannah Rookwood, her cousin, Barbara Babthorpe, and her sister, Barbara Ward. These are the women who accompanied Mary Ward when she took her decisive step in 1609 and returned to St Omer, where she bought a house and in splendid independence opened her first school for the religious education of English Catholic girls.

Now in exile in Flanders, Mary refined and developed her ideas and plans. Church Law at that time demanded that all new Orders should adopt one of the already approved Rules but that of course entailed enclosure. Mary Ward wanted her Sisters to work underground in England and to do this they would have to dress in secular garb and have the freedom to come and go. They could not live in settled, secluded communities but would have to live in ones and twos, in the world, surrounded by heretics and making their own individual decisions. She was impressed by the Rule of Saint Ignatius and the life of the Jesuits and would willingly have affiliated herself to the Society, but Jesuits were expressly forbidden to undertake the care of women religious and so Mary Ward decided that her Institute would follow the ways of the Jesuits while retaining independence in their own government. And so followed another startling conclusion that women should be governed by women.

It is difficult today to understand the howls of horror and storms of protest which Mary Ward's proposals excited in the Church. She was regarded as a dangerous revolutionary seeking to disrupt and destroy the established order. It was said that her views could come only from a spirit of disobedience and a criminal disregard for traditional values. Women religious would not be safe outside the enclosure nor could women be trusted on their own in the world. The idea that women could govern themselves was ludicrous. Who ever heard of women apostles? Were these women trying to usurp the role of the priests? Ridicule was poured on all their efforts and insults freely offered. Mary Ward and her Sisters were laughed at as 'Jesuitesses, Galopping Gurles, Wandering Gossips,

Gad-Abouts' and dismissed lightly and cruelly by one eminent Jesuit with the wounding remark, 'When all is done they are but women.'

To this latter statement, Mary Ward exploded with exemplary vehemence,

> There is no such difference between men and women that women may not do great things, as we have seen by the example of many saints who have done great things. And I hope in God it will be seen that women in time to come will do much ... If women were made so inferior to men in all things, why were they not exempted in all things as they are in some? For what think you of this word, 'but women', but as if we were in all things inferior to some other creature, which I suppose to be man? Which I dare to be bold to say is a lie and with respect to the good Father may say it is an error.

Controversy continued to surround Mary Ward and it saddened her that so much criticism came from her fellow-Catholics in England. Nevertheless within seven years she had sixty Sisters in her company and several schools were flourishing. A London house had been inaugurated in 1614 and Susannah Rookwood installed as Superior with six permanent Sisters. Each year, Mary Ward crossed the Channel to guide and encourage these disciples and join them for a time in their apostolate. It was impossible to keep her presence secret from the civil authorities and Archbishop Abbot of Canterbury grudgingly acknowledged her success when he said that that woman had done more harm than several priests and that he would willingly exchange six or seven Jesuits for her. Hearing that the Archbishop wished to see her, Mary had the temerity to call on him at Lambeth Palace. When she found he was not at home she made her point by engraving her name with a diamond on a window pane. Later, on two occasions, she was captured and imprisoned and even had sentence of death passed on her but each time she was released unharmed.

In 1616, with the help and encouragement of her friend, the Franciscan Bishop Blaise of St Omer, Mary presented her plan to Pope Paul V and sought his blessing on her enterprise. In reply, Pope Paul commended her Institute and held out high hopes of eventual recognition and confirmation but even this papal support did little to quieten the vociferous opposition which surrounded her on all sides. Mary waited with patience for more information from Rome but as time went on it became more and more evident that the Church authorities were not prepared to commit themselves to any further marks of approval. With typical courage, Mary decided that she must press her case personally with the Pope and in October 1621, she set out with four companions to walk the 1,500 miles from Brussels to Rome.

The new Pope, Gregory XV, received Mary Ward with great kindness but many of his advisers in the Curia were shocked that a woman should present her own case. In fact, the verdict had already been given against her. Intemperate letters from enemies in England had poisoned the minds of the Cardinals. Mary was allowed to stay on in Rome but she was fighting a losing battle and in 1625 she gave up the struggle and determined to return to England.

Her journey home became a triumph. At least her friends appreciated her worth. In Florence the Archduchess welcomed her. In Milan, Cardinal Borromeo spoke alone with her for over an hour and placed his carriage at her disposal. At Innsbruck, the Archduke Leopold and his wife received her. At Munich, the Elector Maximilian of Bavaria begged her to stay and gave her the house called Paradeiserhaus in the Wein Strasse where she opened the first of the more than one hundred schools which she and her Sisters founded in that country. A few months later, the Emperor Ferdinand II personally invited Mary to open a school in Vienna where she soon had 500 pupils. Mary abandoned her plans to return to England and devoted herself completely to the development of these schools.

Such success entailed much hard work for Mary Ward and took its toll of her health and strength, but her success did nothing to lessen the general attacks which were still being made on her in England and in Rome. In fact, by 1629, it was clear to her that the authorities in Rome were about to condemn her, and on 13 January 1631 her worst fears were confirmed when Pope Urban VIII signed a bill which suppressed Mary Ward's Institute, closed all her houses and dispersed her Sisters.

At that time, Mary was in Munich and there she was arrested by the Inquisition as a 'heretic, schismatic and rebel of Holy Church'. She was imprisoned in the Convent of the Poor Clares at Anger and lodged in a 'filthy, little room, double-locked and with one small window'. The Sisters soon discovered that they had been misinformed about the prisoner they had been obliged to accept. They said, 'This is a great servant of God; our house is blessed in her setting foot in it.' Nevertheless, they held her in obedience to the Holy Office and the harsh conditions of her incarceration brought Mary Ward so close to death that she actually received the Last Sacraments.

In Rome, Pope Urban VIII knew nothing about Mary's imprisonment and as soon as the news reached him he immediately ordered her release. With freedom, her health improved and once more Mary set out to walk to Rome in order to plead her own case. The Pope received her kindly and allowed her to live and work in the Holy City in a private capacity but after six years of constant pleading it was evident that the forces ranged against her were too powerful and Mary determined that she had no alternative but to acknowledge defeat and return to England.

Mary Ward arrived in London in May 1639 and settled with her Sisters in St Martin's Lane. With the help and protection of Queen Henrietta Maria a small group of children, rich and poor were gathered together to be educated as Catholics. For three years this apostolate flourished but with the outbreak of the Civil War, London became too dangerous a place and Mary took her Sisters first to Hutton Rudby in the North Riding of Yorkshire and then to Heworth Hall just outside the city walls of York.

In the latter months of 1644, Mary Ward realized that her death was approaching. On New Year's Day, 1645 she received Holy Communion for the last time but the priest did not consider that she was ill enough to receive the Last Sacraments. He was then called away and prevented from returning so that when she died on 30 January she died without the ministrations of a priest, but at least she died surrounded by her loving and loyal Sisters. She was buried in the Protestant churchyard of the neighbouring village of Osbaldwick by an Anglican clergyman who 'was honest enough to be bribed'. Her grave has since been lost but her memorial stone is preserved in a place of honour within the church and is often visited by her religious daughters of the Institute of the Blessed Virgin Mary and the Loreto Sisters.

More than two hundred years after her death, Mary Ward's work was at last recognized by the Church when in 1877, Pope Pius IX formally approved and blessed her Institute. Today, almost 5,000 of her Sisters throughout the world recognize her as their Foundress and pray in gratitude that her heroic virtue and extraordinary holiness may soon also be officially recognized by the Church to which she so loyally dedicated her life.

MARGARET POWELL

Margaret Powell was born about the year 1612. According to a manuscript of 14 October 1642 in Father Christopher Grene's Collection M, she was a daughter of Sir Henry Browne and therefore a member of the great recusant family of the Montagues.

From other sources it would appear that Margaret had been married twice. La Sieur de Marsys in his '*Histoire de la Persecution en Angleterre*' (1646) refers to her as Margaret Parkins, the wife of Mr Powell, and then goes on to describe her as, '...allied through her parents with one of the most noble Houses of England but greatly impoverished through the continual persecutions that she had suffered for God's cause'. He also adds that she had an only son, whom she had educated herself as a Catholic because her husband was a Protestant.

La Sieur de Marsys also describes Margaret Powell's way of life. She was engaged continually, he relates, 'in acts of piety, prayer and fasting and especially the service of the sick priests in prison. She willingly shut herself up with them and helped them with such diligence, care and kindness that even the most hardened heretics could not refrain from respecting such an extraordinary virtue.' (Book 1, p. 57.)

Mrs Margaret Powell lived in London with her husband in their large house in Saint Peter's Lane, near Cow Cross in the parish of Saint Sepulchre. As a busy housewife she was fully occupied with domestic affairs but nevertheless she found time and opportunity to welcome several priests to her home and Mass was frequently celebrated for her servants and friends. Every precaution was taken to ensure the safety of the community and for some time all was well, but in September 1642 an unreliable maidservant saw her opportunity to make money by betraying her mistress to the pursuivants.

The unfaithful servant approached Captain James Wadsworth, the leader of a little group of professional priest-catchers, and asked him how much he was prepared to pay her if she conducted him to a priest actually engaged in celebrating Mass. Wadsworth had been brought up as a Catholic but had renounced his Faith in 1625 to make his living from the rewards paid for the capture of priests. He was later to be described by Sir William Sanderson (1655) as 'Mr Wadsworth, a renegade, proselyte turncoat, of any religion and every trade, and a common hackney to the basest catchpole bailiffs'. It was this unsavoury character who agreed to pay £5 to the maidservant as the blood money for her priest.

On Sunday, 11 September 1642 the trap for the priest was made ready.

The servant conducted Wadsworth and his men to the inn next door to Mrs Powell's house and there established them in a room which overlooked the room where Mass was to be celebrated. There she pointed out a certain window and told them that when she drew the curtains on that window it would be a certain sign that Mass had just begun.

The priest-catchers waited patiently and as La Sieur de Marsys has recounted (Book 1, p. 60) used the opportunity to refresh themselves on the readily available drink. Nevertheless, they were careful not to miss the signal when it was given. They moved quietly to Mrs Powell's front door where the servant allowed them to enter without disturbing anybody. Then they rushed the room where the priest, Father Thomas Bullarker, had just begun the Gloria of the Mass. The priest, a Franciscan, looked at the intruders and showed no emotion and then he raised his eyes to heaven and said, 'Alas. If only you had waited until after the Consecration then I would have had the Sacred Body of my Saviour to strengthen me against the violence which you have prepared for me and under which my feebleness might lead me to succumb.'

Father Bullarker was arrested at the altar and paraded through the streets in his vestments. Margaret Powell gave herself up without a murmur and surrendered also her twelve-year-old son who had been serving the Mass. All three were taken to different prisons.

Father Bullarker was first examined by the Sheriff of London but the priest expressed himself so forcibly and eloquently that he was taken before a select committee of Parliament where he once again acknowledged his priesthood and produced the most powerful arguments in his own defence.

On 5 October, Father Thomas Bullarker and Mrs Margaret Powell were tried together at the Newgate Sessions. Again the priest proclaimed his own priesthood and was therefore sentenced to death. On Wednesday, 12 October he was drawn on a hurdle to Tyburn. A large crowd gathered to escort him on his honourable way and Father Christopher Grene has preserved the information that 'as he was drawn to execution, two gentlewomen, his penitents and those, it is said, of good quality, but disguised, accompanied him on either side of his sled through all the dirt, which in divers places was very deep. They spoke with him and several times kissed his hands.' (Collection M, 1642.) Arrived at the scaffold, Father Bullarker tried to preach on the Real Presence but was shouted down. At a given sign, one of his Franciscan brethren gave him absolution and then he was hanged, drawn and quartered.

Blessed Thomas Bullarker was beatified by Pope John Paul II on 22 November 1987. The trial of Mrs Margaret Powell followed on, immediately after Father Bullarker had been sentenced to death on 5 October. The indictment has been preserved and shows that the accusation was that 'she knowingly, willingly and feloniously ... received, welcomed, comforted and helped' Thomas Bullarker, whom she knew to be a priest. She placed herself upon the country, i.e. she agreed to be tried by jury and pleaded not guilty.

A contemporary hostile tract has referred to 'Mistress Powell' as the priest's 'land-lady' and describes how she was brought to the bar and that upon examination was found in nothing to vary from the erroneous opinion of this her holy father, whether by him converted (being formerly accounted so light, that her honesty would hardly be taken with allowance) or seduced it makes no great matter. But she also seemed very willing to die, confessing that her deed was not ignorantly committed, for she knew well enough what man he was, and what power the law had to take away her life if it were known to any that she harboured him in her house; yet nevertheless, she said, she could not but do it out of conscience sake, and this was all she had to say for herself.

From all this it is evident that Margaret Powell was ready to follow in the footsteps of Father Bullarker to the scaffold and she was in fact bitterly disappointed when she was remanded without bail to stay in prison until the next Middlesex Sessions at Newgate. La Sieur de Marsys, who at this time visited her in prison, has expressed his surprise and edification that the thought of escaping a cruel death should cause the lady so much grief. But Margaret Powell yearned for martyrdom and wished to be with Father Bullarker as he gained his heavenly crown.

At the next Session on 7 December 1642, Margaret Powell seemed to have achieved her heart's desire when she was sentenced to be hanged but a memorandum was added to the record of this verdict in the Gaol Delivery Registers and once more she was deprived of martyrdom. The memorandum was an appeal to higher authority and is worded thus, 'It is thought fit and so desired by this court that Mr. Serjeant Phesant do attend the House of Lords to acquaint Their Lordships with the proceedings against one Margaret Powell, convicted for the felonious receiving of Thomas Bullarker, a popish priest, (who was executed the last session) knowing him to be so, and to know Their Lordships pleasure whether she shall be executed according to the judgment given against her or be reprieved.'

She was in fact reprieved but the reprieve was given to her in a most cruel manner. On the day appointed for her execution she was taken out of prison and La Sieur de Marsys has described how she was actually on the scaffold preparing for death and martyrdom when she was told at the very last minute that she was to be pardoned and set free. King Charles I and his gentlemen of Parliament could not bring themselves to countenance the execution of a woman, and so Margaret Powell remains a martyr by intention only.

When La Sieur de Marsys published his book in 1646, he could report from personal knowledge that Mrs Margaret Powell was still practising her Faith and assisting priests and that she was living in Oxford.

HENRIETTA MARIA STUART

As the Queen Consort of King Charles I, Henrietta Maria was in a unique position to help her fellow Catholics and she did not hesitate to use her power and influence on their behalf at every opportunity. Perhaps, she was not called upon to demonstrate the same bravery as other Catholic women but she was aware of the fate of some of her unfortunate predecessors and the eventual execution of her royal husband was proof indeed that she herself was not immune from such danger.

Henrietta Maria was only fifteen years of age when she first came to England. The daughter of King Henri IV of France and his Queen, Marie de Medici, she was married, on 1 May 1625, by special papal dispensation to the Anglican Charles Stuart who had been King of England for only five weeks.

It was not a popular marriage in England. The bride was very young and immature. She was no great beauty. She had been poorly educated and spoke no English. But to the English people she had two overwhelming faults: she was French and she was Catholic. On these grounds her presence in England was resented. Insults were hurled at her in the street and howling mobs gathered at the gates of her palace. From the very beginning the young girl was put to the test but her frail form concealed a powerful spirit and she did not fail her cause.

Henrietta Maria brought with her from France a determination to help her fellow Catholics in England and to do what she could to alleviate their distress. The terms of her marriage contract ensured that she was to have her own chapel and priests in London and a promise had been made by King Charles that English Catholics would be free to practice their religion, provided that it was done in a private and peaceable manner. Unfortunately, at first, the new Queen misjudged the temper and the sensitivities of her Protestant people. Her French courtiers, her French attendants and especially her French priests upset the local citizens who objected to their numbers and to their behaviour. There were just too many chaplains performing their duty in too bold and ostentatious a manner, and at the stern request of Parliament, King Charles was obliged to expel more than sixty members of the French party in August 1626.

The Queen at once demanded her rights and made protest to her powerful brother, King Louis XIII of France, who indulged himself in such warlike noises that King Charles was obliged to acknowledge his responsibilities. A compromise, wholly advantageous to the Queen, was arranged. Her French entourage was to be restricted but she was allowed a bishop and twelve priests as her chaplains and a new chapel was built for her in London.

Perhaps the greatest Catholic achievement of Queen Henrietta Maria was the establishment of this powerhouse of religion in the very heart of an alien city. At her first coming she had been served by Oratorians, who had been lodged 'in the suburb of Saint James, in sight of the royal residence, to which access was not obtained of the sentries without extreme difficulty by the Catholics who repaired thither to attend divine service'. But now she replaced her Oratorians with a community of ten Capuchins and sited their convent at Somerset House which was much more open to the general public. The Friars, for their part, generously placed their chapel at the disposal of the London Catholics and engaged themselves in secret pastoral work throughout the city.

Father Cyprien de Gamache, one of the Queen's Capuchins, has described their work in his book, *Memoirs of the Mission in England of the Capuchin Friars, 1630-1669*. In this work, he has reported how the Queen herself laid the foundation stone of the Chapel Royal on 14 September 1632,

> at Somerset House, which belongs particularly to the Queen and is the finest palace of all England. When this chapel was opened, Her Majesty's Capuchins served it thus: from six o'clock in the morning there were successively Masses and General Communions until noon. Not a day passed without bringing some penitents to the confessionals. On Sundays and festivals, the throng was so great that one could not get in without difficulty. Persons were obliged to wait two or three hours before they could enter a confessional. On those days, a controversial lecture was held from one o'clock till two, immediately before Vespers, which the Capuchins and the musicians, placed in two galleries opposite to each other, sang alternately. When Vespers were finished, the preacher mounted the pulpit, and preached for the space of an hour or three quarters on the Gospel of the day, touching occasionally upon certain controversial points. Compline was then sung. Then followed various conferences, some of piety with Catholics, others of religion with the sectaries, who came eagerly to be instructed in our creed and to have their doubts resolved. The Christian Doctrine was publicly taught in French and English on three different days in each week. Not a week passed but there were two or three conversions. (quoted by Father John Morris SJ in *Troubles of our Catholic Forefathers*, First Series, p. 203.)

It is indeed remarkable that so much Catholic activity should be going on in the city of London while religious persecution raged on unabated, but much of the responsibility for the Capuchin success must be attributed to the patronage and protection of Queen Henrietta Maria.

Henrietta Maria also had a profound influence over Court life, especially after 1630 when her husband seemed to grant her all she wished. Her practice of her religion was sincere and wholehearted but was not specially attractive. She indulged herself in petty devotions and paid much attention to the relics of the saints, miraculous stories and unusual scapulars. Such practices and approaches made little appeal to the stolid English. But what did appeal to them was the exquisite good taste of the Queen's manner of religion. For her, nothing was too good for the service of God, and for Him, she demanded the very best of everything. Her chapel at Somerset House was designed by the best architect of her day, the Catholic Inigo Jones. She patronized the genius of the Catholic composer, William Byrd. She cultivated the artistic talents of the Flemish Catholic, Sir Anthony Vandyke and brought him to settle in England. She imported Richard Dering from Brussels to be her chapel organist. Her household became a salon where artists, musicians, composers, writers, poets and wits congregated and found themselves recognizing the high standards and values of the Catholic approach. Henrietta Maria herself did no direct proselytizing but she placed her Catholic ladies and her priests in strategic positions amid the company and by their conversations they converted to Catholicism an amazing number of the ladies and gentlemen of the Court and their guests.

Queen Henrietta Maria was loyal to her friends and always ready to defend her priests. When one of her gentlemen-in-waiting, Matthew Savage, was discovered to be in reality Father David Codner, an English Benedictine monk, she rushed to his aid immediately. Three times in 1631 he was arrested for his priesthood and three times his release was secured by the Queen's personal intervention.

The Queen took a keen interest in Catholic affairs and was always ready to help the missionary priests in their difficulties. At her intercession, many were released from prison and others reprieved from sentence of death. Among her special friends was Father Henry Morse SJ, the Priest of the Plague. She helped him with money for food, medicines and nurses and made some of her donations from her own purse. In September 1636, Father Morse himself contracted the plague but shortly after this he was betrayed and arrested. He was tried at the Old Bailey and sentenced to death for being a priest but the King intervened and granted him a pardon 'at the instance of our dearest consort, the Queen'. Saint Henry Morse was eventually hanged drawn and quartered as a Martyr on 1 February 1645, but by that time his Protector the Queen was in exile in France.

In 1639 Queen Henrietta Maria took the lead in a great Catholic enterprise. The Scottish rebellion of that year caused enormous additional expenses to the Royal Exchequer and in any case the King was always short of money. To help to relieve this burden on her husband and to establish the loyalty of the English Catholics, the Queen invited them all to raise for the King's use some considerable sum of money 'freely and cheerfully presented'. She promised that anyone who would 'employ themselves towards the success of this business' would be protected against any 'Inconveniences' as a consequence of their efforts on behalf of the King. (Article: 'John Crosse of Liverpool' by R.G. Dottie, Recusant History, vol. 20, No. 1, p. 38.)

Another very important contribution to the Catholic cause in England was made by Queen Henrietta Maria in 1633 when she sent Sir Robert

Douglas to Rome as her personal representative to the Holy See. With the approval of King Charles, Sir Robert became a direct channel of communication between the Pope and the Court of Saint James. The contact was too informal to be regarded as the resumption of diplomatic relations but it was at least the forerunner of such relations and gave England a link with the European diplomacy of the Holy See as well as affording to English Catholics a more intimate connection with their religious superiors. In response to this initiative of Henrietta Maria, a succession of papal agents was sent to London on the same informal terms but all these agents were accredited unofficially to the Queen and not directly to the King or the Government. Dom Leander de Sancto Martino and Gregorio Panzani came to London in 1634 to represent Pope Urban VIII in this way, and they were followed by George Con and Carlo Rossetti. All these arrangements were terminated in 1641 at the insistence of Parliament but by that time the reports of these agents had given the Roman authorities a much clearer picture of the state and condition of the English Catholics.

Queen Henrietta Maria was obliged to flee from England when the regicides captured her husband in 1644 and she was at the French Court when she heard the devastating news of his execution. She could only return to England in 1660 when her son, King Charles II, was restored to his throne, but her health was not good and she returned to France within a few months.

In July 1662, Henrietta Maria as Queen Mother returned to England with great determination. She re-established her chapel at Somerset House and restored her Capuchins to their old convent. Once more they embarked on their pastoral activities as they made their daily Masses available to all Catholics and fiercely preached their sermons for all the citizens of good will. In a very short time, the Queen's Chapel was again recognized as the centre of Catholic life in the capital.

The Queen herself lived an exemplary life and applied herself to her devotions. In an age of extravagance she lived well within her income and her frugal style of life demonstrated her love for evangelical poverty. According to Mr Joseph Gillow,

> She paid all her accounts weekly; she had no debts. She had, as her contemporary biographer quaintly expresses it, 'a large reputation for justice'. Every quarter, she dispersed the overplus of her revenue among the poor, bountifully bestowing, without consideration of difference of faith, her favourite charity ... releasing debtors confined for small sums, or for non-payment of fees; likewise sending relief to those who were enduring great hardships in prison.

But the Queen was not a strong woman and suffered much ill-health. Her constant concern for the suffering Catholics, the years of anxiety during the Civil War, the cruel death of her husband, and the strains of widowhood and exile, all exacted their toll on her physical and psychological condition. She was advised by her doctors that a return to the quiet life of France was essential for her recovery. In these circumstances she consulted her son,

King Charles II and told him very plainly 'that she would recover if she went for a time to breathe her native air and seek health at the Bourbon baths, and she would do so, if he would not close her chapel to his Catholic subjects; but if it was closed for one day on account of her departure, she would stay and live as long as it pleased God, and then die at the post of duty.' The King granted his mother's request and she left London in June 1665.

Henrietta Maria never returned to England. She died in her sleep at her country palace at Colombe on 10 August 1669 and was buried with her royal ancestors at the Abbey of Saint Denis near Paris. She may not have played an important role in English history as such, but she was the power and the strength behind her beloved husband in all his misfortunes and her extraordinary services to the struggling Catholic community have secured for her a place in English Catholic history which demands further recognition.

INDEX